Praise for *I Am Diosa*

"Gutierrez's words are at the same t[...] and modern. It's exactly what's neede[...] ate. *I Am Diosa* is for every modern woman who craves a wisdom that's been denied to us for too long. Read and USE this magical book." —Rebekah Borucki, mother, author, and advocate

"Christine Gutierrez is a brilliant and powerful force who embodies everything she teaches. *I Am Diosa* walks you through the inner process of understanding your past and healing your wounds so that you can live a vibrant, authentic, and empowered life. *I Am Diosa* is for those who are ready for serious transformation."

—Yung Pueblo, author of *Inward*

"Finally, a book that beautifully and effectively combines a psychologically grounded perspective with ancient wisdom for cultivating self-love, self-care, and deep healing. *I Am Diosa* is a step-by-step guide to true transformation and authentic empowerment."

—Terri Cole, licensed psychotherapist

"*I Am Diosa* is the book we all need right now. Christine masterfully weaves psychology, soul, and her compelling personal story as an offering to come back home to our true, unbroken, and Diosa selves. Christine's gift is that she speaks from the wholeness of her truth leaving nothing out—shadow, trauma, or addiction. She has worked hard to heal, she has earned her scars, and her journey is our initiation." —Robyn Moreno, author and curandera

I Am Diosa

A JOURNEY TO HEALING DEEP,
LOVING YOURSELF,
AND COMING BACK HOME TO SOUL

Christine Gutierrez

A TARCHERPERIGEE BOOK

tarcherperigee

an imprint of Penguin Random House LLC
penguinrandomhouse.com

First trade paperback edition 2022
Copyright © 2020 by Christine Gutierrez

There's a Hole in My Sidewalk: The Romance of Self-Discovery by Portia Nelson.
Copyright © 1993 by Portia Nelson. Reprinted with the permission of
Beyond Words/Atria Books, a division of Simon & Schuster, Inc. All rights reserved.

Cycle of Change, socialworktech.com, adapted from a work
by Prochaska and DiClemente (1983)/Ignacio Pacheco

"Wolf and Woman" by Nikita Gill. Taken from *Wild Embers*, first published in 2017 by Trapeze, an
imprint of the Orion Publishing Group Ltd.
Copyright © Nikita Gill 2017

"Shedding Skins" lyrics by singer-songwriter Fia Forsström: fiasmusicofficial.com

Most TarcherPerigee books are available at special quantity discounts for
bulk purchase for sales promotions, premiums, fund-raising, and educational
needs. Special books or book excerpts also can be created to fit specific needs.
For details, write: SpecialMarkets@penguinrandomhouse.com.

The Library of Congress has catalogued the hardcover edition as follows:

Names: Gutierrez, Christine (psychotherapist), author.
Title: I Am Diosa: a journey to healing deep, loving yourself, and coming
back home to soul / by Christine Gutierrez;
Description: New York: TarcherPerigee, an imprint of Penguin Random House
LLC, [2020] | Identifiers: LCCN 2020005370 (print) | LCCN 2020005371 (ebook) |
ISBN 9780593086650 (ebook) | ISBN 9780593086643 (hardcover)
Subjects: LCSH: Self-acceptance in women. | Self-esteem in women. |
Self-actualization (Psychology) in women.
Classification: LCC BF575.S37 (ebook) | LCC BF575.S37 G87 2020 (print) |
DDC 158.1082—dc23
LC record available at https://lccn.loc.gov/2020005370

ISBN (paperback) 9780593421437

Printed in the United States of America
4th Printing

Book design by Ashley Tucker

I dedicate this book to little Christine. You did it. You were always worthy. You were always loved. You are seen. You are heard. You are divine. We made it.

To my mom and dad, for believing in all of my wildest dreams and being willing to grow.

To my husband, Fernando, you are the manifestation of my deepest soul's work. Thank you for existing—you are moving art, and I am ever grateful for your love, inspiration, and support in my life. *Te amo my twin flame.*

And to my Diosa community, you are the blood in the veins of this medicine and work. You are the dopest, most fierce, loving, and raw community of souls. This is all for you.

Contents

PART I

The Darkness: Exploring Trauma & the Original Wound

Beloved Mother

Creator of the Heavens and the Earth,
you are my heart of my heavens,
my heart of the Earth.

Mother you created us in your image.

Diosa de Luz
I am the light and you are my Guide,
my heart hears your voice in the Wind
as I walk throughout your Earth beloved mother.

Cleansing and clearing myself with your sacred waters,
Sweet water, Salty water, Bitter, and Sour waters.

Spirit of the Grandmothers of the Four Directions,
In prayer asking the spirit of the Fire to clear my way
so that my words can be received.

Help us Beloved Creadora y Formadora,
I am sending my cries to you spirit of grandmother moon
as you move us throughout the ages.

Standing here before you with my arms extended,
connect us, you are the center of the Universe
as we are the beings of the Four directions.

Hear us, all of us that represent all the colors of the rainbow.
We are your children in the name of the Great Mystery.

Bless each and everyone Diosa mia.

Abu Flordemayo
February 2020
Love and Light,
Grandmother Flordemayo

Querida Madre

Creador de los Cielos y la Tierra,
eres mi corazón de mis cielos,
mi corazón de la Tierra.

Madre nos creaste a tu imagen.

Diosa de Luz
Yo soy la luz y tú eres mi guía,
mi corazón escucha tu voz en el viento
mientras camino por tu Tierra amada madre.

Limpiándome y limpiándome con tus aguas sagradas,
Agua dulce, agua salada, amarga y agria.

Espíritu de las abuelas de las cuatro direcciones,
En oración, pidiendo al espíritu del Fuego que me abra el camino
para que mis palabras puedan ser recibidas.

Ayúdanos, Amada Creadora y Formadora,
Te mando mis gritos espíritu de abuela luna
a medida que nos mueve a lo largo de los siglos.

Parado aquí ante ti con los brazos extendidos,
conéctanos, eres el centro del universo
como somos los seres de las Cuatro direcciones.

Escúchanos, todos nosotros que representamos todos los colores del arco iris.
Somos sus hijos en nombre del Gran Misterio.

Bendice a todos y cada uno Diosa mia.

Abu Flordemayo
February 2020
Love and Light,
Grandmother Flordemayo

I Am Diosa

INVOCATION

I AM DIOSA is not merely a book. It is an initiation. An activation. A call back home to Soul and your true in-your-bones divine Diosa Self. Listen to the voice of your soul and come back home to you. You deserve to feel the power and the magic that awaits in the depths of you. Divinity incarnate—in flesh—is your birthright. Stars are what you are made of. God/Goddess in each cell. Earth in your feet. You are the cosmos.

Let us gather around the fire, in the medicine of the soul's night.

Let us dive into the oceans of one another's heart longings.

Give me your demons. Give me your wounds. I open my arms, wide, embracing all of you. I will kiss each wound tenderly. I will rock you and whisper you *cantos del alma* . . . Until you remember a time before your wounds bled. Until you remember a time before you cried. I will hold you until you heal and become whole . . . Until the fragmented pieces of your shattered soul come back home to you.

Hand in hand, let us go deep on the journey inward—back home to the true you, to the soul you, to the fully embodied Diosa, in-your-bones you.

In . . . in . . . in—inward we go.

Your pain is welcome here. Your brokenness is welcome here. Your woundedness is welcome here. Your rawness is welcome here.

Your discovery is your own. And your pace, honor it above all.

This is merely a framework, but your flow is always best.

Remember, on this soul journey to healing, nothing is black-and-white. Nothing is merely fear or love. We can hold a multitude of feelings at once. It is in the holding of the tension of these opposing emotions that the true medicine is found. It is not in the villainizing of more difficult emotions—anger, revenge, pain, jealousy, fear—that we find peace. On the contrary, the rejection of these emotions is the very rejection of the universe itself. The world is made of darkness and light. Pain and pleasure. You too are made of both. The sooner you accept this, the more deep the healing journey becomes.

Healing is a weaving, a dance, a learning, an unlearning, a constantly unfolding process. And, my darling, you have your own unique soul's journey. So let this be a map, but let your soul be the compass to guide you along the way. Your soul always knows, but perhaps the voice has been hidden. This is why you are here to uncover and reclaim the soul.

I wrote this book for you. For the ones that have been broken down. Whose sense of self has been shattered, sometimes while in the arms of men or women, too wounded to recognize gold was upon them. This is for the ones that still flow—with soul in the cracks of their pain and their shame. Who, despite it all, choose to rise, rise, rise and grow, grow, grow. This is for you.

Repeat This Mantra Out Loud:

We call ourselves back from all time and all places.
We call ourselves back from all time and all places.
We call ourselves back from all time and all places.
We are here now.

We call ourselves back home today from however far away we have
strayed.

We call ourselves back home today.

We call ourselves back to the place of our Soul Home. Soul Home.

This place of love, divinity, and peace that exists and has always existed and will always exist.

We call ourselves back home today.

Let us be guided to lift the veils that block us from seeing the truth that holds us back.

Let us be guided to carry the sweetness of divine nectar and comfort as we navigate tough terrains.

Let us be compassionate and kind to ourselves as we go on this journey.

Let us be guided back home to Soul, to Self, and to deep, deep-in-our-bones healing.

I am home in me. I welcome the Soul Journey.

We open this circle of healing with an energy of love, truth, sisterhood, and deep soul transformation.

And so it is.

PREFACE

Every creature on earth returns to home
—Dr. Clarissa Pinkola Estés

I spent the majority of my life looking for ways to abandon myself and escape the pain that existed within me. Most of the time I was running, I didn't even realize it. I wasn't aware of the deep sorrow that lived in the center of my belly. I wasn't aware that I was walking around like an empty vessel—shattered, with a broken heart.

I remember when I first heard the term *God-sized hole.* I felt a sense of relief that there was a phrase to encapsulate what I was feeling for so long. I had a God-sized hole within me. I felt this immeasurable amount of pain and, more than anything, loneliness. Loneliness had me looking for love in all the wrong places. It was a kind of deep soul aching feeling, and I couldn't fully locate it—it seemed as though the loneliness was in my cells and in my bones. I imagine that I was running from something that was too much for my mind and body to comprehend. I ran far, far away . . . from me.

When things are scary, we run. It's a primal reaction that comes when our brain registers fear and sends a signal to our nervous system. I learned later that trauma will do that to you. Trauma creates what we therapists call dissociation. It is the disconnect from self that comes as a response to the traumatizing event. And I had many traumatizing events.

It was as though I was running through dark alleys looking for a hit of something to make me not feel the deep agony my spirit and mind were in. Along the dark path, I sought shady characters for just a hit of love. I would do anything to feel that comfort, despite the consequences. I knew it was wrong, but I couldn't stop going back. Drug dealers had become my type, and the chaos of the life that came with it. Growing up in Bushwick, Brooklyn, I had both the hood and the private Catholic-school life in me. But the ache inside me had me going to the shadiest corners.

Trauma builds our tolerance for pain in an unhealthy way, and so without realizing it, I was accepting abuse because I was good at holding it—I had my entire childhood. But I couldn't take it anymore. And thank God for that.

My love addiction and heartache were leading me to a new door—an opening within my psyche and soul that would inevitably heal me.

I heard a voice within me trying to get my attention. A voice that was reminding me that things weren't normal, and something was wrong. This internal soul voice was asking and begging for me to question the life I was living and who I was allowing in my life.

"Do you want to stay in this abuse forever?" "Do you want to be lied to and cheated on and called names?" "Do you want to step into your full potential, or do you want to stay here in misery and settle?" They were serious questions that were begging me to remove the veil of denial.

That voice saved me. It is what I call "the soul voice," the voice that is connected to "the more," to God, Goddess/Diosa, Source, Divine, or whatever name is aligned for you.

This is the SOUL CALL. It is the call from your soul for you to return back home to your true self, to your soul, to your wholeness.

For the next decade, I went on a journey to healing, and I still am. I think we all are, really. Doing our best and healing one day at a time.

It wasn't just one moment that led me to heal, and I won't set an unrealistic expectation that everything is perfect now. *I am a living, breathing woman with a sea of emotions. I am like the waves, and I rise and fall like the tide. To minimize my experience to a simple before and after is a disservice to the multitude of colors and emotions that are complex like the universe herself. Like me, like you.* But I will say that tiny moments added up and led me on a journey to what I call healing. I learned some things along the way that saved me from living a life that was once a dead-end road. I gathered tools that opened new doors and that gave me the gift of choice again. I share these tools because they might also be helpful for you on your journey of healing. I don't share it for you to do it all, without question or thought, but instead to find what resonates with your truth, with the unique soul voice guiding you.

This is what *I Am Diosa* is all about. It is a journey and an initiation.

This book combines the spiritual with the psychological so that you are equipped with tools to heal. You will explore the pain and trauma you have experienced and how it affected your sense of self, your relationships, and your daily choices. You will explore the ways you act out, the ways you are triggered, and the ways to use your wounds to find wisdom and purpose. Through that exploration, by untangling the webs, you come back home to you, to the healthy version of you.

This book is another expression of the work I do every day. Whether I am sharing online, speaking onstage, or meeting with a client one to one or on one of my retreats, I remind people of their worth, remind people of their Diosa divinity, remind people that their trauma can never make them less than. I aim to hold people and guide them through the pain and darkness, because it is there that we need the most love.

Dr. Clarissa Pinkola Estés, author of *Women Who Run with the*

Wolves, says, "I've not forgotten the song of those dark years, *hambre del alma*, song of the starved soul. But neither have I forgotten the joyous *canto hondo*, the deep song, the words of which come back to us when we do the work of soulful reclamation."

This work is about soulful reclamation. The rejoining of soul back into our bodies, into our primal selves, and from there remembering who we are—beyond the wound, beyond shame, beyond the pain.

I don't take this responsibility lightly. For we are breaking not only our internal patterns of pain and suffering, but the lineages of abuse and pain that have come before us.

It is time for us Diosas to rise.

I Am Diosa is meant to guide you through this process of deep healing. It gives you the opportunity to get to know yourself and love yourself—not on a superficial level, but at the core of you. For we go our entire lives looking for love—but it is the love for Self that will determine the rest of our lives.

This is an initiation that we can't skip. Nothing and no one out there can give us the soul nourishment we seek unless we have positive regard for the self. The rest will be add-ons, but it must start with us. To intimately know the self and the soul is a gift of a lifetime. It is a romance. To be your own beloved. To kiss your shoulders and hug yourself and hold yourself when you are wanting to escape. To learn to love yourself that deep allows you to know who you are and what you need and what you don't need.

No matter where you are in this journey, I want you to know there is hope and there are even more miracles awaiting you. Whether you have been doing this work for years or just beginning— so long as we are alive, we get to revisit this work and keep peeling back layers. Shedding like a snake, old conditioning, and revealing soul skin in its place.

I remember going to bed each night with a thousand bricks in my heart. I remember when the road led nowhere. Every corner I chose, a dead end. I remember how empty I felt. I remember how I crawled out, bloody knees and fear seeping through me. Even as I crawled, I remember some part of me lit up. Some part of me came alive. Amid the pain and the breakdown was an inkling of a breakthrough. My soul knew. Change was coming. Worth was growing. My Diosa soul light began to flicker on.

It's not the biggest steps that begin the change, the transformation, the alchemizing—it is the slightest willingness. Do what you must.

We deserve to heal. We *deserve* it. We owe it to ourselves to experience the change, to fall in love with ourselves because we have done the work to live a life that is soul aligned. No matter the heartbreak or fear in your heart, your soul is rooting for you.

Treat this journey with reverence and honor. Be committed to going deeper than you have before. Give yourself the gift of going all in and being radically honest with yourself. Reveal secrets that you have hidden in chambers so that you may free yourself. There is nothing within you that can hurt you if you face it, but what you keep locked in can hurt you. Remember you have your soul there to guide you, so do not fear. You were born to do this.

Because your soul led you here, I know you are ready to dive deep. We will do this together; I will be here every step of the way. It is time to own that you are Diosa.

Repeat to Yourself or Out Loud:

I Am Diosa

This begins our sacred journey back home to you. I am excited for the transformations that will occur. I stand with you hand in hand and heart to heart.

You are so loved. You are worthy. Let us begin.

Te amo Diosa.

xx

Christine

I Am Diosa

INTRODUCTION

> "Be gentle with yourself for you are meeting parts
> of yourself that you have been at war with."
> —Unknown author

Welcome, Diosa. I am so grateful that you are here. My heart is full, knowing that we are here on this journey back home to self, to soul, and our true Diosa (Goddess) divine self—together.

I consider the soul to be the part of us that has always existed. The part of us connected to the "more," to the dimensions beyond this mundane world. The soul that is part of God, Goddess, *La Diosa*, Source, and limitless infinite life energy.

We are being called to return to Soul. We are being called back home—to our Soul home. We are living in times when people, more than ever, are realizing the need for soul growth. People are being called to go beyond the surface world into those dimensions of depth and true healing.

We have disconnected for far too long from the feminine, from Shakti, from the mother, from the cosmic womb, from the roots. The pain has become too much. But our soul always remembers—there is more.

This book is about reminding you that there is more. Beyond the pain, beyond the suffering, the trauma, the self-sabotage. But first we must look at the soul wounds. First, we must dive to the root. First, we must do the heavy lifting so that we can connect the dots. Witness the patterns that no longer serve you. Then—with soul-work, patience, community, and love—healing can occur.

The deepest soulwork is usually the darkest and grittiest. The moments when you feel like you can't go on any further . . . where the air thickens and your knees wobble from exhaustion. When you lose faith that there is light beyond the tunnel of black. Sometimes it's a faint prayer, whispered between sighs and cries of desperation. And with what you think is your last breath, your prayer is answered. And the soul of the sea, and the stars, and breeze come with a gust of wind within your lungs—animus—resuscitating you back to life.

The darkness is a place that offers an opportunity for a new life to begin. Like the womb, which is dark, and also a passageway to another world.

Perhaps you are in the dark night of the soul. A moment when you can't see what is ahead, but all you know is that something is changing or has to change. Perhaps you have picked up this book in one of those "FUCK, HOLY SHIT, NOT THIS AGAIN—same cycle, pattern, trigger, or self-sabotage" moments. Or perhaps you are numb and soul exhausted and looking to remember the passion, the joy, the peace, the calm, the healthy, the empowerment.

All of this is a normal part of life. One that we must not avoid. The sun rises and it sets. In these moments, you must not escape it, but instead allow yourself to be with it.

We don't want a superficial light. We want a light that rises from the depths of the darkness—one that glows as a result of your soul's growth. In the womb of darkness, it is the universe begging you to be the cosmic child again. To float in the womb of the Great Mother, La Diosa, Ma, Mama. To float surrendered in the darkness, not knowing. There is nothing to do but be. Because we are conscious of those dark moments, we fear them; but what if we can add depth and understanding so that you can be comforted in this moment of darkness. There is a holiness in the dark womb of change. You are being stretched and grown, just as the embryo is nourished by their mother. And though you may be tempted, don't rush. Be with the rhythm of the lessons of your soul, for your soul is intelligent and there guiding you to the highest version that is specific and unique for you. How sacred you are, divine Diosa, to be guided by Source on a path that is just for you.

Learning to connect to your soul voice, to heal your soul wounds, and to come back home to Self and Soul—these are breakthroughs that can make every area of your life healthier, happier, and more aligned. In working with people for more than a decade, I have seen the power of this soulwork and the transformations that occur in people's lives. The first step is always the hardest, but if you are here, it's because you are ready.

Wherever you are on your journey—you are welcome to unpack your emotions and stay for the ride. To still yourself enough to hear the rumbling in your belly and daggers in your heart. Place your luggage, your coat, and the weight of the day to the side for just a moment, and come sit with me and chat, *pláticas del alma*—soul chats.

I am here to take you on a journey, to help you to heal the wounded soul and guide you back home to you—to the true you. I will help, alongside spirit, to untangle the webs of your pain, shame, and trauma. By sharing stories from my own life and those of other Diosa clients that I have had the honor of hearing and helping. We will do this by sharing songs, prayers, tools, and inquisitive questions. There is nothing off-limits when it comes to soul healing—let the soul guide the way for this journey. This is your time to heal. You deserve it.

In the book *Woman Who Glows in the Dark*, Elena Avila says that "Curanderas help to build up a person's energy system and self-esteem, and teach them how to break the vicious cycle of depression and hopelessness." This description depicts how I view this process of helping someone to heal their soul wounds. I help you build your energy, remind you of the power and magic that has always been within. Under ruins and fragmented pieces, but always there—the soul and the divine Diosa within awaits.

Who Is a Diosa?

Diosa is the Spanish word for Goddess. The Diosa is a representation of the Soul Self who sees with her spiritual sight and smells with her soul senses. She is deep and raw—broken and whole. She lives in two worlds simultaneously: the world of the day and the mundane, and the world of the night and the mystery of soul. *La Diosa* lives in between realms. She has access to the gates of the psyche's temple. She is resilient. Born of the ashes, she puts her bones back together piece by piece through it all—she always rises. And she doesn't just rise, she dances as she rises. Naked, raw, whole, free. She is the music in the beat, the elements of fire, water, air, earth. She is Shakti—primal core energy. She is snake in the spine, activated. She is MA, Mother. She is ready to do the soul-work required because she is satisfied only when living her deepest soul truth. She has always been and will always be. She is you, she is me, she is all.

A Diosa is willing to go deep and heal.

A Diosa rises from the ashes time and time again.

A Diosa is fierce and loving.

A Diosa is connected to her shadow and her light.

A Diosa is connected to her soul, and if she isn't, she won't stop until she comes home to her soul again.

Diosa goes beyond male or female. Diosa is about invoking the feminine energy that we all have. Cis male, cis female, transgender, gay, straight, nonbinary—all are welcome to use the word. For all can activate the Diosa energy within. Diosa is the primal core energy of the universe and is open to all. I will be writing and using words like *women* and *she*, but this is for all. Feel free to make this book your own and cross out pronouns as needed to make it yours! If you are here, you were guided here. Your soul brought you here. And so you too, are Diosa.

About This Work

Before we get started on this journey, I want to share how I approach healing and provide a framework for what's to come. I believe that too often, we go into the healing journey without understanding the context. There are many healers who have not earned their life initiation to guide others through soul reclamation work. It is deep and profound and dangerous if not done with skill, tact, integrity, and care.

There is an invisible bridge from this world of form and ego to spirit and soul. Both sides are necessary and sacred, and it can be a wonderful communication system if we are tuned in to both.

From a young age, I questioned the mundane and tried to reconcile it with little cosmic Christine. To me, humans seemed like robots—doing the same thing every day out of habit, without realizing there was more to life. I didn't know how children were going hungry when money was only a piece of paper. I understood from an early age that money was only money because we assigned that value to it. I knew on an intuitive level that children shouldn't ever go hungry because of a piece of paper. I questioned the mundane world constantly. At the same time, I was connected to aspects of my Boricua culture, which allowed me to tap into the world of "the more." I was taught, for instance, to share my dreams—I was taught by my mother and my *abuelita* that I call my Gega, that dreams hold medicine, warnings, healings, foreshadowings. They were considered sacred. I remember learning that whenever I had a bad dream, I should share it to make it less powerful, to understand it better. We would sit and analyze our dreams together. These moments allowed me to honor that my deep gut feeling—that the mundane world was not the only world that existed—was correct. The world of spirit too existed.

This call to heal came from the call of my soul, from the lineages of *curanderas* and healers in my family. It was only a few years ago that my mother shared with me that my maternal grandmother who is now in the Spirit realm, Maria Luisa Garcia, wore all white for me for a year before I was born. She had a baby-blue tassel around her waist. She did this as a "*promesa* with God" for me. It was a spiritual devotional practice to bless me. These practices live within me now. I am here because of the work of my ancestors. I am grateful for their work beyond words. I was blessed within this lifetime to be used by the divine to serve—becoming the hands and feet to help the divine do the sacred work. I don't do this work because I went to school and took workshops. That was only in response to the call from my soul.

Following that call led to my work as a licensed therapist, eventually focusing on trauma and abuse. It also led me to study more holistic approaches of spiritual wisdom, like energy work, meditation, tantra, and studies of the divine feminine—la Diosa—the Goddess. On an intuitive level, I felt that the clinical world was starved for soul and for more of a warm heart, and so I continued to explore the two.

I remember learning that the word *psychology* means "the study of the soul." I was shocked because I had never heard that in grad school, and I was relieved that there was more to this path than the study of the mind. I had always sensed that, but to finally know what the word meant was a powerful moment for me. Dr. Clarissa Pinkola Estés says: "The word *psychology* literally means the study of the life of the soul. The word *psyche* is derived from the ancient word *prushke*, which is related to both the image of *la mariposa*, the butterfly, and *la alma*, the Soul. The word is also related to the essence of the breath; in other words, to the animating force without which all of us would lie dead upon the ground. Psychology in the truest sense is not the study of behavior per se, but the study of the animating force."

And so I believe in a mind-body-spirit approach. I believe that it is not merely that your internal world affects the external world, but also that the external world impacts the internal world. I believe that things are deep and complex and multidimensional. I believe we know a lot and know nothing. I believe we can't place an affirmation over trauma; it must be untangled with support, reverence, patience, time, mourning, integrity, and counseling. I believe that our cultures have been severely ignored in this spiritual lexicon. I believe that sexuality has been deeply ignored and that the sexual energy that runs through us must be cherished and nurtured.

I don't believe that spiritual slogans like "Everything is a reflection of you" are healthy or provide the depth needed to help someone heal in a grounded and integrated way. I instead believe that as we heal the wounds and the daggers in the mind, spirit, and body—through dedication and soulwork—we become more whole and embodied. And in that space, we heal the subconscious and have a healthier life. I don't believe that everything that triggers you is just some unhealed part of you. Actually, I think that sometimes you just don't like a bitch because your intuition is telling you that there is something dangerous that actually does not reflect who you are. I don't believe that we need to escape the ego, for there are healthy ego functions that protect us. We need to embrace every nook and cranny and emotion, we must mourn and cry and bitch—to come back home, to the true soul whole you—reclaiming all the parts of self and soul.

I teach from a sisterhood level, as an *hermana*, a friend. I share my opinions and my experiences, and I pour passion in each word because it comes direct from my gut, from my yoni (vagina—sacred portal), my bones, *mis raices*. And still, I want you to know that your soul is in control. If something I say doesn't resonate, explore it, and trust that you know what is for you and not for you. There is no right and wrong. This is a journey for soul healing and returning to *your* true Soul Self state—that is beautiful and unique for you.

In my work, these are just some of the traditions, approaches, and teachings I pull from:

- Shamanism
- Tantra
- Cognitive behavioral therapy (CBT)
- Jungian therapy
- Culturally sensitive therapeutic approach
- Mindfulness-based cognitive therapy (MBCT)
- Somatic therapy
- Transpersonal therapy

This is a book about healing patterns of destruction, self-sabotage, soul wounds—and learning a real integrative approach to sustainable healing. Even without specifically calling out each one of these approaches (or the others I use in my work), know that they are all present.

Because, once again, I don't believe in quick fixes. I don't believe that life is about escaping life. I believe it is about flowing and "accepting life on life's terms," as they say in twelve-step rooms.

Healing is fucking hard, but I believe it's always, always worth it.

I say this all to say that depth matters and the ways of the soul go beyond words. So even as I share tools and techniques, please understand that there is not one way and all soulwork requires an individual path. I honor and cherish the healing of the psyche and soul, and to do my best to not reduce it to simply wrong vs. right, fear vs. love, or ego vs. soul. This path is the path of all things and all emotions. All of it is part of your soul's journey. The more real and raw you get, the deeper the healing of the soul wounds. So let's get raw and real and go to the core. You got this, boo.

How to Flow Through This Book

This book is meant to be a sacred companion. A Diosa's map to healing deep soul wounds, returning to true Self, to Soul Self, to your Diosa Divine Self. It is meant to share stories that inspire you, that sometimes warn you, and that always guide you to come back home to you. Through each chapter, I have included soul affirmations that are meant to soothe you and give you a centered point for your mind and heart to focus on. I also share resources from my own life and other resources that have supported the Diosa community throughout the years. On this journey we will need many sacred soul companions that help us. This is a "we" thing.

This book is about helping you heal the root of the pain, the trauma, the self-sabotage, and all the patterns that are blocking *you* from your *true self.*

You will also have soulwork in each chapter, which is essentially homework for your soul. They are deep inquiry questions designed to help you get to know your wounds and desires better. It is an opportunity for you to dive to the core of your psyche and soul and uncover what lies there. In the discovery, you can gain deeper insights into how you are feeling and what self-sabotage lives there, and connect the dots that will inevitably be a key in your transformation. Each soulwork is a companion to the chapter that you are reading. This way you are able to integrate the lessons in a practical way and have real-life results.

As Carl Jung said, "Who looks outside dreams; who looks inside, awakens." This is your time to look inside—to explore your innermost terrains of psyche and soul. To notice the quality of the soil in your heart and sex organs. To see where the shadow of shame lives and love up every single part of you. Give yourself permission to go deep and be raw and real. I always remind my clients that they are the only ones reading their soulwork unless they decide to share it—so gift yourself the gift of honesty. In Alcoholics Anonymous, they say that it is only through "rigorous honesty" that we can save our lives. And I couldn't agree more.

As we go along this journey, you will have aha moments and moments of questions and emotional purging. You will have new desires born on the other side of the purge. And one of the best ways that I have found to help you along the way is to write it down, old-school style, on pen and paper. I recommend getting a sacred journal that you dedicate to this process. Make it a ritual. The more heart and soul and intention you pour into the process, the deeper the healing goes. So let's go all out on this journey back home to self, to soul, and to our true divine Diosa selves. Give yourself the opportunity to get to know you and rise so that you can have the life that you deserve, based on your whole authentic badass self.

You deserve it, *mama*. The intention is to treat this book experience like a spiritual retreat. In essence it is a retreat in a book: a process, an unfolding, a learning and unlearning. This is a sacred pilgrimage.

Key Resources

Throughout this book, you'll find a wealth of resources to tap into and explore, but I also wanted to share some resources to start with so that you feel supported on this journey.

Meditation is a key part of this process. It is a time to be held and nurtured and to be able to tap into higher dimensions of spiritual support. Meditation is scientifically proven to help reduce anxiety and depression, and it is also a wonderful coping skill to add to your healing toolkit. Whenever you feel you want to be guided and reminded of peace, of centered groundedness, and a love bubble of comfort, I highly recommend listening to guided meditations. I have my guided meditations available on Simple Habit; simply search my name, "Christine Gutierrez," and get access to my meditations. There are also myriad other meditation guides there for you to explore.

I also encourage you to seek outside help from a trained and licensed therapist throughout this process, if needed, and especially if you have trauma. There is nothing more powerful than doing this work with someone who can help you process the feelings that come up. You can sign up for therapy either in person or online. A wonderful resource to find a therapist in your area is psychologytoday .com. A quick Google search with "licensed therapist" and the name of your country and state will also be useful. For those that are busy or prefer this form of teletherapy, I highly recommend trybetterhelp .com/cosmicchristine and Talkspace to find qualified and licensed therapists. And of course, if you ever feel suicidal or like hurting yourself or someone else, call 911 or the National Suicide Hotline (1-800-273-8255). It's always better to be armed with a suitcase of tools and resources than to not know. It's always better to have a prevention plan than wait until the depression hits to start researching. The National Suicide Hotline number is a free and confidential service available 24/7 and on holidays as well. I am so grateful for all these resources that have saved my life and so many people's lives around the world. Finally, I highly recommend joining the Diosa Tribe community. It is a place where you can connect with Diosas around the world doing this work and going along this book journey with you. The Diosa Tribe is a global community of like-hearted women that come together to heal, to share, to grow, to rise, and to lead. It is a sacred space to bask in the medicine of other dope, fierce women. Life gets chaotic and busy. It's hard enough to be a human in this busy world, but to be a woman (and even more to be a Latina woman/women of color), and a conscious woman is a lot! It isn't easy, but it's worth it to invest in our healing. The world is waiting for the unique truth that we have to offer. But we need the space to be loved up when we can't love ourselves. A space to be inspired and share our hard days and our biggest dreams. This is your place to get loved up and supported. You can find out more about this raw, powerful, transformational group of Diosas on my website: christineg.tv. It takes a village, let's build it together, Diosas.

Soulwork

Let's explore what I call "soul intentions," which will essentially be the north star for this journey. They might change or might not, but they give a starting point for the goals you want to experience on the other side of this process. Using your journal, write down your responses to the following questions:

1. Tell me a little more about yourself . . .
2. Tell me a little bit about your childhood, your life in general, and the main memories that you believe have impacted where you are today . . .
3. What do you know to be true in your gut about where you are in your life right now?
4. What is no longer working in your life?

5. What brings you here today, to this book and this healing journey?
6. What are three blocks and challenges that you are currently going through that have you tired and wanting to change?
7. What are three soul intentions or soul goals that you have for this journey?

Here are some examples of soul intentions from my clients:

- I want to learn to feel myself again and trust my gut.
- I want to truly love myself and get to know myself, the real me, again.
- I want to connect to my soul and spirituality and feel guided again.
- I want to heal the root of my toxic relationships and claim healthy relationships once and for all.
- I want to learn to own my voice and feel empowered to speak my truth and set boundaries when needed.
- I want to create new healthy coping mechanisms.
- I desire to feel self-confidence, self-assurance, and self-worth.
- I desire to heal my childhood trauma and the patterns that stemmed from it.
- I desire to let go of all the toxic relationships in my life and feel worthy of healthy relationships.

What a gift it is to do this work. Remember, Diosa, this is your soul journey. And the healing journey is unique for each soul. Take with you the qualities of gentleness and compassion—for they are key as you proceed. Encourage yourself for being here and reading this book. Because healing deep like this ain't for the fainthearted. And you, beloved, are blazing with a fierce heart. You have already taken a massive step by being here. The chapters will build on one another and support you in your soul's journey back home to soul, to self, and to your Diosa divinity. In the next chapter, we will explore how we have disconnected from our soul and how to reconnect. For it is here, in the world between worlds, that keys are given.

A woman that is connected to her soul heals not only herself, but the planet.

#iamdiosa

The Darkness: Exploring Trauma & the Original Wound

CHAPTER 1

A Return to Soul

"My child, where have you gone? I long for your presence. It's me, your soul. Where are you? Are you home in you? Or have you strayed away? I am here waiting for you. Calling you to me. You feel me, but you shun me. I am the wind in your ears, the rumble in your belly. I am here steering you home—the home beyond this world—the eternal—soul home. I will never forsake you. Return to me."

—Your soul

We go through life looking for the way back home to Self, Soul, and Diosa Divinity—whether we know it or not, we are looking and searching to reconnect to that place. It is an instinct that is within us from the time of our birth into this physical world. I think of it as the link between the spirit world and the physical world. This inner knowing that there is an internal soul home of sorts, that is the true place where we belong and come alive.

We often search in places that are ragged with thorned roses and swamps of lost souls. This isn't wrong or bad—for nothing on the soul path is about shaming what is wrong or right—it is instead about exploring what is true and honest for you as an individual soul on this earth. We must travel often far away to find ourselves, both on a practical note and on a spiritual note. I don't know if we can escape the initiation of leaving in order to come back home to ourselves.

The return to soul can be seen as a process of three archetypal phases. This isn't to say there aren't many other phases, but instead to highlight archetypal journeys that are similar overall, though they differ greatly from soul to soul.

Phase 1: The Departure from Soul
Phase 2: The Initiation
Phase 3: The Return to Soul

The phases of this process differ in content, but the form often remains the same. In many ways they are like the bones in one's body. The skeleton represents that which is the same in us all, but we all differ in how we look—our size, our skin color, our hair. These archetypal phases are ancient and consistent throughout time. They tell a story. They allow us to access a kind of soul map so that we may return back home to our true self and our soul self.

In this book, we will be accessing this three-phase healing and initiation back home to soul. It reminds me of the process that Joseph Campbell speaks to in his 1949 book *The Hero with a Thousand Faces*. Campbell refers to the hero's journey and the many phases and tests that one must go on in order to return to and be changed—alchemized from the old into the new.

This is how the energy of *la Diosa*, Shakti, the feminine primal energy, works with us. She is the skeleton, the archetypal story that can be found throughout the ages. The way she chooses to work with us may differ, but there are certain core principles that we can look to and understand that remain the same. *La Diosa* is ancient. The wild feminine call back home to soul has always been and will always be. She is the creatrix. The magic weaver.

The Departure Through the Return

The departure is when we leave the reality that we know into some new, unfamiliar, uncharted territory. There is a sort of soul call. The Soul Call to awaken and change and shift may come in the form of that ancient inner voice within, a traumatic relationship, past traumas, getting sick, accidents, losing someone you love, a moment in nature when you feel moved beyond this realm, through sex. The energy of *la Diosa* will present herself and make herself known.

The energy that I most work with is Kundalini Shakti—*Shakti* meaning the primal feminine energy of the universe. Just like the universe herself, magical and mysterious, so is the energy of Shakti. She is the great teacher and the wild mystery. I am always in awe of her medicine and magic. And when she calls us, she calls us into the unknown, into the dark womb where all is possible—the cosmic womb. And it is here where we can unlearn and learn who we truly are, who our Soul Self is. It is key to have faith and be patient here, for you are leaving all you know. This initiation requires surrender.

Campbell called this phase of the journey the Road of Trials because it is a challenging journey of transmutation and alchemy. This is the rigorous part of the soulwork. This is the part of the path where we must come face-to-face with our own Shadow, with the unknown, with the element of the mystery, with the wounded, unloved, unwelcome, and broken parts of ourselves. We also come to face the ones who stand at the gates. The ones that challenge us. We are met with spiritual tasks and missions that are laid before us. We must meet the ones that trick us on the journey to help us accomplish the spiritual mission. This mission is meant for us to win, but we must go in wise and awake and willing because some tasks are challenging. Not everyone makes it. But if you are radically honest and willing and committed, you will make it.

With the departure, we are stretched to grow in uncomfortable but necessary ways—taken apart like a puzzle to be put back together again with soul as the glue. The death and rebirth that happens within us becomes manifest in the external world as well. It starts within us, though, and it sticks when we do the necessary soulwork. The alchemical fire comes face-to-face with the downloads and conditioning of our childhood, of society, of the identities that we have acquired, of the defense mechanisms, and all the ways we show up in the world. And then the magic of the fire of alchemy and transformation is that it burns what no longer needs to be. From the growth, from the stretching, from the cracking open, we find the precious gems unique for each soul. Gems of hope, gems of growth, gems of consciousness, gems of individualization, gems of trust in oneself and soul voice, trust in Shakti Ma, the Divine Feminine, *la Diosa*, and a heart within that has broken open and pours forth love as never before. A life beyond our wildest dreams emerges from the ashes left by the fires. Kundalini Ma, Mama Diosa, provides everything that is needed to support us. As my tantra teacher Amma says, "The Mother always provides. You need not worry. Make time to do the work and show up, and she will provide the sweetness and the nectar."

Our initiation is complete when we return *home*, literally or symbolically, and arrive in our new life. I call this returning home to Soul. The Soul Home. Coming back home to our souls and our true Selves. Here, we come back transformed. We come back with new understandings and teachings. Here, we have shed old skins like a snake and have come back in soul skin.

It reminds me of my journey back home to myself after hitting my knees and knowing I needed a change with my relationship to alcohol. Going on a journey, getting help—both spiritual and human support, and finally returning home to myself, sober, happy, joyous, and free. I removed shame, I removed the darkness. I hit my knees and said, "My life is unmanageable." I didn't know for sure if

I was an alcoholic, but I knew I had a problem every time I drank, and I was willing to change. Through my journey, I was healed and made new. Along the way, I learned and applied the lessons, and it showed. This initiation allowed me to take off the glasses of pain and dead-end roads and instead put on the glasses of love and see and feel hope. The old life was transformed and made new. It was all there, and all of the parts of the journey were needed to bring me back home to me and to soul.

Then the integration of the initiations and its medicine occurs. There is an integration with self and soul. From this integration, a reemergence occurs.

There is a new soul skin and a new life in the world. This is the integration of the light and the darkness—the wholeness in moving form in the world.

I invite you back home to yourself. To unlock doors within you, for there your inner temple of majesty lives. To dive deep, knowing you are never alone, and that I am rooting and holding space for you, alongside the other Diosas and souls on this journey. I invite you to go to those shadows and places that might have been too much hassle to revisit, until now.

If at any point anything becomes too much, pause and remember that outside help, such as therapy, can be a wonderful tool to integrate along this process. This work is not meant to replace therapy. And if you read a chapter and it triggers a memory that is emotionally overwhelming, I encourage you to pause, breathe, ground, and perhaps bring it into your session instead so that you may be supported. As a licensed therapist, I highly recommend integrating therapy into your life. Therapy is a valuable resource when digging up bones of the past and doing this sacred healing work. You have the right to your own journey, and slow and easy might be your pace. Listen to your heart and your gut.

This work is about coming back to your soul and your truth. So often we spend our lives looking for peace in the wrong places . . . looking for ourselves in the wrong places, but ultimately we are looking for how to feel more whole, more complete, and more authentic with oneself and others—we just don't know where the true source lives, so we go on a hunt in all the places that it is not.

When we go inward, we can explore and navigate, recognizing the truth from the untruths within us. Noticing the patterns that are inside of us passed down from lineages of trauma and pain that are not ours to carry anymore. Each of those pieces of ourselves that have left us due to trauma. With this book, it is my intention that you begin to reclaim some of those pieces of yourself one day at a time. For once we reclaim those lost soul pieces, you become healthier and more whole and can see better. The veils are lifted. You begin to be who you were meant to be.

This process back home to self and soul reminds me of something my soul brother Yung Pueblo said: "Serious transformations begin with two commitments: the courage to try new things and act in new ways, and the honesty needed to no longer hide from or lie to ourselves."

This is your time to no longer lie or hide, but instead to reveal and heal.

In *I Am Diosa* we will explore the parts of you that you have lost—that have been taken away, reclaiming the soul pieces, and reconnecting to the primal feminine essence within—Shakti, Diosa energy to heal you and guide you. You will be guided to untangle those parts of you that are knotted to release the stored energy within each block. In doing so, you will learn practical tools and more ancient wisdom tools that you can take with you throughout this journey called life. This book is meant to be practical and real because life gets real. It's not meant to spiritually bypass our problems, world politics, or the deep complexities of healing real traumas. But it is meant to say that no matter what, we deserve to heal—not by escaping the realities, but instead by embracing and understanding the realities that have occurred to us and around us so that we may heal from the root up.

Starting the Journey

Let us step into the Unknown, where everything begins . . . the initiation.

Take a moment to pause.

Inhale. Place your left hand on your heart and your right hand on your belly or sexual organs. Perhaps close your eyes if you are able to or simply soften your gaze. Feel into your body and this moment. Inhale through your nose, feeling life force enter your body and letting the breath dance through your cells and every nook within your flesh and bones. Count 1-2-3. Keep it in. Then exhale it all out through your mouth with whatever sound wants to come out of you. Continue to do this, breathing in—feeling connected to the source, Shakti, that lives in the breath. Hold the breath. Count 1-2-3. Exhale through your mouth. Count 1-2-3-4-5, allowing it all to flow through you. With each exhale, see if you can soften your body. Relax your forehead. Let your tongue rest in your mouth. Let your shoulders drop away from your ears. Allow yourself to surrender and come back home to yourself.

Now pause and see where you are. Take a moment to scan your body and notice how you feel. We think we are always here in ourselves, but sometimes we aren't. At times we are far away from ourselves. Far away from our body. Far away from our emotions. Far away from our soul. And when we are far away from ourselves, we don't know who we are, and if we don't know who we are, we can't know who we become in the world—and who we want next to us. The closer we come back to our soul self, the more soul-aligned our lives become.

And so, when we breathe with this intention of coming back home to ourselves, we begin to unlock the door.

I am so grateful you are here, *Diosa*. Wow. I have dreamed of this day. During teary nights, acting out and hitting up that asshole guy yet again, there was an inner voice that knew that beyond the chaos existed peace. I heard that inner voice say:

1. There is more to life than this.
2. You deserve more.
3. As you heal deeper, you will help others heal deeper.

That was my soul voice calling out to me.

To be honest, I still can't believe it. And at the same time, I can, because I wouldn't stop putting in the work and getting help. But the truth is in the beginning of the journey, I didn't know for sure that this day would come. I stepped out with faith, knowing that anything would be better than what I was living. I was desperate for change. Terrified but desperate. Seeing myself fall and get back up again and fall and repeat the same mistakes was discouraging, to say the least.

I had this vision of healing myself and being empowered and healing others, but I couldn't quite get there. I desired more than anything to feel good and make loving choices for myself and others, but I wasn't able to at the time. My self-esteem and the downloaded blueprints of what love was for me were all fucked up.

But I did it, one day at a time. And as we start this journey, I encourage you to do this one day at a time. Sometimes, one moment at a time.

There are certain principles to remember as you go on this journey. Because how we approach the process is sometimes even more important than the process itself.

1. Be open-minded.
2. Be openhearted.

3. Be compassionate to yourself.
4. Practice loving self-talk.
5. Trust that there is more peace and joy and freedom on the other side of the pain.

And if you can't believe any of these things quite yet, that's okay: Let me believe it for you and let the countless other women who have risen from the ashes be your roots and your support. Stand knowing that your ancestors and all the women who have passed through this journey are rooting for you.

You are supported and held, Diosa.

This is our space to gather energetically and connect on this spiritual journey back home to soul and self. This is our chance to get raw and messy, and to share the real things that live within us, including the shame that comes with that. For so long, I craved the permission to share in this way and to hear others share as well, so I could know that I wasn't alone.

And so, before we begin, I want to share key things that have impacted me so we can get to know each other, and I want to hear from you too. Please visit my website to find out more about the Diosa Community: christineg.tv.

By connecting and coming together as a community and sisterhood, we can shed light on all the darkness as we make our way through this journey together. Let's begin.

The Soul Call

We have all heard it (and if you haven't, I promise you will if you listen close enough). The soul call. This call is a deep internal call. It is a siren from the soul, beckoning for you to come back home to your truth, to your worth, to your peace, to your serenity, to your health, to your soul, to your divinity.

It is sometimes a whisper within you, a gentle nudge that you feel in an inspired moment.

Some of us hear a loud voice telling us, "Leave that relationship," "Give up drinking," "Quit that job," or "There has to be more than this."

For others, it is a bodily sensation, a rumbling in the middle of the night when we least expect it.

Sometimes it needs to speak through others because we are too removed to see or hear anything other than the suffering we are in. In that case, it can take the form of someone else saying, "Hey, I think your soul is trying to tell you something."

This soul call is there to save you. It is there to guide you. It is the compass through the shady and scary parts of the forest that are inhabited by characters that seek to harm you. Your soul voice warns you when needed and encourages you toward the good, always.

Your soul voice is ancient and placed within you from the divine. The soul call pulls you toward the good, toward your truest self.

The soul call is what saved me. Remembering that my soul was in charge saved me. The voice of the divine within me, which lived beyond what my current life and actions were doing, and managed to survive through it all, that was what saved me.

I heard the call many times and ignored it. Perhaps you can relate. I would hear it and be like, "Not now, girl, I am too busy getting a hit of love from this toxic relationship that does not serve me at all but feels so much better than the loneliness I will feel when I let it go. *So no*, not now. Leave me alone."

When you ignore it, that inner voice fades, but it always remains.

Eventually, I listened to that voice. It isn't that I heard it once and it all got better. *Nope!* I wish. I would hear it, pay attention for a little bit, and then relapse. I would go back to that fucked-up drug dealer or the job I promised myself I wouldn't go back to anymore. The voice would tell me to run when I got into an abusive relationship (again), or get sober, or to look at my codependency issues. It was a constant up and down.

In a lot of ways, that was the theme of my life: breaking promises to myself. I was incapable of taking care of myself, and often did just the opposite. I put myself in massive danger, both emotionally and physically, because I just didn't love myself. I thought I did, but I didn't. My inner darkness and pain were on the hunt for their matching eternal darkness. On the outside, I had many things that were going fine, so it was hard to see just how much pain I was in. It would be good for a while and then it would all crash and burn. But then I would forget how bad it was and go back out there and do the same shit all over again. I had become a pro at lying to myself. I had become a pro of living a double life. Sometimes it's easier when everything has gone to shit because it's harder to lie to the self. But for me, my double life had me hiding behind the façade, the front—that some things were okay—but I was crashing, crumbling, spiritually dying. That's the danger of emotional pain, it can hide—but only until it can't. Eventually it became too much. Either I would live in chaos for the rest of my life or I would finally admit to myself that I had a problem and I wanted more. I was scared to be alone. I was scared to do the work. But I could not keep going the way I was going. I felt that I was going to die—either literally or spiritually—but either way, death was looming over me. The scent of dead carcasses and black ravens flying over me. I was irresponsible with my life; placing myself in dangerous situations was wearing me down. The façade of the double life started to crash. The chaos and pain were starting to bleed everywhere. I was exhausted, and it was actually my exhaustion that saved me. I was so tired of lying. So tired of keeping my front up. So tired of hiding and lying. I didn't have the energy anymore. Not having the energy and being at my wit's end was actually a positive thing. 'Cause it got me to be honest with me. I wasn't okay and I needed help.

So many times, the façade keeps us blocked. It keeps us keeping up with the frame of things instead of looking at the content within it. This soul life is about the content in the frame, not the frame. It is not about projecting perfection or lying to fit a mold. It is about being real—even if that means things have to get messy first.

Remember that the ego will have you think that when you are getting honest about how shitty things are or how unhealthy things have become, it means you are taking a step back. It will have you try to cling to the comfort of "faking it," "keeping it together," and keeping up the illusion of "I'm fine," but when you are making soul shifts, things might get harder before they get easier.

Let's say you have a beautiful big apartment with a toxic partner. You hear your soul say, "It's time to leave." You know that financially you will have to go to your parents for a bit till you get back on your feet. Your inner critic might tell you, "Look at you, look at your age, look at how pathetic you are, moving back in with your parents. You are going backward." The form was previously prettier, but the content there was rotten—your soul was rotten, the love was rotten, the content was empty. In this case, you leave, and the form may appear less "together," less big, less attractive, but your soul is aligned. Living in your parents' home is filled with soul, and thus the content is full of healing.

Be aware that the way of the soul is always concerned with the truth behind the form. The soul is concerned with the content. Focus on what is soul aligned and you will be guided.

Little by little, things started to stick. Every time I would listen to my soul voice, my life got better, and the voice got louder and stronger. On the outside, things got messy. I was single, I was more emotional, I was no longer keeping it together. But the content of my life was shifting—it was no longer a lie. Truth had become my new priority. Slowly, it became easier to notice when I was in alignment with my soul and my truth, and when I was stuck in a pattern, a story, or a harmful situation. I could observe the situation and work my way out of it.

The soul call is like a siren that guides us back home to ourselves. And as we are guided back home to ourselves and our souls, we heal in our bones. That's what you'll do as you read this book.

This journey is about getting real and raw and accessing parts of our psyche and soul. It is about exploring our lives and seeing the fragmented or injured parts and repairing them.

It's not easy to go there, but it's harder to live a life that's out of alignment with the soul.

If you're here, it's because some part of you desires the healing that is possible for you. It is messy and difficult to go to those places we often want to forget, but it's always worth it. There are massive miracles and healing transformations beyond the wound that needs tending.

These emotional wounds are no different from the wounds we have on our physical bodies. If we get a cut on our skin, we must clean it and let it heal and scab and repair. Some wounds are deeper than others, and yet all deserve to be cleaned and tended to.

You have doors that open when you tend to your wounds.

Your wound is a door.

Your trauma is a door.

Your addiction is a door.

That toxic relationship is a door.

Your fear is a door.

Your secret is a door.

Your anxiety is a door.

Your desires are a door.

These doors lead to healing, new beginnings, deeper knowing of soul and self, and thus others and life itself.

Our emotional wounds often stay hidden because we can't see them with our physical eyes; instead, they play out in self-destructive ways. It can show up as feeling shut down, numb, frazzled, or lost. It can look like overeating, overspending, overdrinking, overdrugging, overfucking. It can come through in relationships that destroy the soul and the Self.

And so I invite you on this journey. On this journey, we say, "No more! I am ready to look at the wounds and ready to do the work to access my healing."

This book was created with the intention to empower you and remind you of you—the true you. This book is a chance to reconnect you to your soul and your divinity. It will lead you to a deep-down-in-your-bones type of unshakable worth.

Remember, though, this is not a race. This process of healing is lifelong. Be easy on yourself and be gentle as you travel inward and back out and in again.

This reconnection to your soul and primal self is your birthright. You deserve it. Your soul is within you and around you. The healing has begun. The remembering started. The doors opening.

As you begin this book, play the song "Shedding Skins" by Fia. You can find this on my Spotify list, but if you can't access the Internet, below are the lyrics to the song. Sing them to yourself in whatever hymn comes to you.

Fia, "Shedding Skins"

I am open I am free
And my life is breathing me
As I surrender to the will of the Divine
No more stories of the past
I am shedding skins at last
And I realize I'm already in Heaven
The moment I stop running from the demons in my head
And instead I choose to love them
When saying yes to life both shadow and light

My suffering is done and I come alive
I am born and I will die
By each breath, a final sigh
It doesn't matter where I go, I cannot hide
But when I find my sense of peace
I can walk through Hell with ease
I might fall a thousand times but I shall rise
And the moment I stop running from the demons in my head
And instead I choose to love them
When saying yes to life both shadow and light
My suffering is done and I come alive
I want to feel it all
I wear my heart on my sleeve, saying
Here I am, can you see me?
Oh I am beautiful and fucked up, in the most glorious way
When standing in my truth, who cares what people say
'Cause the moment we stop running from the demons in our heads
And instead we choose to love them
When saying yes to life both shadow and light
Oh, our suffering is done and we come alive
Oh, the moment we stop running from the demons in our heads
And instead we choose to love them
When saying yes to life both shadow and light
Oh, our suffering is done and we come alive
Oh, the moment we stop running from the demons in our heads
And instead we choose to love them Oh when saying yes to life
both shadow and light Oh, our suffering is done and we come alive

It has been said that as we sing, we pray ×3. Let's sing over ourselves today. The bible says, "In the beginning was the word." For
me this means that *words* are powerful; they can bring life or death
energy over us. As we sing songs of love and speak words from *la*

alma, the soul, we bring life back into ourselves. We heal our wounds. I consider myself a spiritual archeologist, helping to guide you in digging up the bones of the past and uncovering what lives within the hidden realms of the subconscious and within you. As we dig and discover what lives there, we access the medicine we have been waiting for. Let's get digging.

What are the blocks that are currently showing up in your life? Where are you feeling lost, hurt, confused?

I encourage you to write down the blocks. Then, write down the desires that live on the other side of them. Let's pick three. I love the number 3; there's something magical about it.

For example: I feel like I lost myself in my last relationship. It broke me. It was toxic and I don't know who I am.

The intention on the other side of that would be perhaps: I desire wholeness and to love and honor myself completely.

Another example can be: I feel stuck with my self-esteem being so low.

The intention on the other side of the block might be: I am confident and allow myself to be seen and loved and honored.

Now your turn: What desires and intentions live on the other side?

These soul intentions may change, but this gives you a starting point and allows you to know where you are going in this soul healing journey. It is like a compass beginning to point you to the healing and reclaiming of parts of you that have been lost. This is your soul's wisdom guiding you.

This is a type of meditation, this self-inquiry: to go inward and explore what parts are torn, fractured, scarred, and hurting. We can tend to ourselves like a garden, seeing the parts of us that are ready to die, and from that death, new life is born. For we are part of nature, and as we allow the cycles to move back into their natural state, rhythm flow returns.

Soulwork

Let's set a baseline for this work, as you embark on this journey. Using your journal, write down your responses to the following questions:

1. What are the top three blocks you're experiencing right now?
2. What are the desires and intentions on the other side?
3. In order to get to those desires, what in you must die for something new to be reborn?
4. What within you needs to be shed?
5. What hurts within you that needs love?
6. Where is there stagnation that is begging for new life to be poured over it?

Mantra

I listen to the soul voice calling me home.

Ceremony

Creating a Diosa Soul Altar

An altar is a special location where you place your spiritual totems and items. It is a space of reverence, a place for pause, prayer, and connecting to spirit. This will stand as a spiritual center in your home. A place for focusing, centering, and connecting. I highly recommend that on this journey, you begin by adding this element to your home. You can even have a "traveling altar" so that you may travel and find a moment to connect to your spiritual center even when you are away from your physical home. The altar, in essence, is your spiritual home.

This has been such a pivotal part of my spiritual practice and ritual. It is where I begin and end my days. You can get as creative as you want with your Diosa Soul Altar. This is absolutely unique for each person and should be a place that lights you up and makes you feel calmer by being around it. Some keys in creating your soul altar are:

1. Find a special place in your home. It should be a place that is clean and sacred for you. You can place it somewhere that you feel you will be able to connect with it easily. Some of my favorite places to have my altar are in my bedroom and in my living room. Have your altar elevated off the ground; I usually use a section of my dresser.

2. Have a theme or intention behind the altar. You can change it depending on your needs, desires, the moon phases, or specific times in your life. I recommend constantly refreshing the energy by tuning in to your needs with your soul altar. A theme for this journey perhaps is: healing core soul wounds, connecting to the voice of soul, and boosting self-worth. This can be your Diosa Soul Altar, that you dedicate to this healing journey.

3. Find sacred objects that are special and meaningful for you. I love this part of the creation process. Creativity heals. Let yourself find flowers or leaves on your walk. Buy your favorite incense (being mindful to use herbs that are not endangered) and place a bowl of water, perhaps blessed holy water from your local Botanica, or bless it yourself by praying over the water and saying something as simple as "I bless this water in the name of the divine. May it serve to heal me and clear me and connect me to my soul's highest destiny. And so it is." Another idea is to place photos of family members that are living or that have passed that mean something to you. You can also place photos of spiritual beings or angels that mean

something to you. For example: Jesus, Mother Mary, Mary Magdalene, Archangel Miguel, Santa Clara. When you do this, you bring in their divine support to the earthly plane. In addition, you can place crystals, seashells, powerful words in a frame, books, poetry, feathers, candles, and so on. This truly is your creative playground, so allow yourself to be guided in creating this Diosa Soul Altar for your sacred spiritual journey.

Great work going to the core. In many ways you are now a spiritual archeologist—digging up bones of your past—and uncovering stories from your life. As we do this, we navigate our inner landscapes. Next, we will go to the root. You will explore the blueprints that you downloaded from childhood, so that you know what messaging you were modeled—that no longer works. In this process, I will guide you to become aware of how those messages affected your psyche, your soul, and your way of relating to self and others. When you see the scripts that you learned, you learn to unlearn and change the script. Stay open to your process, for though the process is often grueling, there is medicine in every step of the journey.

Remember to come home to
your soul when you go astray.
Your soul shows you the way.

#iamdiosa

CHAPTER 2

Getting to the Root of It

"The wound is the place where the light enters you."

—Rumi

In the next few chapters, we will explore the root of it all. We will explore your core wounds. We will explore the blueprints that you downloaded as a result of those soul wound experiences. For as we connect the dots, we begin to see patterns. As human beings, we all have patterns: some which are healthy, and others which are not healthy and no longer serve us. The patterns that are healthy can stay, but the patterns that cause you harm must be healed and reprogrammed. We want patterns that allow for growth, alignment with self, and a life that leads to freedom, joy, connection to the wild primal healthy feminine, and peace.

The truth is that our patterns become ingrained, and when they become ingrained, we must learn to reprogram them. We have been born into a world where suffering exists. Many times, we learn these patterns from our family of origin. We learn to cope in ways that aren't actually helpful, but that perhaps were needed due to the home life that you grew up in. This can lead to maladaptive behaviors, which are behaviors that aren't helpful and stop you from adjusting in a healthy way to your environment and situations. Some examples of maladaptive behaviors are:

- substance abuse
- attention-seeking behavior
- sex addiction
- love addiction
- aggressive outburst
- workaholism
- Internet addiction

These patterns usually stem from a wound that is begging to be healed but has been covered up, avoided, shunned, or numbed. Here, we are saying: No more. "I will no longer avoid that which needs to be seen and healed."

And remember, as you move through this work, that you are not alone. I am here with you, holding your heart and rooting you on this journey back home to loving you. What I know for sure is this: You must get to the raw, messy, dark root of the pain in order to alchemize and heal it. As a therapist and as a woman that has risen from the ashes, I know that it isn't easy to talk about these things. It's hard to face the parts of us that hurt. However, it is in these exact places where we must look. Why? Because when we don't look to these original wounds, they run the show. The wound then becomes the driver of your life. That can't be good, right?

Imagine a literal wound, a bloody scab driving a car. A wound doesn't even have eyes! Definitely not cute and not a good idea. Your wound won't get you to your destination safely, but your eyes will. As we heal, we lift the veil of illusion off our eyes. We begin to see with spiritual sight.

I invite you to use your spiritual eyes to view this story. Allow yourself to explore as a spiritual archeologist. You are exploring your life story to uncover the parts of your psyche that need some loving.

You are strong and brave, my love. If you are here, you have survived. I have survived too. And those with scars to share their lessons learned are the bravest of all. Let's dive deep, explore your story, and start this amazing and transformative journey.

Diving deep and getting honest is hard, and yet it is empowering and necessary work.

One way to get deep and honest is to reveal your shadow "dark words," and instead of running from it, lean in to it. Embrace it.

The Shadow is what we cannot easily see about the Self. It is also known as the "disowned self" and the unexamined or disowned parts of our personality. Carl Jung said, "To become conscious of it involves recognizing the dark aspects of the personality as present and real. This act is the essential condition for any kind of self-knowledge." For it is running from the wound that grows it and leaning in to learn and love it up that heals it. This is a technique that I have incorporated in my Diosa Retreats and has provided deep insights for hundreds of women around the world. It is my gift to you here in this book to meet your shadow word.

On the next page, you will find a list of words in the shape of an infinity symbol. Instead of choosing a word from your mind, I want you to trust in the guidance of your soul. Soften your gaze so that you aren't able to read the words on the page. Place your finger or pen on the symbol and gently trace around it, like a sigil, which is a magical symbol imbued with power. Do this ten times, as you breathe deeply. Stop when you feel ready. Wherever your finger or pen has landed, you have found your shadow word. Remember that this isn't who *you* actually are. This is meant to highlight the area that has perhaps been hidden in the shadows and that has been running the show.

Work with this shadow word and reflect on how it has a part of your life. Understand that as you do this, you are facing the shadow and this is a pivotal moment for the deepest kind of healing.

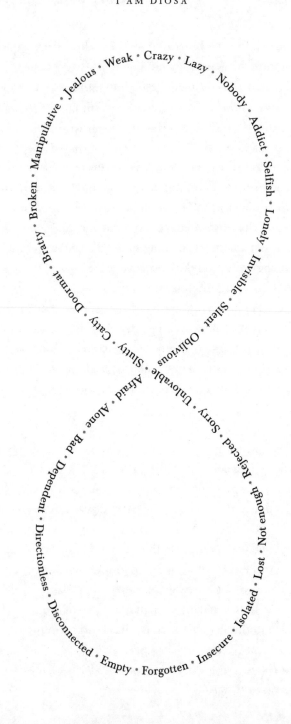

I wrote the following words one day when I was feeling down and depressed about the soulwork that I still had to face: "Real self-love requires you to meet your shadows face-to-face." Real self-love is looking inward at the things that no longer work. Allow yourself to work with your shadow throughout this journey. Release the shame and instead embrace that which has been trying to run the show. What you embrace and face, you deeply heal. Give yourself a moment to ask yourself, "How has this shadow word shown up in my life?" "How do I relate with this word?" Journal your thoughts as you reflect. This is the real self—love. Embracing the shadows leads to the light.

Your Tikkun

In exploring the patterns, maladaptive behaviors, and wounds present in our lives, we encounter the one particular wound that is our greatest wound, one that continues to come back time and time again. In Jewish mysticism, they call this tikkun: that which you came to earth to repair. You know your tikkun because it is a pattern that continues to repeat itself over and over. In Hebrew, the word *tikkun* means fixing or rectification. So, essentially, your soul comes into your body to have a spiritual and human experience, and part of this experience is to recognize the tikkun that you were born with and that you are therefore meant to repair or heal. There is medicine and light hidden in the broken parts. Brokenness in some ways is required for us as humans, woundedness is required for us as humans; instead of fearing it, let us own it and embrace it, finding our brokenness and woundedness so that we may love it up and heal it.

So, what is your tikkun? What is one of the main negative patterns that you have seen in your life? Let's say you have really fucked-up relationships, that you have gone through many relationships, and time and time again, you see that they are not healthy or happy. What is the fear underneath this pattern? Perhaps it is "I am deeply scared to be alone. I am scared to be abandoned. I feel unloved." In this case, healing requires learning to be alone, to love yourself, to feel safe with the arms of the divine and not rest your worth and protection and safety in the arms of a man or a woman. To feel loved within yourself would then be one of your soul missions.

Some people say that they have no trauma, that nothing big and terrible ever happened to them, and so there are no wounds that they carry around with them. The truth is that we all have trauma, we all have wounds—some are just deeper or bigger than others, more obvious. Whether they travel with us from childhood or other major events, they live within us, affecting our work, our relationships, and other aspects of our lives. Regardless of how big or small these wounds are, we all deserve to explore our inner emotional terrain so that we can have more choice in life rather than a life full of reactions.

The beautiful thing about this is that as we begin to make conscious choices to repair the wound, we access more light. In essence, we access the fallen sparks of light.

Let us uncover your wounds to access the fallen sparks of light.

Wound Exploration

Our root wound is usually a wound from childhood. This is something that takes away a piece of our soul essence or in therapeutic words—that impacts our self-esteem and sense of self. This wound influences our choices and how we perceive ourselves and the world, and it generally comes from our parents or primary caregivers.

Our original love wound is oftentimes where we download our love blueprint. Our love blueprint becomes the map by which we choose how we view ourselves and how we view love and relationships. If we have a dysfunctional or traumatic experience around love as a child, it will highly impact and influence our relationships as an adult. The love wound also gives us access to other wounds, and so it is a powerful place to start.

I know that it's sometimes difficult for people to understand some of the concepts I delve into in this book, starting with their "greatest wound." It can feel abstract or out of grasp, something that you know holds the key, but you aren't even sure what it unlocks. Because of that, I want to share my greatest wound and my process of discovering it by catching myself in a pattern over and over again.

For most of my life, I tried everything possible to escape the flesh and bones of myself. The burden of feeling the pain of my traumas was too much to bear. I didn't know it at the time, though. I wasn't conscious of the desire to not be in myself, but it was showing up all over the place.

Mr. M was the campus bad boy, and I had picked him. It happened so fast. From crush to crushed. "You're just a fucking slut." "You just like attention, just like your slut friends."

I abandoned myself in the hopes that by conquering *him* I would somehow feel good enough—then and only then would I feel complete in myself. He was my obsession, and the pursuit of him loving me became my only goal.

We were in college, though I can't remember what year, because being with Mr. M was all a blur. I went back so many times that it all started to become a strange nightmare. While I created a show of pretending to leave him, I was plotting how to stay. I felt like a piece of shit, stuck in a hellhole of getting him to love me like I always dreamed of being loved.

Have you ever looked at a fire pit right before the fire is about to go out? That was me, maybe one spark left, but slowly fizzling out.

I went to his phone, and with every single text I read, I felt more and more powerless, like I was falling into a pit of lava. I was burning with fury but also felt weak.

Even as I read through their exchanges and sweet emojis, I

wasn't just upset that he was cheating, but that it meant I had to put on another show. I would have to show my anger and pretend to break up with him, when I knew that I wouldn't actually leave. Because leaving meant facing reality, and I much preferred to live in fantasy.

It was the most fucked-up feeling in the world: to know I should leave and feel completely and utterly incapable of loving myself enough to do it. My fear had me stuck, and the more he fucked up, the more I felt I needed to stay. When I was in fantasy mode, I didn't have to face the deep wounds that were oozing and festering. Reality made me have to deal with shit that I was just unequipped to fix at the time.

When he came home after selling weed and making deliveries, I was sitting in his room with the proof. I started yelling.

He remained calm. He told me the girl was crazy and nothing happened. Slowly, I started to doubt all the proof I had just seen. Slowly, I started to doubt my gut instinct. I wanted to believe his lies because the truth was too hard to face.

My inner voice was yelling even more loudly than I was: "Lie to me, please! Lie to me so I don't have to leave you. Lie to me so I don't have to be alone with me. Convince me that I'm wrong. Convince me that my gut is wrong. I'm too weak to leave. Convince me that you're telling the truth, so I don't have to face me."

Desperation filled me and encouraged me to stay.

Time and time again, I stayed. The evidence of him cheating faded. The objective of confronting him faded. My new mission became to make things peaceful as fast as possible so I could justify staying with him again.

I wasn't ready to leave. I couldn't.

Never in a million years did I think I would end up on the floor of an apartment, begging him to take me back. But I did.

"Please, let's stop the drama. Let's make it work. We can do it.

Let's do it. Stop fucking up." It wasn't anything different from the love that I saw growing up.

I started to make the connections to my childhood. I was brought back to my original primal wound. My first heartbreak: when my dad left us. And then other wounds began to flood my memory. The food shoved in my face, the pillow over my mouth when I wouldn't get up in time for school, the broken doors, the name-calling, the abuse.

The year was 1989. Tears rolled down my face rapidly, like a waterfall after a day of strong rains. "PLEASE! PLEASE! DON'T LEAVE ME!" I thought if I shouted louder or if I begged more, it would somehow make him change his mind. I thought that if I cried with more conviction, I could touch the right strings on his heart and inspire him to stay. My heart was beating out of control. My nerves felt as though they were being electrocuted. I was no longer safe in my body. I was no longer safe in my world. I was terrified. "I want my daddy!" I screamed. "I WANT MY DADDY!" The door closed and my world changed forever. I yelled for months after my father left.

My heart was broken in that moment. My world of safety shattered at age four. Stuffed animals and lullabies were not able to soothe the void of my father leaving our home.

I shoved my feelings away, convincing myself that I had it good. This was way better than the other little Latina girls on Hart Street—their daddies left for good. Theirs were in jail or in another country with another family. My daddy just left the house, but he was still in my life. I tried to convince myself that it wasn't so bad, but my shattered heart would rattle in the silence of the night, reminding me that I was still heartbroken. My heart longed to feel whole. How ironic: I grew up on Hart Street, the street where my heart first broke.

Mr. M was a replay of my first heartbreak with my dad. Both

love *and* abuse were common in my home. There, I was also called a slut and stupid. I was constantly scolded for things that would be small to someone healthy, but to an angry parent unable to process their emotions, it was the perfect reason to act out and make me feel like I was nothing.

I remember being eight years old, doing homework and using an eraser that had left a red mark. I was an A+ student, but nothing could escape the wrath. My homework was ripped up into pieces. He didn't like that the eraser left a red mark. Even as I write this, I cry. I remember being in shock. "I didn't do anything wrong. Why are you ripping my homework?! I am a good girl. I do good in school. What did I do so wrong?!" I was terrified, angry, and confused, feeling like I was in a weird alternate universe. A part of me knew that it was wrong for him to do this, and yet I was stuck, powerless, a young girl who had no choice but to soak up the abuse.

I was taught that I didn't deserve patience. I didn't deserve healthy communication. I didn't deserve support. And I was especially taught that I didn't deserve respect.

Mr. M reminded me of home. It felt familiar to my nervous system, so I knew how to endure the heartache.

That image left a startling imprint on my psyche; fear imprinted in my nervous system.

I learned a few key messages from that original love wound:

1. I am not safe!
2. People leave me because I am unlovable.
3. If I beg enough, maybe he will stay in my life.
4. Relationships aren't safe.
5. I am unworthy of love and respect.

I let this inner script run my life and my relationships for years. I let that inner voice dictate all the choices I made. It was as if that little four-year-old girl on the floor begging and pleading for her daddy to come back home was the one calling the shots in my teens and twenties. The aching void inside me felt so scary to sit with that I became obsessed with filling it at all costs, no matter the consequences. I just wanted the pain to go away. I wanted the aching loneliness to stop. I wanted the fear to subside, and I did just about anything in an attempt to make the wound stop bleeding.

I share my love wound because I want you to know you are not alone. We all have a story. Our stories are filled with darkness, light, and many shades in between. What is your love wound? What are the key messages that you learned? It is behind this wound that the gem of your deepest and most profound healing is found.

What we keep in the dark grows like mold. The darkness loves when you ignore it, because that is where the darkness thrives . . . in the shadows . . . away from the light. It is common to numb from it, to run from it, to try and escape it, but all this does is replicate the wound with new people, new situations, and new interactions because you are not healing the wound.

The moment you begin to explore these forgotten stories, these painful memories, these experiences tucked away, that is the moment you can begin to heal them.

What we feel into, we can heal.

Working with Difficult Emotions

Since we are all energetic beings, we are most definitely affected by our emotions. We must begin to become completely aware of our emotions and recognize what and who affects them. We must become spiritual archaeologists: exploring and digging into the depths of our psyches and spirits to see what is there. Once we become more familiar with our inner emotional terrains, we are able to flow with the emotions without resisting, suppressing, or acting out on difficult emotions. We learn to work with our emotions instead of against them.

The first step is to recognize that difficult emotions are a natural part of life. Difficult emotions include sadness, anger, jealousy, abandonment, fear, despair, loss of hope, and betrayal. Let's not demonize these emotions by calling them bad. Difficult emotions are just *different* emotions than happiness, peace, confidence, and joy. All emotions have their own medicine and texture.

Roger Walsh, a professor of psychiatry, philosophy, and anthropology, says that we have three major errors in how we respond to difficult emotion:

1. judging or condemning difficult emotions as bad or evil
2. ignoring or defensively pushing painful emotions out of awareness
3. indulging or inflaming them, for example, by nursing feelings of resentment toward someone who hurt us and gleefully plotting revenge

By doing this, we become shackled and led by the emotions. We trap ourselves in a hellhole of emotions, where instead we could honor them, work through them, and process them. When we do so, we allow them to pass through us. Judging them, ignoring them, or indulging in them *traps* the negative emotion within our body, heart, and mind. We don't want that, do we? We must learn to be more mindful and more artful in our response to our emotions so that we can be the emotionally intelligent and psychologically savvy people that we are meant to be. The key here is that if we continue hoping and praying for life's ups, downs, and struggles to go away, we will be painfully disappointed, because life changes just as nature does. Like nature, we have our seasons—emotional states and stages in our life, each with a different temperature, affecting us in different ways. Even though we are more sophisticated creatures, we are nevertheless part of nature and subject to having life change on life's terms. We can choose to accept the ebbs and flows of life. In accepting our emotional seasons, we will have healthier expectations and thus a healthier relationship with life. Our emotional health depends on our ability to work with our difficult emotions. Learning to do so will bring many blessings to our lives.

Fear and anger are like the monsters of the psyche when you don't know how to work with them. They come out from the dark and scare you. The fearful voice is cunning and convincing. It even sounds rational and wise at times. But underneath it is an energy of anxiety when you really tune in. Just as a child is often scared of the dark and of the monsters in the closet and under their bed, we too are often scared of the monster of fear and anger. After all, we aren't usually taught to cope in a healthy way with these feelings.

Emotions are not the big bad wolves, but our response to them often is. Let's explore fear and anger so we can learn to more healthily respond to these emotions.

Fear gives us many signals, some of which begin in our body. We feel a queasy stomach, tightness, perhaps anxiousness, we freeze, our hearts race, we get sweaty palms or cold palms. All of these are natural responses to fear; they are intended to protect us from harm. Much of our life is dedicated to running in fear of getting hurt. Fear can sometimes make us feel as if we are dying, when in reality the only thing dying is the old self, and though it's scary, it's also beautiful to learn, change, and grow.

We must learn to sit with both actual fears and perceived fears, and to distinguish the two and honor the two. A real fear can be going to the forest and knowing there are bears active in that area; you see a bear approaching you and growling. This is the same response that we have when an internal trigger is being activated in the present—whether the threat is real or perceived, we feel as though it is as real as the bear. In some ways, it is that real—to our nervous system.

But we must sink into the feelings and comfort them until they reach an equilibrium, and then, from that space of calm, ask it what it needs to be comforted. Then and only then can the intuition function return to distinguish if a situation is actually a threat for you or not.

Our fears and fantasies are all about what could or could not happen. We must recognize the illusion within our fears. Of course they are valid, they scare us, but we can climb our way out of them by realizing that there are gems hidden within the fear when we look for them.

Take, for example, if you have been cheated on in most of your relationships. Now you are within a healthy relationship with someone transparent and loving who has shown you that they are honest and loyal. Still, you can't help but look through their phone. Your mind is constantly racing and creating stories of being lied to and cheated on. You are living in a projection on a movie screen of fear not based on reality. In some cases, perhaps you are getting cheated on and you look because your gut guided you. But we must not live in this constant state of fight or flight. There is another way. The observation of these emotions will help you break this pattern of obsession and instead give you a tool to work with the feelings to gain clarity.

Now, what about anger? I have been an angry person before, so I know the heat, the fire, and the pain of this emotion. Can you relate? Growing up in a home with lots of yelling and emotional outbursts introduced me to anger at a very early age. I also grew up in Bushwick, where the culture was real and raw but also aggressive and wounded. I downloaded some of that and it took me time to really shift into expressing myself versus attacking and protecting myself. This is also important to note—that I had to be out of the unsafe environment in order to not have to protect myself.

Who are you angry at? Write it and explore it. List the names and situations below that are heavy on your heart.

Then, ask the Divine to guide you on practical ways to release the anger for yourself. A simple prayer:

"Great spirit, guide me to release the anger surrounding this person and situation for my own health and sanity. I surrender this for you to handle so that I can exchange the bricks of burden for the lightness of your peace."

This doesn't mean you condone bad behavior or go and speak to people that have no place in your life. This simply means you gift yourself the peace of releasing anger that is hurting you and not helping you.

Emotions are our teachers; let us be good students and learn from them. Anger affects not only our minds but also our spirits and our bodies. We must allow the anger to be heard. Rage is sacred. At times we will have to yell, scream, and curse. *Do it,* get it out, but do it in an environment where you are safe and others are safe from it.

To work with the difficult emotions, you must move from Victim to Creatrix. It's seemingly easy to be the victim; it's a completely different path to be the warrior, to be the creator. This is different from being an actual victim of crime and abuse. This is about how we move through our lives, when we are ready to go from a life of "Life is happening to me" to "I am deciding to be an active participant of my own life." There are many factors that affect life, and therefore I want to be very clear that if you are in an environment that is actually dangerous to your mind, body, spirit, etc., claiming you are a victim is a powerful act of self-love. I am a survivor of domestic violence and first I was a victim to violence. True violence and abuse is oftentimes watered down in a dangerous way in this field, and it's important to me to make that distinction. When you are in a safe environment but are still feeling like a victim, there comes a time when you need the alchemical fire back to get your butt motivated to shift and choose. I want you to be the Diosa creatrix. Shift your attention from "Oh my God, this cannot be happening *to* me" to "Thank you, this is happening *for* me."

As time goes on, even the worst situations can become moments to shift and learn from. Imagine that the divine specifically created this very moment for you to learn from. It might not make sense to you yet, but trust that there is indeed a divine and higher order at work. There is something more. Not everything is what it seems. Sometimes it appears that the worst situation in the world brings nothing but negativity. In fact, the obstacles that come with tears and blood are usually filled with golden wisdom. The moment you realize what your situation is revealing, you shift from victim to creatrix. Being in the position of a victim is draining. Eventually we are ready to move forward. Oftentimes, we carry our story for far too long and allow it to bring us down, making us feel unloved and stuck in the past. As an adult, we have the responsibility to heal— even if the wound wasn't our fault. In my own life, I was a victim of abuse and I needed to honor my innocence. When I was able to say, "I am a victim and I did not deserve what took place," I finally learned that I am not victim to my life now. Perhaps I couldn't control it before, but to my best ability I will create the life I desire *now*. Through accepting this, I allowed myself to release the old story and walk toward an empowered new story.

Witness the moments where you find yourself playing the role of a victim. Where, even in a moment when someone did something fucked up, you dwell or allow your life to be worse over it. What can you shift? How can you tend to your own mental and emotional sanity better? Ask yourself from this empowering perspective: "How can I learn from this?" Remember, you are the creatrix! Anytime you find yourself stuck, give yourself something that you can sink into that allows you to shift emotionally to a healthier space. It can be as simple as saying to yourself, "How can I become wiser because of this?" You can't control others, but you can control yourself. Placing yourself in the position of the creatrix allows you to be empowered and make conscious healthy choices. When you are in the position of the victim, you are disempowered and at the mercy of others. Choose wisely.

I want to make it very clear before we move forward that healing difficult emotions is a process that takes time and cultivation; this is not something you can just do and be healed. It is an art that has many layers to it. Be gentle, be easy, and take it slow—step by step, day by day, moment by moment. This book will serve as an inspirational guide offering tools for you to practice and incorporate into your daily practice of self-care.

We don't have to eradicate fear, anger, or sadness, we just need to respond appropriately to them. This is the key to being a true spiritual student. Not looking to gloss pink fluff over everything or using an affirmation to eradicate fear. Affirmations help, but they can't be a Band-Aid. We must always go to the root. Fear is part of life; the key is to respond in a positive way in spite of it.

Instead of making your feelings your enemy and running from them or attacking them or avoiding them like the plague, befriend them and get to know them. Ask them: Who are you? Where are you coming from? What do you like to do to feel happy and have fun? What do you need to be heard? Embrace them, just as you would a dear friend in real life.

Let's further explore your fears by taking a Fear Inventory. In this activity, you will have the opportunity to learn about fear and which fears are prevalent in your life. In addition, you will learn how fear has affected your life.

Take a sheet of paper and pen and on the left side of the page
write down these top fears:

- I am afraid of being alone.
- I am afraid of never finding love.
- I am afraid I am ugly.
- I am afraid of dying.
- I am afraid of being abandoned.
- I am afraid of being lied to.
- I am afraid of losing loved ones.
- I am afraid of never finding my purpose.
- I am afraid to lose control.

Then write down any others that come up for you. Keep going
until you feel complete. On the right side of the page, write the
Emotional Cost.

For example:

FEAR—I am afraid of being abandoned. // EMOTIONAL
    COST—I am super-controlling with my man.
FEAR—I am afraid of being alone. // EMOTIONAL COST—
    I stay in dead-end relationships so I never have to
    be alone.

As you do this, keep going and be proud of yourself as you continue to write and feel complete. Spend at least ten minutes doing
this. If it helps to set a timer, do so.

Next, I want you to write on another page: On the other side of
this fear, what is the lesson for growth?

For example: "I am afraid of being alone. I must learn to love
and be with me. I am never alone if I am one with me."

You are here because you want to heal your insides and cope in a healthier manner so you can lead a happier life. By understanding your emotions, you will be able to fear them less. Instead of stuffing them down, it is my intention that you embrace them.

Below you will dive into some more soulwork. Be gentle with yourself. If you can answer only one question for today, that is beautiful, honor yourself for anything that you do. All in its time. Gentleness is better than any assignment that you can do. Be sure to take it easy and do what you can.

Keep in mind as you dive into this chapter's soulwork:

- The moment you feel pain, the healing has begun.
- Your job is to connect to the feeling, not run from it.
- Know your soul wound story.
- Befriend your feelings.

As you bring up the truth, you might experience difficult feelings. Remember to be gentle with yourself. Remember to breathe deep and take your time. This is all about progress, not perfection. Healing is an individual journey, and there is no deadline to complete the work laid out in this book. So take your time. Get additional support if you need it, and nourish yourself by drinking lots of water and eating healthy foods. It's essential to take care of your vessel as you do this kind of healing work.

Soulwork

Let's get to exploring some of your wounds. Using your journal, write down your responses to the following questions:

1. What is your tikkun?
2. Who was the first person that broke your heart?
3. What was their name or names?
4. How did they hurt you?

5. How old were you?
6. Where were you when it happened?
7. How did it make you feel?
8. From 1 to 5, 5 being the most painful and 1 being the least painful, how painful was that experience for you?
9. What did this experience teach you about love?
10. How did this experience impact other areas of your life (communication, self-esteem, emotions, etc.)?
11. What are your top fears?
12. What lesson lived on the other side of the fear?

Mantra

All emotions are sacred, and I revere all as my holy teachers.

Ceremony

Becoming the Wound

This chapter is about going to the root of your pain. In shamanic traditions, rituals and ceremonies were done understanding that there is medicine for the psyche and soul in ceremony. This is especially true in soul retrieval—the regaining of the soul back into the body after a traumatizing event. In this ritual and ceremony, you are going to *become* the wound and speak as the wound to really give voice to how the wound feels.

This ceremony welcomes sound—specifically, a drum sound and poetry. You will write a poem that is from your wound. This will be the wound speaking to you, so you can understand your soul wound's voice and pain. Creative expression is key in accessing the deeper feelings that hide behind more overt language. Poetry accesses the deeper realms of feeling and speaking that go beyond talk.

An example of a poem from my own emotional wound:

I, the wound of abandonment, live in the bones of your ancestors.
For the fear I carry is not only my own.

I was left many times on the ground to fend and stand on my own.
And so I am scared and afraid. Lead me to heal.

Once you have the poem, you will drum as you speak the poem out loud. If you feel inspired to sing the poem, you can as well. If you do not have access to a drum, go on YouTube and search for "shamanic drumming" and play the one that most speaks to your soul. Do this ritual for five minutes total.

When you are finishing, thank the sounds of the drums, thank your guides and ancestors, thank your soul, and thank yourself. Bow to your wound and imagine light pouring over it. You are tapping into the medicine woman within as you add ceremony to your healing journey.

Doing this soulwork allows you to heal and live a different life. We do this work because it works. Because it hurts too much to stay living trapped by the ghosts of violence, pain, and shame. Because our soul remains like a bright light—shining amid the chaos of the wounds. Beautiful warrioress you are—diving to the core. I always remind myself that in order to have a beautiful home, I must have a strong foundation. In many ways, my foundation of home growing up was shaky—and I had to return to heal what caused me harm and reprogram the thoughts I downloaded and heal the nervous system affected by the harm, in my body. I had to slowly change what was holding me back from my true self. If you are doing this work, it's because you are not here to fuck around. You want to go to the core and see what must be healed. Now that we have explored some of the shadow and wounds—let's connect the dots. Let us explore how your past is currently affecting your present. When you do this, you begin to shift into the life and person you want to be with the gift of conscious choice. You are gifted the power to make choices. Again, when you see how your past affects your present—it is there that you can adjust, shift, modify, and reprogram to create the life you actually desire and not the life that is on repeat due to our family and life programming. Open your heart and mind to the dots in your life connecting. Ask your soul for guidance, and let yourself be guided. My hope and desire is that in doing this you can begin to make different choices and have shifts internally that allow you to remember *your worth* at your core.

*You, beloved, are not more
lovely when you are smiling
than when you are crying.*

Your tears are sacred rivers of healing.

#iamdiosa

CHAPTER 3

How the Past Affects You Now

I walk down the street. There is a deep hole in the sidewalk.

I fall in.

I am lost . . . I am helpless.

It isn't my fault.

It takes forever to find a way out.

I walk down the same street.

There is a deep hole in the sidewalk.

I pretend I don't see it.

I fall in again.

I can't believe I am in the same place.

But, it isn't my fault.

It still takes me a long time to get out.

I walk down the same street.

There is a deep hole in the sidewalk.

I see it is there.

I still fall in. It's a habit.

My eyes are open.

I know where I am.

It is my fault. I get out immediately.

I walk down the same street.
There is a deep hole in the sidewalk.
I walk around it.
I walk down another street.

—Portia Nelson, *There's a Hole in My Sidewalk: The Romance of Self-Discovery*

Recognizing emotional triggers is key to healing soul wounds. You know that feeling when you don't get a text back from the guy you like after you thought you had an incredible date? Your wheels begin to spin, and you go into that dark, insecure space? Or the feeling when someone says something casually, like, "You know, you are so emotional!" And immediately you feel shut down, small, and upset? It's as though a raw, tender part of your insides gets touched with a hot iron rod.

It throws you off-center. And you feel out of control. Your emotions all rise to the surface and you are flooded with feeling anxiety, depression, shame, and a whole other cocktail of difficult emotions.

Before we go further, let's first define what an emotional trigger is. A trigger is when a situation occurs that pokes at you emotionally or psychologically and reminds you of an earlier memory, feeling, or situation that hurt you. This may be conscious or unconscious.

The wound is raw and the wires of the nervous system are often exposed when trauma occurs and pain happens. Those wounds then learn to survive and adapt. And thank God for that, because we needed some of those defense mechanisms and tactics to survive—especially in the face of abuse or danger as a child. However, as we move into the phase of our adulthood, it is here that we want to recognize the effects of the wounds in our life.

We want to see how that wound shaped us—our thoughts, our relationships, our feelings, our fears, our triggers, and how we respond to those wounds being touched.

Imagine, let's say, the wound of abandonment.

You were left as a child by your dad, who had a drinking problem, and due to his addiction, he was unable to properly keep you safe or stay in partnership with your mother, and so he left. When he left, you were left with this hole in your heart and a deep subconscious belief that said, "I am not worthy. I am easily forgotten. Easily leaveable."

Now imagine you are twenty-eight years old, two years sober, and dating again after being celibate for a year. You meet a guy you like. He has qualities that you love. He is a "normal drinker," doesn't do drugs or smoke, is physically active, and loves the same music you do, and the conversations flow and there is just a fire and a click romantically.

You realize you really like this guy. Suddenly, you start to flood yourself with fear. The risk level heightens as you project your fears onto this current situation.

The fear says something like: "You like him and you're going to mess it up. He will leave. You will be abandoned and heartbroken. You're not enough for him to stay."

Your heart rate goes up. You go from super in flow and joy to super crazy and in fear. This, my friend, is what I call the "cray zone," when you begin finding the most catastrophic way for this to implode.

You create the best novella in your head: "He actually doesn't like me. I know he was sneezing nonstop the last time I saw him, but he probably was lying. He made up the fact that he was sick. He probably took acting classes and is well adept at faking sneezes. Perhaps, he took a class specifically for how to fake illness. Yeah, I think that's it. He's lying. He hates me. He never really liked me anyway. He probably noticed something about me—something wasn't good enough for him, and now he's leaving me. They always leave me. My dad left me. I'm easy to leave."

Why does this happen? Why can a seemingly "small thing" throw us off-center so far and so deep?

Well, because we all have childhoods and life experiences that leave us with emotional wounds that carry weight and pain. Many times as a child, you didn't have the proper space or guidance to tend to that wound. The wound goes unhealed and remains inside of you. And imagine leaving a wound open and not having any protection over it, no medicine, no healing salve, no bandage. Raw and exposed. Anything—even the wind—might make it sting, hurt, and potentially infect it.

The seemingly small joke about you being "so emotional" that might have been said without any ill will can bring you back ten years to the moment when you were crying hysterically, begging for your mom to listen to you and her laughing in your face and saying, "I am going to ignore you now. Just stop. You are so emotional." That verbal abuse and emotional neglect now leaves that wound there.

Anytime that any person or any situation resembles your original wound— though it may be different—the wound is activated. The emotional trigger occurs.

There is a saying that says if it's hysterical, it's historical. There is a historical reason why you are responding this way.

Exploring Your Emotional Triggers

Emotional triggers are often hard to identify because they are hidden behind reactivity or buried under stones that have been untouched for years. But you must get to know your wound immediately—get cheek-to-cheek with your wounds. To own them and know how they smell, how they move, how they get triggered, how they respond, what they need to be calmed. This is your time to bring them to the surface, nurture them, pour salve over them, and slowly begin to deactivate their ability to overthrow you into unhealthy situations and reactions.

My personal emotional trigger, for example, is emotional distance. Growing up, I was a perceptive and sensitive child. I felt the pain of the world and of my family. I felt their stress, their anxiety, and the broken family dynamic. Although they both did their best, my parents didn't really have the space to process their own childhood wounds, and as a result they had maladaptive coping mechanisms that caused them to shut down or act in rage. My mother would close up and ignore me when in emotional situations, while my father would lash out, attack, and abuse. Both showed love and also abuse. The feeling of safety and consistency were not available for me, and thus I felt emotionally unsafe and unstable.

For many years, when someone shut down at all or wouldn't respond, I would freak out and go into a spiral of panic and fear. Out of nowhere, the feelings of intense rejection and abandonment and unworthiness would appear. And I would do *anythingggg, and I mean anythinggg,* to avoid the feeling of emotional distance or nonresponsiveness. I felt lonely, powerless, ignored, and unseen a lot as a child, so feeling any degree of loneliness or rejection or nonpresent emotional connection as an adult was a huge trigger for me. By learning to identify this wound/emotional trigger, I began to slowly nurture the inner child that felt this way. I would speak to the wound, listen to my wound's needs, know when my wound was being poked/triggered. This is the goal for you too: to come close to the wounds, not to run from them and shun them into a shadow that will inevitably come back in uglier and more destructive ways.

For the wound can't be ignored. It will always beg to be healed. The more you ignore, the more it festers and grows.

Compassion is needed as you go through this process. To go inward and to develop a level of "observer," connecting with the pain you experienced as a child. Remember to practice loving self-talk as you do this work.

The inner child within you deserves your safe and loving adult validation. Your inner child deserves to know that your original wounds and emotions and pain mattered, that your feelings of rejection, loneliness, all mattered. If you didn't get the nurturing you needed, your job as an adult becomes to cultivate that nurturing with the self.

A common emotional trigger that many of my clients go through is the "no response from a guy you like" trigger. (Remember to change gender, pronouns, or other specifics at any time—this is your book.)

If a guy doesn't respond, no one is going to love that. We all want to have loving responses, so it's normal to be upset. Sometimes you might even be feeling an intuitive gut feeling that something is off.

The problem comes in when the emotional trigger is activated like a bomb, and your response is at a level 90 out of 100, with 100 being the highest emotionally activated state and 1 being the least.

This happens because some part of you feels like the situation has that much power over you. You feel out of your center, feeling you are unworthy, that you caused it, and that you're broken. You're feeling as though this is just like when you were abandoned before.

How do you recognize it's an emotional trigger?

- You feel super-thrown off.
- You feel off center
- You might feel upset without knowing why.
- You react in a way that, in hindsight, seems exaggerated, given the situation (but in the moment it feels very intense and even unbearable).
- You feel crazy, angry, small, insignificant, anxious, depressed.

- You feel out of your body or like you blacked out.
- You begin to have catastrophic thoughts.
- Your body rises with heat, fear, panic, worry.
- You feel sick to your stomach.
- You assign meaning to the situation that might not actually be there.

Once the triggers are located and identified, the wound can be healed. Step by step, with patience, grace, courage, and work.

You know that you are healing the emotional trigger when it occurs and instead of having it activate like a bomb, you get to engage with it. Sticking with the example of the guy who doesn't respond, perhaps you don't like it! This is a normal, healthy human response, and it's actually important to know your needs and what you want. So, cool—you know you want someone to text you and be conscious and expressive of his desire for you. There is nothing wrong with that. You deserve to have high standards, emotional needs, and beautiful desires.

By shifting from reactive to proactive, you gift yourself the grace to observe what you don't want and you get your power back by saying, "I don't want to be with someone that doesn't text me after a date that he had a great time. And if he didn't, I only want to be with someone that equally likes and expresses his interest in me." Therefore, I deactivate the trigger by not believing that I am being rejected, ignored, abandoned, because I'm easily unlovable, easily leaveable, and unworthy. So instead I say "I love myself enough to know what I deserve, and I choose to not be with you."

This is an opportunity to deepen your worth and stop placing external validation on your internal worth. By repeating it over and over again, each time that the obstacle or seeming obstacle occurs, you work on healing the trigger. You continue to show up to the emotional trigger by calming yourself, speaking to the self-sabotaging, insecure voice that emerges from the wound that is there to shred you to pieces and remind you of why you are unloved, unworthy, unseen, unimportant, etc. Speak to the insecure gremlin. Say no in a voice of authority: "NO! I refuse to listen to these attacking thoughts. I refuse to listen to you. I command you to stop."

A lot of this won't make sense until you are in the actual situation that triggers you and you practice this in action. This is not something that you can do just reading this book. This needs to occur in real time in real life, with real motherfucking triggers that make you feel like motherfucking shit. So practice it and use it when you actually get triggered. Don't just read this part. Do this part. *You must work this soulwork for it to work.*

Will it be fun? Fuck, no! It will actually feel like a tiny death. You will feel awful and disoriented. But it will be empowering. You will rise like a warrior with a sword to chop away the lies and illusions, and access the bliss of your truth and your worth. By practicing this through action, it will become wisdom and knowledge in your body and bones, rather than your simply remembering it on a superficial level in the mind.

And the more you do it, the stronger you become at not believing the lies that the obstacle means something awful about you. The more you do it, you turn that reactivity into proactivity and there is space between you and the trigger. And in that space, you have the power, the prana, the presence to choose from your empowered self and not your wounded, fractured self. Because the wounded self is coming from a place of desperation and panic, and in that state you can't see what you need to do to make yourself feel safe. Essentially, in those triggered moments, you feel unsafe. This soulwork is about learning to make yourself feel safe.

And, of course, if you are actually in an unsafe external situation with an abusive person, you need to get professional help immediately to help you get out safely. Beyond that, this is about nurturing yourself so the wires aren't as exposed, the wounds are not oozing, and the wise, whole self rises with wit, intelligence, swag, power, and truth and says, "Cool, I trust me. I will observe and see what happens, and if he doesn't call, cool, because I want only present men anyway. And you know what, you can't abandon me, because I'm a grown-ass woman who has me. I got me. God has me. I can't be abandoned by anyone other than me. I choose me. I choose to comfort my wound and not react to it."

So what are your triggers? Do any of these situations trigger you? And if others come up, write them below these. Think about situations that really make you spiral.

- someone rejecting you, ignoring you, or being angry at you
- someone not wanting to resolve a problem
- someone saying "We have to talk"
- someone calling you "sensitive"
- someone not being overly loving or expressive of their love
- someone leaving you or threatening to leave you
- someone calling you lazy
- someone pulling back or shutting down
- someone not saying you did a good job after you worked hard on something
- someone not saying "thank you"
- someone giving you a disapproving look
- someone blaming or shaming you
- someone being judgmental or critical of you
- someone being too busy to make time for you or prioritizing work over you
- someone not appearing to be happy to see you
- someone needing you only in a sexual way or saying they see you as just a friend
- someone kissing you or going down on you
- someone trying to control you

- someone being needy
- someone changing their pattern—they usually call daily, and then one day they don't
- someone telling you something about your body
- someone complimenting you
- the smell of alcohol
- someone that looks or sounds a certain way

When we are discussing healing soul wounds and triggers, we must understand that oftentimes it is the untreated wound that is acting out and choosing for us. And we don't want our unhealed wounds choosing for us. As we heal the wound, we reclaim our power and can choose as healthy empowered adults.

In addition to acting out of the wound, you may also be suppressing them, avoiding them, shoving them into the dark closets hidden in the back. What are some ways that you avoid your triggers?

- I get super-anxious.
- I get needy.
- I ignore my emotional needs and become a people-pleaser.
- I say yes when I mean no.
- I threaten to leave so I am not left.
- I shut down and withdraw from the other person.
- I blame someone else for my pain.
- I turn to an addiction—drugs, food, alcohol, sex, porn, shopping, work, gambling, and so on.
- I ignore it and pretend it isn't happening.
- I fight, but I don't actually share how I am hurting.

I want you to know your emotional triggers like your new best friend. So you can be like, "Bitch, I *see you*!" "You ain't gonna trap me this time." "Let me love on you before you self-sabotage and burn the whole shit down." (Said lovingly to yourself, of course.)

Proactive Formula

As we discuss wounds and emotional triggers, an important concept I want to introduce is the concept of *klippot*, which in Jewish mysticism is defined as a shell made of your darkness, or tikkun. By facing and overcoming those obstacles, you crack the shell open and are then able to access the light.

This concept came into my life when I needed it most and truly helped me to place a framework around why, on a soul level, this repeated pattern—wound—was occurring in my life. I imagine the wounds as the *klippot*, and inside the hard shell of the wound is light, healing, emotional growth, miracles, and soul growth. As you heal, you reclaim those lost soul light sparks. The goal, then, is to constantly face the obstacle as it arises and know that there is a deeper spiritual meaning. The emotional triggers, the situations that throw you off, are there for you to heal the wound and gain back the lost light in those areas.

You are a vessel, and the more you fill the vessel with the truth of who you are as divine, as Diosa, the more you live your life and choose empowering soul wholeness vs. the wounded, fragmented self.

To help you with this, I recommend trying the proactive formula, which is based on Kabbalistic principles.

When you are experiencing a triggering behavior, thought, or feeling, instead of jumping to a reactive state, you insert a PAUSE. By pausing instead of reacting, you can take time to shift back into your empowered state where the divine can help you CHOOSE from a proactive space—a centered space.

This is a way of self-regulating, so that your nervous system is calm before you respond. You are able to reduce anxiety and fear and be in a good feeling place. You see things that you wouldn't otherwise see. You *notice* red flags and are able to choose to go the other way vs. retraumatize yourself by walking into it.

So, what is your tikkun? Let's say your tikkun is "I am abandoned and leaveable. Everyone leaves me." You've just started dating someone and things are flowing and going well. Then you receive a text message: "Hey love, I have been sneezing nonstop and feeling super-weak. Would you hate me if I rescheduled tonight's dinner? I would love to take you out Monday, Tuesday, or Thursday. Do any of those work for you when I'm back to 100 percent? So if you don't see me in the gym tomorrow, you know why. Lying in bed in fetal position."

Your immediate reaction? "So this is how it ends, right? You don't like me, do you?"

Here is the trick about this: You never fully know if someone is lying or not—except by trusting your gut and by trusting your intuition and observing how someone shows up. In this case, the guy happens to actually be honest. But let's say, for example, the guy is a two-timing liar and is actually canceling to go on another date. It doesn't really matter, because whether he's telling the truth or not, the wound being triggered still needs to be healed in the same way.

So the problem or the obstacle here is not the guy canceling the date and potentially not liking you and being flaky and a liar. The obstacle is actually your response to the wound, because you must learn to soothe the internal trigger, become an observer of the situation, and have enough sense of self to trust if someone is lying or not.

Essentially, the healing of the trigger must go from reactive to proactive. Here's what you can do:

A challenging situation or an obstacle appears in your life . . .

- **Step 1:** Pause. Observe your reactive nature.

- **Step 2:** Become aware that your real enemy is not the challenging situation or obstacle that has arisen in and of itself. Your *reaction* to the obstacle is the problem.

- **Step 3:** Realize that this obstacle is being given to you by the Divine to grow in some way.

- **Step 4:** Ask the Divine for help in being led to the most proactive solution to the situation. For example you can say something like: "Higher power, help me to have the patience and the grace to walk through this situation differently. Give me the strength and the clarity to handle this in a way that feeds my higher soul self. Fill me with your strength and your wisdom. Help me to choose proactive over reactive. Thank you."

- **Step 5:** Then, take a proactive action step once you feel calm and guided.

This proactive formula saved my ass so many times. In moments of reactive triggers it really allowed me to pause and to choose to calm my nervous system and insert a proactive solution over a reactive behavior. Another tool that is helpful in moving from proactive to reactive is:

Bonus tool: Speak out loud or to self what you desire on the other side of the emotional trigger. For example, "I desire to feel safe and it is my intention to share in a way that makes me feel safe and heard. I am scared, but I am here for myself. I am simply scared, but I desire to feel calm. I desire to have a conversation from a grounded space that makes me feel confident, cool, and collected.

I desire to be a woman of grace. I desire to be a woman that speaks her truth with both vulnerability and honesty. I desire to speak with ease." In this way, you are reminding yourself how you actually want to be and feel versus giving in to the trigger and feeding the trigger.

And lastly, repeat the mantra "Then is not now." To take it further, say, "Even if this situation is familiar, I can call on the new tools that I have today to handle this in a new way. I choose to handle this in a new way that brings me more peace." If a triggering situation is similar, you will have to respond to the trigger differently so that it heals. Otherwise, it will loop and repeat until you do.

I offer you these steps, but I also want to remind you that this is a journey. Why? Because far too many self-help books lean too much into the direction of "If you do these steps this way, you will be happy all the time." That is a lie. That is psychologically damaging and can be really destructive to someone struggling with trauma, pain, abuse, poverty, mental illness, racism, etc. I'm interested in helping people find a sustainable way to manage their emotions and be all of who they are, and sometimes that means feeling sad or depressed or anxious, but still wonderful and joyful and perfectly imperfect. And so, it is important to keep this in mind particularly when you are exploring your soul wounds and emotional triggers.

Still, the benefit of the proactive formula is that it allows you to pause, interrupt the feeling of chaos, and switch up the negative pattern.

- Breathe
- Get a glass of water
- Listen to a song
- Do something, anything, other than feeding your triggers

This pattern-interrupter allows you to invite in the light, the Creator, God, Source, and in this pause, the healing can occur. You have time now to shift into a new space and *choose* not from compulsion and not from the wounded, fragmented self, but instead from the healed self. You gain more clarity.

This is also what meditation does. It allows you to come to center, to come to yourself, to have your soul come back into your body. It gives your nervous system a chance to calm down, to move from a state of fight, flight, or freeze into a more neutral state where you are able to have some choice again.

Create a list of your positive pattern-interrupters that you can do in a moment when you are triggered.

You can't fully delete a traumatic experience, but you can learn how to cope with it better. So my goal here in teaching you about the wounds, the emotional triggers, and some of the tools you can use to nurture the wound on a psychological and spiritual level is not that you can try to be happy or untriggered all the time. It's about being in tune with yourself, knowing yourself and your pain points and how you typically respond, so you can accept all of who you are. From there, you can continue to become healthier one day at a time. One moment at a time.

Becoming the Divine Parent to Your Inner Child

As we become adults, part of the work is reparenting and nurturing our inner child, becoming the parents we wish we had in most cases. (Trigger warning for following page.)

One of my clients is a woman whose dad raped her when she was younger. (I call all acts of sexual molestation to a child *rape* because it is a better word to encapsulate the act of violence to a child.) She grew up feeling such deep shame and self-hatred because she internalized the rape to mean she was undeserving of love and that somehow it was her fault. When she finally had the courage to share what happened to her, she was told she was lying. She was brushed off and ignored. All the shame she felt intensified. She felt crazy and so embarrassed for sharing. She had to see her dad for years after the incident and act like nothing ever happened. She went on choosing men that reflected that original pain. She criticized herself so many times. She called herself the worse names. She called herself "dumb, insecure, crazy" and more. "This is just because you're fucking wounded. Your father raped you and that's why you aren't trusting. You're so fucked up."

Thinking of all the women that I have met throughout the years, including myself, that have berated themselves and covered up the wound brings tears to my eyes. So much pain. So much hatred. So much self-attack.

Imagine that instead of being shunned and rejected and not trusted for her words and her story, she was met with unconditional love and honor. Imagine instead someone scooped her up and hugged her tightly and said, "I believe you. Oh my God, I am so sorry this happened. Let's get you help. Let's press charges and let's get you safe and away from him. I am here for you. I love you. I believe you. Let it all out. Cry, scream, release it all. You're allowed to be angry—he's a sick man and you didn't deserve any of it." Imagine that kind of love and validation.

Then perhaps she would have been able to meet herself with that kind of love and self-acceptance and trust too. But if we are met enough times with that kind of rejection, we create pathways internally that then have us rejecting and punishing and abusing the self. Leaning into the pain and the feelings isn't easy but it's worth it. Leaning inward to our wounds and triggers and becoming the healthy parent to our inner child is key. Meeting the pain with love is how we heal.

In this process, take note of what your inner child is feeling.

Step 1: Recognize the Cries of Your Inner Child

We can't help our inner child if we don't tap into our inner child's needs and wants and feelings. Since so many of us are numb, and, as I said in the beginning of the book, have run away from ourselves because the pain was too great to bear—we must take steps to recognize and tune inward to see what our inner child is feeling.

"Baby love, what are you feeling?" Tune in to the body—the body is the messenger of the feelings of the soul. Is your stomach tight? Does your heart ache?

Step 2: Be the Loving Parent You Always Wanted

I call this embodying the divine parents—the mother and father—the divine mother and father that goes beyond this realm and embodies the healthy ideals of the mother and father archetype—therefore, whether or not you experienced healthy parents in this lifetime, here is your opportunity to dream up the ideal. What would I have wanted to hear? What would make me feel safe, heard, seen, comforted, loved, nurtured, held, protected, honored, peaceful?

Imagine those emotions that you would want in these ideal loving parents. Embody them as you speak to your inner child. Whatever your inner child expressed, they felt. Speak to them. Respond to their needs, their feelings, their emotions. Look into your inner child's eyes and say, "I hear you. I see you. I am here for you. It's okay and it's going to be okay." Be curious and loving toward little you. Little you needs your love as you explore your core wounds.

Step 3: Confront the Core Shame-Based Wounded Beliefs

Here's an example of a shame-based belief: I am unloved because my dad abused me, and if he abused me it's because I'm unworthy and not good enough to be loved, and if I am not good enough or worthy enough to be loved I will be left by all men. I am easy to not love. I am hard to love.

Now you can speak to the shame-based belief as the loving parent. Here's a scenario:

Maria Sofia is going on dates, and after swiping left on multiple dating apps, she finally meets a guy she is drawn to, Julio. On their fourth date, Julio begins to share that his ex-girlfriend got him the job that he currently has, and while he is happy that they aren't in a relationship, he is grateful that she helped him grow professionally.

Immediately, Maria is triggered and begins to compare herself. Her inner thoughts begin to go rapid-fire. Her body closes up and tenses; she feels frozen. "Do I need to help Julio professionally? Maybe he will not get a lot out of dating me. Does he still like her if he mentioned her? I wish he hated her, but he seems to be grateful for some things."

Here we see that Maria Sofia is triggered by some deeper core beliefs. She needs time with her inner child to speak to the core wound as a loving parent.

Inner Child Maria Sofia: I don't like it when he talks about his ex. It hurts me and makes me scared he loves her more than me.

Loving Adult Parent Maria Sofia: Why does it hurt you when he talks about her?

Inner Child: Because it makes me feel like I'm not good enough, and if he's speaking about her, then clearly he still loves her, and if he still loves her, then he doesn't love me. I can't handle that feeling. It hurts too much.

Loving Adult: Why does it hurt so much? Do you think him mentioning her means that he doesn't love you?

Inner Child: Yes.

Loving Adult: Does it remind you of anything from your childhood wounds in the past? Anything that reminds you of your relationship with your mother or father?

Inner Child: Yes, my dad always compared women, and then would end up cheating. He even cheated on the love of his life with her own cousin. He regretted it afterward, but he didn't care in the moment and cheated. I'm scared. If my dad did that, then Julio can too.

Loving Adult: Julio isn't your dad, and him sharing that his ex did something good doesn't mean he wants to be with her. He is able to express that while he doesn't want to be with her, he is still grateful for some parts of their dynamic, and that doesn't take away from the gratitude he has for you right now.

Inner Child: What if he leaves me?

Loving Adult: Your dad cheating on someone had to do with his inner self-esteem and his seeking validation outside of himself. He was wounded, and his pain caused him to act out of integrity. Has Julio ever been out of integrity with you? Or lied?

Inner Child: No, he hasn't lied, but I am scared he will.

Loving Adult: Even if he left, you would still be good because if he did something like that your truth is you wouldn't want to be with him. The fear and anticipation of the pain is what is hurting you and driving you mad. Instead of waiting for things to go wrong, be present to what is being presented. Has he actually been honest? Has he proven trustworthy? Is he aligned with his words and actions?

Inner Child: He has, but I'm scared he won't be.

Loving Adult: No matter what, you are safe with me. I love you and I'm here for you. You are safe in you no matter what. Your gut guides you. Allow yourself to keep showing up to that and trusting your gut one day at a time.

Inner Child: Okay, I do feel safer knowing I am safe in me and I have my loving parent within taking care of me.

Step 4: Ask Spirit for Guidance

This is a necessary piece, and I want to highlight that here. That no matter what has happened to you, I believe in the power of the spirit that lives within you—your soul—strong and vibrant like the sun. I believe in our innate capacity to heal from the incomprehensible and horrible crimes done against us. At times you might feel as though you don't want to do the work. Because let's be real, doing emotional labor of this kind is not for the faint of heart. But my guess is, if you are here, your heart is blazing with fires from your ancestors— beating with the blood of desire for change. You are stronger than you know. So just keep on keeping on, one step at a time.

Soulwork

It's time to dig deeper and get to know your emotional landscape better. Using your journal, write down your responses to the following questions:

1. What are your main emotional triggers?
2. What does it feel like when you are triggered?
3. What area of your life are you most triggered in?
4. What was your original wound that relates to this emotional trigger?
5. What are your unhealthy ways to cope with your emotional trigger to the wound?
6. What are the healthy ways you cope with your emotional trigger to the wound?

Mantra

I am allowed to have my emotional needs met. I am safe to be loved and held and seen. I got me.

Ceremony

Solar Plexus Healing

When you are being triggered, it essentially pulls you away from your core, from your gut, from your solar plexus. The solar plexus is associated with the color yellow. The mantra associated with the strengthening and healing of the solar plexus is the sound "RAM." This is a beej mantra, and beej means the seed. What I love about seed mantras is they go to the root.

As we are going to the root healing, we want to work with sounds and colors associated with these parts of the body and energy centers. This ceremony will combine the color yellow, a candle, and the beej mantra sound and chanting of "RAM."

Buy a yellow votive candle, and if you can find a nontoxic one, even better. Once you have the candle, before you light it, I want you to get a Sharpie and write on the glass, "I am strong and secure. My self-esteem is glowing like a bright light." You can also feel free to write anything that you are inspired to, as this is your sacred ceremony.

Intention is key before you light your candle. Breathe, consider your intention, and allow yourself to infuse the candle with your prayer, intention, and energy. The energy you put in your intention is where the magic occurs. This candle will represent your self-esteem and healing your triggers. Light it and put it in a safe place, perhaps on your altar.

Take a comfortable meditation seat and repeat the words "RAM, RAM, RAM." Set a timer for three minutes or five minutes—either is a great period of time to get into a rhythm and flow. Remember that as you repeat the beej mantra RAM, you are healing your self-esteem. You can also place your hands at your solar plexus—touch adds an extra element of energetic healing. The solar plexus is the area right above your belly button, beneath your ribs. And as you touch your solar plexus, you can continue to chant the mantra "RAM."

You are healing yourself with these ceremonial tools that you can continue to use on your own whenever you need to. Be proud of yourself for doing this work. When you are done, thank yourself, thank your soul, and thank your guides. Breathe in through the nose and exhale big in full surrender through the mouth. Come back to this exercise as needed throughout this process.

Honor yourself, Diosa, for the soulwork you are doing! Get excited for every small step you take, for they all add up. We live in a world obsessed with external success, but the soulwork is done in the darkness, in the moments with you and the silence of the night and your pillow—with tears dripping down your face and the glimmer of hope as you commit to doing this hard but rewarding work. Connecting the dots and seeing how your past is currently affecting your future is powerful and profound. I hope you see how, as we do this, lightbulbs light up. Neurons shooting and making sense of things—consciousness expanding and awareness growing.

During this process, remember to ask your soul, your guides, your guardian angels to assist you in your healing. This is a grounded and practical healing based on psychotherapeutic foundations and a soul spiritual experience. For me, they must go together. Ask to connect even more dots as you go forward: "Spirit, lead me to connect the dots in my psyche and soul to make the shifts you would have me make to be my highest self in this incarnation. Thank you and so it is, Amen."

Next, we will explore soul traps. This is one of my favorite chapters, for I believe it essential for us to recognize the ways in which we are usually trapped so that we become awake to these traps and can smell them from afar. I want you to be able to sniff out what is not soul aligned to then know what is soul aligned. Off we go.

I am allowed to have my
emotional needs met.

I am safe to be loved and held and seen.
I got me.

#iamdiosa

CHAPTER 4

Recognizing the Soul Traps

"Practice listening to your intuition, your inner voice; ask
questions; be curious; see what you see; hear what you hear;
and then act upon what you know to be true. These intuitive
powers were given to your soul at birth."

—Dr. Clarissa Pinkola Estés

It's important as a woman that is coming into her Diosa—her wise,
whole, intuitive self—to learn to smell the traps that are meant to
capture our wild, creative, full, vibrant soul. It is important to smell
danger before it approaches and as it is nearing. To sense, like an
animal in the forest can sense when a predator is coming. For being
captured psychologically and spiritually is a death too.

We, like a rabbit about to be eaten by a fox in the wild, can get
caught by predators and traps. Some traps are people, some come
in waiting too long past an expiration date, some come in denying
to ourselves our true soul's desires, some come in giving in to the
mundane way of the world and not listening to your own unique
soul's drumbeat, some come in sacrificing the way of the soul for the
way of the world.

In reading this book and doing the work, your intuition is being
repaired and healed. This allows you to now be on the lookout for

traps meant to keep you away from living as the most aligned version of your soul's highest expression of itself. For when we ignore the signs and the traps, we lose our color. We lose our vibrancy. We lose our purpose. We lose hope. We lose Shakti. We lose that light switch being on. We lose ourselves.

Seven Common Soul Traps

Let's break down some common traps and give examples for each. As we do this, take notice of the traps that are currently at play in your life. Becoming aware of the traps is the first step in not staying in it or falling for them again.

Trap 1: Comfort

Comfort is luring, for it smells of the familiar. Like a soup from your childhood home. Even if the soup isn't that good, if you ate it every Friday after coming home from school, there is something comforting and familiar about it. Comfort has its place. A cozy, comfortable, and healthy familiar is different from the comfort that I speak of here. The comfort that I am referring to is the comfort of playing safe and settling, but not because you actually desire it and want it.

Here's a common scenario with the women in my therapy and healing practice: "I am dating a guy. He's been in my life for ten years. We recently broke up for a little bit. I actually enjoyed being on my own. But I started getting scared. I am thirty-two, and I have no baby and no family. I am desperate to have a family and meet a husband. I want to be a mom. I am terrified it won't happen and, well . . . I know he isn't exactly emotionally healthy, and it is a bit toxic, but I think, 'We *can* make it work, maybe?' I can maybe just have a baby with him and raise it on my own? I can just use him in a way, since he is there. Maybe we can figure it out somehow?"

In her gut, she knows she is settling. Oftentimes, my clients will even share, "I think it's just because I'm comfortable." But the fear of having no proof that they will meet their husband and have a baby keeps them hanging on to something tangible. What is tangible is the guy that's already there. Even if it's toxic, it's something she knows. Memories. Years together.

And so the comfort keeps her dying a slow internal death. One that is leading her to be trapped, perhaps like her mother and grandmother were trapped—repeating lineages instead of breaking them—but she is too scared. How can she trust that internal soul voice that says, "Be alone, go travel, this is the next step"? She is holding on so tight, fearful that she won't have the family and the baby. She wants to make anything work, even if it doesn't really work in her heart. Forcing something is a sure sign that it is not of the soul way. Comfort has overtaken her, and she is trying to make herself fit something that isn't life-giving and soul-nourishing. In fact, it is life-taking and death-producing. It is stagnant and fake. In this way, she is surrendering to not live her real soul life. She is taking a counterfeit life for a temporary safe comfort.

As empowered Diosas, though, we are learning to smell this trap and know this trap, in all its ways. To be aware and wary when it comes to rear its head.

Speak to the trap: "Oh, hey, there, comfort trap. Trying to make me settle and play small. I see you. I know you. You won't give me the life I want. I am not fooled by your cunning ways. I know you just want me to stay comfortable, but my soul is not comfortable with this choice, only my fears. My soul wants courage, not conformity. I refuse to stay. I will leap. I will do the difficult but good thing for me. This way of settling is a dead end. If I choose the way of my soul, it might be hard at first, but in the end, when I tune in, that is what gives my soul life."

Here, the job is to choose courage over comfort. To send that goodbye text, to block on social media, to cut ties with the guy, the ex, the job, the friends that no longer serve you. To make the leap. To sign up for that art class because your true dream is to be a painter, or a writer, or travel the world, or date, or be alone. Do the thing that is hard but good for your soul, not easy and good for just the moment.

Soul Lesson: "I choose courage over comfort."

Trap 2: Counterfeit Gold

This next trap is perhaps one of the most luring of all. It comes dressed glowing. Light oozing from every crevice. It is the sexiest and most attractive of all. It calls you by your name and knows your every desire. But when it shows you your desire, one tiny thing is off, and it can be so tiny that sometimes it is not even detectable.

Imagine putting every single thing you want on a vision board— a board with photos that you want to manifest to life. You have a guy with dark skin, green eyes. Next to it you have a hospital because you also want him to be a doctor. There is a photo next to that of Jamaica, because you always dreamed of meeting your husband on vacation, in a whirlwind romance.

Now fast-forward two months, you are on your trip in Jamaica. You did the vision board, you wrote your ideal husband list, and from the corner of your eye, you see a man that looks shockingly like the man in your vision board. As he comes closer, he smiles. You smile back, shy but confidently. Your heart begins to beat. You think to yourself, "This is too good to be true. I think this guy is the one I have been imagining." You feel the heat rising in your body. Before you know it, you notice his steps are nearing you! He is coming to say hi to you. You compose yourself, take a breath, and lock eyes. "Hi." "Hi," you respond. He says, "I couldn't help but notice how stunning you were, and I just wanted to say hi. I am not sure if you have a boyfriend and I usually don't approach women, but I just had to say hi and give it a chance." You respond back, "I don't have a boyfriend, and I am glad you said hi. I was also looking at you." You both smile and begin to chat. You look down mid-conversation, and you notice his shirt has a hospital name on it! You ask, "What is that shirt?" He responds, "It's from my job. We did a charity fundraiser and we all got one. I work as a doctor, pediatrics." You try not to let your panties drop . . . But you are LIT THE FUCK UP! Your mind flashes forward to your beautiful wedding in Italy and two kids in a gorgeous, massive house. You can't believe it. You knew it . . . Just like your vision board. You continue to talk and what do you know, he is sober just like you! I mean, it is just getting better and better. You end up getting a bite to eat and one thing leads to the next and you end up going dancing. He has some moves on him and you are falling for him every second more and more. As you part ways, you kiss, and he gets a bit grabby, but nothing too much. You smile and grab his hands and say, "I love that, but not so soon. I don't like that kind of touch in public." He says "I am sorry. You're right, I got too excited." You invite him to hang out and are clear that you don't want to have sex. He says he is totally okay with that and so you head to the villa. When he arrives there, he says, "I think I shouldn't come up. I like you. Let's instead hang tomorrow." You are confused, but you agree. You think, "Maybe he is really polite. Wow. He must like me. I mean he was all hot and heavy two seconds ago and now he isn't coming up; that's weird. But what a gentleman." You give a final kiss and you part ways for the night. He texts you as soon as he gets in. "It was so good meeting you, beautiful. Speak to you in the morning. It was hard to not go upstairs. I kind of regret it. But I'm glad we had that kiss. Sweet dreams."

The next morning, the first text in your phone is his. You are glowing. You feel this might be something more than a vacation fling. He writes, "Good morning, beautiful sunshine." You smile and respond back, "Good morning:)" He says, "How about we meet up and go hang with your friends and my friends on the beach tomorrow maybe?" You respond, "That sounds great. Message me and we'll plan it!" The next day comes . . . and no text. At this point, you feel in your gut that something is off. He was so eager and then didn't come over. He said he wanted to hang instead during the day, and then no response. It is starting to feel like there is a missing piece of information. You don't want to make a big deal of it, so you don't say anything. But you are sad and disappointed—he wasn't true to his word. Finally, you decide to message him in the evening before you go to bed: "Hey, I am going to be transparent—and while I normally don't do this, I wanted to share because I really felt we clicked. We kissed, it was amazing, and we spoke for hours. You said you would come stay and then changed your mind last minute and suggested we go out during the day instead and then no word from you. While we just met and you don't owe me anything, I felt a cool and transparent vibe from you. But this isn't my style of communication. Hope you understand. I wish you the best and enjoy the rest of your trip." You immediately regret sending it, but your gut is feeling super-confident and proud that you were clear and confident and honest. A part of you is so scared that you fucked it up and that you were too rash.

He responds the next day. "You're right, I owe you an explanation. I really like you and I have never met someone like you. I know I just met you, but you have all the qualities I have ever wanted so far. So many things in you I just feel are so me. But it scared me. I just got out of a relationship a month ago and I promised I would be alone on this trip." You respond, "Thank you for your honesty. I really love speaking honestly and clearly and transparently. While I appreciate your words now, I wish you would have told me something prior to us kissing. It was mixed intentions. Either way, I respect your honesty, and I too have taken the time after breakups to be alone, so I fully encourage you to do that. It was the best thing I ever did for myself. Enjoy your trip and may you heal your heart and find peace here in the island. Be well." To your surprise, he responds. "I am sad though, I don't want to miss out on not speaking to you. I like you. Maybe we can still hang out before I go? I don't know, I don't want to not see you." Already you are noticing a back and forth, but you go along with it. You too want to see him. You know no one is perfect—again you notice something off, but you give it a pass. Everything else is perfect. You do a Google search and realize he is also an entrepreneur and a millionaire; he loves animals, children, and volunteer work; and he even has a blog where he wrote a review on one of your favorite spiritual books. You take it as a sign, and you go for it. But day after day, there is a lot of talk and no action. Before you know it, the gut feeling is growing. Something is off and you don't know what it is. But the gold and the shine of everything being perfect on paper lures you to keep talking. Your gut is nudging you that something isn't right. A month goes on and few calls, just texts and no plans to meet up and see if this could ever be a real thing.

Here is the trap: Do you keep chasing the gold, the perfect on paper, or do you trust that slight nudge in the gut that something is off? It's easy to stay and keep on with the lure. The attraction blinds you. But we must trust the gut over the shine.

Eventually you connect with someone else. He is someone that has been in your life for years; you never thought you would marry him or date him, but you have always been drawn to him. You aren't future tripping, you are simply enjoying and feeling safe. So safe that you tell him the story of the perfect-on-paper guy. And he lovingly reminds you, "Don't you always say the gut does not lie? Trust your gut. If you feel something off, then trust it." You say, "You're right. I feel safe with you, so I guess something is off, because I don't feel safe with him."

In that moment, there is a choice, a decision that must be made to choose the soul gold and not the counterfeit gold. It's hard because there is seldom big proof. It is a stirring in the belly, a nudge in the heart. And here you must be brave enough to not let the riches blind you, but instead wait for the true miracle, for the true soul gold.

The best part of this story is that it is based on a true story, though I've changed some of the details for privacy. And in the end, that guy I felt safe with that encouraged me to trust my gut and not be lured is my husband. I call it my final test. The perfect-on-paper guy to the perfect guy for my soul. I'm so grateful that I didn't give in to the trap because for years, I would have tested it out more and more to try and disprove my intuition instead of just trusting it. This time, I trusted it and I was rewarded beyond my wildest dreams.

Soul Lesson: "I choose soul gold over counterfeit gold."

Trap 3: "What If?"

What if he changes? What if he is the one? What if she is the one? What if I wait and they come back to me? What if we go to therapy? What if I give them another couple of years to decide if they want what I want? What if I can make it work?

What-ifs are a trap for so many of us. Coming up with 1,000+ imaginary scenarios of "what if" instead of looking at "what *is*." Fantasy can keep us waiting around for something. Feeding the illusion of "what if" is a trap that often has us waiting for years for something that isn't coming, and in that wait, our bones get brittle, our glow disappears, and we sell our soul dreams for a pipe dream. Take a moment and get really brutally honest with yourself. Where are you playing the "what if" game? And remember, this applies not just to relationships but to other areas of your life as well, like your career.

I had a client that was in a high-powered nonprofit for years. She had stability, but her soul was withering away. She wanted to venture into more of a healing profession, but she constantly was thinking, "What if it won't work?" "What if my job does get better?"

"What if I wait longer?" The what-ifs had extended her soul's expiration date. Look at the facts to break out of this trap. What is actually going on in your job? Have they given you a raise? Do they value you and appreciate you? Does it nourish you and light you up? Is your romantic partner doing the actual work? Are they invested in their spiritual and mental health? Do you see results? Remember the danger of fantasy world vs. reality world. Getting caught up in fantasy worlds is particularly common for love addicts, who build this ideal in their heads for fear of taking the leap and doing the real work to have the real relationship.

You deserve to focus on the truth of the moment. It is important to remove the veils from the illusion of what you wish would happen and show up to what is happening. There is a difference between dreaming up your future and fantasizing in an unhealthy way. The key here is to look at reality and be empowered in moving.

Soul Lesson: "I focus on what *is*, not what-*if*s."

Trap 4: Trap of Being Too Nice

In our culture, women especially are trained to think that it is either/or. We are either the virgin or the slut. We are either a saint or evil. The way of the wild woman is the way we get to be both. We get to be grounded in the reality of being loving and fierce.

We are sold the illusion that being "good" is what society needs. Perhaps we were told as a child, "Be a good girl/boy and be quiet." "*Los niños no son para hablar. Escuchan y ya.*" "Kids are not to speak. They are to listen and that's it." These messages get ingrained in our mind and then we believe that if we step into our voice and our power, we are wrong and bad. We feel guilty for calling a thing a thing. Well, not anymore, Diosa. It's time to reclaim your voice and power.

One of my clients, Clarissa, recently decided to stop talking to a guy who she was in a casual relationship with. They would have sex and hang out, but he was not willing to commit to her. Eventually, she realized they didn't align in their goals and that she needed to move on. She sent him a powerful, loving, and clear text stating something along the lines of "Thank you for the times we have had. I have grown and learned a lot through our times together. I have realized that we are not on the same page about our desires and goals. I am looking for commitment, and that is something you cannot offer me. I respect where you are at and now I am going to respect where I am at. I want more, and more is not available here, so I must move on. I ask that you honor my space and don't reach out, as I want to focus on myself and really move forward. I wish you the best in your life path."

He understood where she was coming from and agreed that he couldn't give her more. That he would miss her but that he understood. So far, all was good. He then asked, "Can we be friends?" Clarissa, then, had to tune inward and see if that truly was in alignment for her. She checked in and her soul said, "I am not open to a friendship. What is healthiest for me is to move on and have no contact. A friendship would be too hurtful. So for the foreseeable future, the answer is no. But I thank you for all this has shown me. No hard feelings. It just isn't a fit for me. Take care of yourself."

She was clear and to the point and confident. He then responded, "Okay, I understand. I will respect that."

A few weeks went by, and Clarissa was in Paris enjoying herself. Feeling strong, Diosa-like, and empowered for listening to her gut, cutting ties, and being clear and direct. She was fierce and she was feeling herself as a result. He texted her, "I miss you." She ignored it. Then again, a few days later, "I know I am not supposed to reach out, but I miss you a lot, Clarissa." No response; she was staying true to herself. The third time, "I hope you're okay, wondering how you are. You mean a lot to me. I am sad that we can't be friends. Is that possible at all? Maybe grab some lunch when you're back?"

At this point the temptation came in. Two times she was strong and aligned with soul, but that third time she caved. She began to rationalize, "I shouldn't be mean. He is being nice, and how bad can it be to just be friends?" She responded, "Okay we can try that. That sounds good." She went with the nice girl.

When she returned, they had lunch and within ten minutes he was telling her about the other woman that he had been seeing and how he chose her over Clarissa. He shared how he always would have chosen her because she never wanted a relationship. He broke her heart in ten minutes on their lunch meeting. Clarissa got to see the darkness. He lured her, and then once he had her, he suffocated her soul and tried to capture her spark, her power, her confidence. She had been so clear and secure and walked away so easily and with grace that his insecurities were triggered. And remember, wounded men like this are dangerous—they prey on you and wait until you are strong to try to take you down. It's a power dynamic. Thankfully, Clarissa and I had been working together, so she knew better than to believe it was her. Part of her self-esteem was of course hurt, because, *hello*, who wouldn't be? But she gathered herself and said, "You're really fucked up and I should have never come here. You're right, you always would have chosen her, because I didn't choose you, I left because you aren't for me. I never want to see you; please do not contact me."

Sometimes we need to be tested a few times before we get it. It's part of the process. So if this happens to you, know that it's normal and just pivot back to soul center. Clarissa booked another session with me to get back on track, and on our call, I joked with her that I like to imagine this team of sweet angels all cute, giving light messages and whispering, "He isn't for you. There is more out there." They try to get you to listen, and then when you don't, the gangster tatted angel comes like, "NO, MAMITA! This ain't working, boo boo. You got to get your shit together, mama. This motherfucker is an asshole, an energy vampire, and you about to get trapped! Get your butt out of here."

Soul Lesson: "I honor my soul's directions."

Trap 5: Thinking You Are "Too Much"

It is scary to speak our truth, and thinking that we are "too much" can cause us to ignore our intuition and stop our communication. This trap is common when I speak to women about dating.

Jasmin shared during our coaching session, "I don't think I should tell him that I didn't like that he made me wait till last minute to give me the details of the restaurant and the time and location. Maybe it's too soon to say that, and if I say something, he will think I am too much and crazy and then not like me. I should play it cool and just respond 'Awesome, see you there.'" The problem here was that her date didn't confirm plans until one hour before the time of their date. She wasn't able to plan her day. It takes about forty-five minutes to arrive at the location, and she was in suspension all day without her date communicating.

Many times, there is a fear that speaking up is not sexy or not an attractive quality. On the contrary, speaking up is like a force field that protects our spirit, our energy field, our needs, our truth, our confidence.

How we say something is far more important than what we say. And most are not taught how to say it or that we deserve to say anything, so women are left waiting, feeling insecure and giving their power away. The Diosa way to date is to be the one that is choosing and that is empowered to lovingly but securely speak her truth. Why waste time? This noncommunication actually makes you accept bad behavior for longer than what it would be if you were able to call it out.

Instead, I coached Jasmin to say, "Hey, I was looking forward to hanging with you tonight, but since I hadn't heard from you with a time and a place, I made other plans." This showed her date that she honored her time and boundaries. Either he steps up to the plate or he doesn't, but this brings the truth to the surface. Here, truth can appear sooner versus being in the "play it cool" cloud of illusion and accepting behaviors that don't align with her soul.

Be aware when you are scared to speak up to behaviors that you do not like. It is key to break the trap by speaking your truth in a loving and direct way.

Soul Lesson: "I speak my truth when something doesn't align with my truth."

Trap 6: The Law of Attraction

There have been a lot of psychologically ungrounded spiritual teachings based on the Law of Attraction that have made many spiritual seekers believe that if something comes into their life, that they should simply accept it and believe that they attracted it and "deserved it" somehow. This thinking can be very dangerous. It is more helpful to ask yourself, "Is this situation or relationship or thing in my life aligned with who I want to be? Am I staying longer in this situation, thinking I must learn something by staying but suffering as a result?" If you are suffering emotionally, mentally, psychologically, etc., you do not have to stay. Sometimes the spiritual lesson is learning to *leave*.

The law of attraction has certain principles that are attractive for many and some parts of it are relevant, but it lacks the psychological meat that empowers people to ask questions and be curious, to support them in making empowered choices. It makes people believe they are so important that they made all happen to them. No one is that powerful to make all happen to them. Life is life, and we must understand there is a bigger force at work. In this way, we are not bound by the trap of the Law of Attraction. We are able to analyze, choose, and accept that not *all* is because of you . . . but once something arrives, it *is* your choice in how to handle it.

Soul Lesson: The universe is mysterious and not all is because of me. I instead ground and I am intentional about choosing what to do when situations arise in my life.

Trap 7: Self-Doubt

As we work on learning how to trust ourselves better, it is very common to experience a lot of self-doubt on the way to self-trust. Doubting that you are worthy enough to have boundaries with men. Doubting that you are good enough to start that business. Doubting that you can and will be okay on your own. Doubting your internal voice.

The trap of self-doubt is one that diminishes your self-worth and swag. It's the voice that is constantly confused. Be aware of when self-doubt comes, but instead of shunning it outright, listen into it and speak directly to it.

When you start to hear or sense self-doubt creeping in, question it and speak truth to it. Often when you are having doubts, it is because you have not had the time to be still with yourself to fill yourself up with your own Diosa power, divinity, confidence. So take some time and space, however small, to listen to yourself before you act. Try not to make decisions when self-doubt is present. Trust yourself to make decisions when you are feeling confident. You can be nervous and confident, but do not heed the advice of self-doubt.

My friend once read to me this bible verse, 2 Timothy 1:7, that she reads when she is feeling insecure: "For God has not given us a spirit of fear, but of power and of love and of a sound mind." When you are not in sound mind, you are in the spirit of fear. Don't trust fear and self-doubt, because that is the voice of darkness. Love and the Divine won't have you listening to the trap of doubt. So call it out when doubt is there. Pray and meditate, and when you feel in sound mind, then listen.

Soul Lesson: I do not believe the voice of doubt. I believe the voice of confidence and sound mind.

Navigating the Traps

The point of highlighting these soul traps is so that you can move forward with awareness. Awareness is your shield through life. It allows you to guard and protect your intuition. Remember and never forget that your intuition is a gift, a divine and sacred guide throughout life. If you know the traps, you will learn to get better at not falling into them, or if you fall into them, you will learn to get out of them faster. Some do stay in the traps for years. We all know of at least one woman who has sold her soul for the lure of a counterfeit-gold job or cookie-cutter man who doesn't fulfill her soul. We all know someone that has put their dream to write a book on a shelf collecting dust for fear they aren't a real writer. We all know someone who has stayed in a toxic relationship and lost all her light in the arms of her energy vampire. Some traps lead to not only spiritual deaths and emotional deaths but actual deaths too. Women who have died in the arms of their abuser or killed themselves because the soul way became too beyond reach. This is not to instill fear, but to place a healthy dose of reality. For grounded spirituality is about reality and magic—not escaping the harsh truths, but instead embracing them so we know what we are working with. We want to break lineages of women who have stayed in the trap.

These soul traps are opportunities for deep growth. They are there to test you. They are there for you to learn from and grow from. Once you learn to sniff the traps and take spiritually aligned actions, you gain access to deeper intuition, as well as a renewed sense of courage, self-esteem, self-worth, and overall soul growth. If we can approach the situations that we face as spiritual assignments designed to grow us, we can get excited to do the work. I remember the moment I started to really get that every time a trap came along, or obstacle where I was confused or triggered or scared, there was a simultaneous miracle waiting beneath the test . . . I started to get excited to conquer the next mission. It is essential for us to stay awake and see beneath the moments that seem most difficult so that we can access the healing there waiting for us. These limitations are key for women in their journey back home to self and soul. When we know this and we speak to this, we have more possibility of not going on the dead-end roads, on the lifeless paths.

Soulwork

To move through the soul traps, you must learn to recognize the soul traps. Using your journal, write down your responses to the following questions:

1. What are the traps that are most prevalent in your life?
2. How has ignoring the soul traps caused harm in your life?
3. What is the feeling in your body when you are ignoring a soul trap?
4. What is the animal that you want to embody to become aware when the traps are there? For example, it might be an owl, for clear seeing in the night, or a wolf, to smell better. There is no wrong choice; listen to your intuition.
5. What do you want to discover on the other side of ignoring the soul traps? For example, on the other side of ignoring the soul traps is an empowered, intuitive woman who senses truth and listens to the truth she senses.

Mantra

I awaken the primal wisdom within. I smell the traps in advance, and I act accordingly to keep myself safe.

Ceremony

Make Your Trap

For this ceremony, choose one of the traps that is most present in your life today. You will create a physical manifestation of what the trap looks like in life so that you can own where you are and choose how to move forward.

I did a ceremony like this years ago, and to this day it was one of the most profound experiences of my life. At the time I was still coping with alcohol, and when I was drunk I would act out sexually. It wasn't that my sexuality was wrong; it was that it was coming from a wounded place. I needed to be coming from an emotionally sober place of conscious choice instead of a fragmented place of reactive behavior. I knew something was off with this compulsive behavior and I knew I wanted to honor myself deeper and heal this relationship with my sexuality. I called on my spiritual adviser and we created a piece of art that represented that "trap of toxic, quick-fix sex" in my life. It was on me to get creative and think of what represented this dark version of my sexuality. I was guided to get a bunch of condoms and thick black tape. I wrapped it all around the condoms to represent being tied up in a mess of different energetic sex strings. I then finished up the piece by hanging different strings that represented all of the uncut cords that I had created due to my acting out sexually. It was a simple exercise and yet so profound. To materialize something that I had been doing really made it real for me. I then bought a card and wrote a promise letter to myself, committing to honoring my sexuality and healing the root of my drinking. That willingness to do this ritual and truly *see* the condoms and the black tape and threads allowed me to own what was going on internally within me. Ritual and art are a powerful practice that allows for deep soul transformation and healing.

Now I want you to practice this ritual:

1. Choose the Soul Trap that is most present in your life today.
2. Create some sort of physical art piece that represents this trap in your life.
3. Write a letter to yourself committing to how you will no longer fall into that trap, and your commitment to protecting, honoring, and revering yourself as the Diosa you are.

Great work! These ceremonies might bring up feelings. And if they do, that is wonderful. Let it all flow. Tears, heart opening, purging—all is welcome here. Continue to breathe and be proud of yourself for doing this deep soulwork.

Yes, mama! Booty dancing in celebration with you. We are waking up our primal feminine powers and beginning to see and smell and taste what is not soul aligned! I love this chapter because it allows us to call the traps out loud and name them. Naming them, and being aware of them, decreases their power in your life. The wolf woman is alive in you—she is smelling the traps that are designed to hold you back, make you settle, and essentially kill *la creatura* (the creature) within—the primal essence. Awakening in your primal awareness, you embrace this reawakened intuitive power—with confidence, ease, wise eyes, and grace. You proceed on this journey back home to true soul and self with something different within. A new knowing. The knowing you feel when a woman that sees with her spiritual sight and smells with her soul-sniffing senses walks into a room. Real feels real. I am proud of you. If any other traps arise, name them, explore them, and activate your wolf senses to know when a trap is near—so that you may avoid them and embrace the gift that awaits as you accomplish your spiritual mission of not giving in to the temptation of the soul trap.

I awaken the primal wisdom within.

I smell the traps in advance, and I act accordingly to keep myself safe.

#iamdiosa

CHAPTER 5

The Body as a Map: Rewiring Our System

"Someone who has experienced trauma also has gifts to offer all of us—
in their depth, their knowledge of our universal vulnerability, and their
experience of the power of compassion."
—Sharon Salzberg

As the Buddha and many others have demonstrated, part of living in the world is opening up to the reality of suffering. It is inevitable that all of us will experience suffering, isolation, emotional and physical pain, and betrayal at the hands of loved ones and those we encounter in our day-to-day lives. This pain can haunt us and remain in our bodies and souls for our entire lives, or it can be something that is limited to specific experiences and moments in our lives. Whatever the case, suffering always brings with it the residue of trauma.

There are plenty of different definitions for what trauma is, but for the most part, you can think of it as a psychological response to experiences that were distressing or disturbing. Whether you were in an accident, going through an illness, moving through a separation or divorce, losing someone you love, or surviving abuse. Even when these experiences are not necessarily life-threatening, they can have adverse effects on our ability to function in our full whole-ness and human being–ness. They can lead us to contract in fear or explode in rage—and because trauma is so layered, it isn't neces-sarily easy to deal with or navigate, much less feel we have any control over.

A trauma-informed approach to our emotional, physical, men-tal, and spiritual well-being is key! As a therapist who has worked to help hundreds of women heal lifelong and ongoing trauma, I know that it takes much more than just talking about it. We can all come up with rational descriptions about what trauma is and how it might play out for us individually, but that isn't enough to actually work through it. Trauma is something that must be healed on a funda-mental level, in the body and in the soul. This is because trauma literally gets trapped in the body after we go through a traumatizing experience. So it is not something that we can merely pour positive affirmations on; we can't just "wish it away" or convince ourselves that the past is the past so we shouldn't dwell on it anymore. Denial or avoidance is a totally understandable defense mechanism when you encounter trauma, but it doesn't take it away.

Clinical psychologist Peter Levine authored a wonderful book called *Waking the Tiger*, which I highly recommend to anyone who wants a better understanding of how trauma works, especially in the body and brain. He writes, "The bodies of traumatized people por-tray 'snapshots' of their unsuccessful attempts to defend themselves in the face of threat and injury. Trauma is a highly activated incom-plete biological response to threat, frozen in time. For example, when we prepare to fight or to flee, muscles throughout our entire body are tensed in specific patterns of high energy readiness. When we are unable to complete the appropriate actions, we fail to discharge the tremendous energy generated by our survival preparations. This en-ergy becomes fixed in specific patterns of neuromuscular readiness. The person then stays in a state of acute and then chronic arousal and dysfunction in the central nervous system. Traumatized people are not suffering from a disease in the normal sense of the word— they have become stuck in an aroused state. It is difficult if not impossible to function normally under these circumstances."

As Levine shares, in the face of trauma, the unsuccessful ability to defend yourself creates stored energy that gets locked inside the body and nervous system. Being stuck in this aroused state means that we are much more susceptible to post-traumatic stress disorder (PTSD) and to being retraumatized by "trigger" events that remind us of the trauma we experienced, even if it was decades ago.

I'm sure you can relate to being in an aroused state of anger or intense emotion, and the sense of not being able to get out of it or simply "shake it off," the way an animal in the wild might after a dangerous encounter with a predator.

From the age of fourteen, I used to suffer from panic attacks and would feel like I was literally dying. In moments of high anxiety and paranoia, it felt as if my mind would disconnect and float around outside my body. It was an out-of-body experience in the worst way possible, and it terrified me.

I clearly remember my very first panic attack. I was walking to the pizzeria, and my body began to feel strange. My thoughts raced, and fear permeated every part of my body. My skin was blazing hot, and my cheeks flushed red. I was convinced that everyone around me could see it. They knew that I was going insane. It was an intense and horrible feeling that I now understand was the consequence of constantly living in a high-stress environment full of yelling, cursing, hitting, and breaking things. That volatility was ricocheting through my nervous system, and because I'd never gotten a chance to process it in a healthy way—perhaps by receiving validation from a trusted adult—my body reacted and reverted to panic attacks as a way to cope with the trauma. The body is a truly intelligent being, and even when the sensations we experience don't feel "good," they are essentially present in order to help us discharge the energy that Peter Levine was talking about.

Sadly, that sense of tension and anxiety followed me for years. I remember the feeling of intense fear in my belly whenever I was around my ex, who was abusive and a serial cheater. It literally made me feel sick to my stomach. My entire body was hot, and my chest was constricted. In fact, this feeling persisted even when he wasn't around, almost as if my body was letting me know that he was out there, cheating on me. He was also selling drugs at the time, and although my body knew it, he would lie and pretend he was on a run. The fact that he was gaslighting my intuition and what I innately knew was doubly disturbing and traumatizing.

I grew up in a household full of lies that never came out in the open but that continued to be covered up by my family members. Throughout it all, my intuition was constantly in conflict with what people insisted was true—which can naturally make it incredibly difficult to trust one's own body. What I was experiencing with my ex was frustratingly familiar. Each time the trigger of hearing his lies came up, it sent vital signals to my nervous system. The trauma was reactivated—and let me tell you, when this happened, it was debilitating. Through the practices that I have shared here and through years of therapy, I was able to slowly work with my nervous system so that I could finally feel safe again.

Through breathwork, grounding practices, and simply receiving some valuable psychoeducation that informed me of the ways in which trauma operates and how it can cause panic attacks, I was able to deeply heal. In fact, I went from having panic attacks on a weekly basis to not even being able to remember the last time I had one.

Of course, I can't say that the panic attacks or the physical sensations I know are directly related to my trauma will never strike again. But at the very least, I have tools that keep my anxiety and panic attacks at bay. Also, with the continuous therapy and support groups that I attend, such as Alcoholics Anonymous, I continue to find opportunities for expressing myself in healthy ways—in a sense, finding effective methods of discharging intense energy and calming my nervous system, rather than allowing it to circulate in my body and keep me in a triggered state.

Some of the tools in this book will become your helpers and companions through life, and others will perhaps fall to the wayside. You might even pick them up again at some other point in your life. Regardless of what you do, I encourage you to give them a try and make them your own. Many of my practices that I have shared have literally saved not only my life, but the lives of countless Diosas I have worked with. They have helped us to persevere and step into our best selves, rather than believing our trauma is all that is real.

The body is your interface between your internal experience and your experience with the world. It's also the site of some really important information about how and where you hold trauma. In the diagram that follows, you will write down where in your body you feel trauma and traumatic memories.

First, however, we will go on a journey inward that taps into your experiences of anger, sadness, and loneliness, all of which are primal emotions connected to our trauma. I encourage you to gently travel into the past and feel into where you experience trapped emotions and feelings that need to be given space for healthy expression and release. Just remember that in this moment, you are safe. You may wish to record yourself speaking the three-part meditation aloud, or go to my website to download the free guided meditation at christineg.tv/iamdiosameditations. If the meditation feels too intense at any point, I recommend for you to stop, breathe to ground and do this with a trained therapist. Only go as deep as you feel safe to.

Somatic Guided Journey in Three Parts

In this meditation, we will first focus on the emotion of anger, how you react to anger, your first memory of anger and, finally, how to move through it. Feel free to read through the meditation once before doing it. You can also record yourself reading it and play it back. I have also have the following meditations available for free on my website.

Part 1

Let's get started by finding a comfortable position, seated or lying down. Place your hands on your lap or by your sides. Just take the next few moments to settle in to the meditation, wherever you are.

Gently close your eyes. Take a few deep breaths here. Slowly breathing in . . . and slowly breathing out. With each exhale, start to let go of any tension you're holding. Relax your shoulders, soften your forehead, and release any tension in your jaw.

Allow yourself to just flow with the natural rhythm of your soothing breath. Breathing in . . . and breathing out.

Let's begin as I always do. Say to yourself, "I call myself back from all times and all places. I call myself back from all times and all places. I call myself back from all times and all places. I am here now. I call myself back home today, for however far I have strayed. I call myself back home today. Back home to my soul home."

Allow yourself to return to your body in this moment. Feel into your emotions. Give yourself permission to explore the feeling of anger. So often, we run from the feeling or act it out. This is your chance to feel into the feelings so that you can face them, nurture them, hear them, and localize where they are living in the body and nervous system. You will get a chance to encounter the trauma that lives below this very strong emotion. As we bring this into awareness, shifts can be made. Healing occurs.

When you learn to breathe into these feelings and navigate where they exist in your inner emotional terrain, you're making a choice to ensure that anger doesn't take the driver's seat. You can become more aware of how it affects you and thus make shifts so that you can alchemize and channel it, rather than allowing it to control and sabotage you.

As humans, we face situations that may trigger emotions of anger that we don't know how to fix right away. Maybe a driver just cut you off in traffic. Maybe your partner keeps forgetting a date you told them to write down. Maybe it's something more serious. Maybe it's extreme anger towards a family member or close friend who has hurt you. Underneath these emotions of anger are colors, sensations, memories.

It's easy to obsess and focus on pushing away anger, so much so that we become more annoyed, stressed, tense, distracted, and even sick. Let us go to the root now, to feel the anger that perhaps you have suppressed.

Allow anger to come forward. If the idea of bringing forward anger makes you feel a sense of panic, take comfort in the fact that this will be temporary. Think back to your memories of anger as a child. Perhaps one memory stands out. Don't think about it too much; just let what wants to come, come. Give yourself permission to breathe and go back in time to remember your first experience of the sensation of anger. Think about the details of that moment. How old were you? Who was involved? Where were you? What did it smell like? What did the air feel like? What particular action made you angry?

Continue to breathe in and out, giving yourself that ease as you do this deep and powerful work. Let the breath nourish you as you go there.

Where in your body do you feel the anger?
What color is the anger?

What are its textures or shapes?

Is it sharp? Is it red?

Go into the feeling and explore the core of the anger and how it shows up in your body.

Allow symbols to come up that represent this anger in your body.

Observe the emotions that arise from this without reacting.

Now imagine you are sitting in front of a fire; the fire brings you back home and speaks to your soul. As large clouds of smoke arise from the fire, visually place your thoughts and emotions of anger into them. Allow them to rise and gracefully float away into the dark starry night.

As you watch them float away, focus on your breath as the anchor that is keeping you grounded.

Meditation is your way of transforming anger into clarity and guidance. This will help you to approach your problems differently, and with greater compassion and understanding.

Allow your thoughts to keep dissolving as smoke into the sky. Let the attachments of fear, judgment, over-analysis, or resentment that arise from your anger dissolve into the vast night. Focus on your deep breath. You are healing. You are coming back to your true soul home.

(Pause for twenty seconds.)

When your mind wanders, bring it back to the fire. Use your breath as the anchor.

(Pause for thirty seconds.)

Breathe in. Breathe out.

(Pause for thirty seconds.)

Before you finish this meditation, take a nice, deep breath. Breathe in for a count of 1, 2, 3, 4, 5, 6 . . . And breathe out for a count of 1, 2, 3, 4, 5, 6.

Call yourself back home from all times and all places. You are here now.

Whenever you feel ready, move your fingers and toes gently.

Blink open your eyes and take a moment to come back to your surroundings.

Congratulations on finishing this meditation. Feel free to revisit this technique anytime you want to feel the anger and localize it to release it in a healthy way.

Part 2

In this next part, we will focus on the emotion of sadness and when the first memory of sadness emerged within you.

Let's get started by finding a comfortable position, seated or lying down. Place your hands on your lap or by your sides. Just take the next few moments to settle in to the meditation, wherever you are.

Let's begin as I always do. Say to yourself, "I call myself back from all times and all places. I call myself back from all times and all places. I call myself back from all times and all places. I am here now. I call myself back home today, for however far I have strayed. I call myself back home today. Back home to my soul home."

Allow yourself to return to your body in this moment. Feel into your emotions. Give yourself permission to explore the feeling of sadness. So often, we run from the feeling or act it out. This is your chance to feel into the feelings so that you can face them, nurture them, hear them, and localize where they are living in the body and nervous system. You will get a chance to encounter the trauma that lives below this very strong emotion. As we bring this into awareness, shifts can be made. Healing occurs.

If you've recorded this or are listening to my guided meditation, gently close your eyes. Take a few deep breaths here. Slowly breathing in . . . and slowly breathing out. With each exhale, start to let go of any tension you're holding. Relax your shoulders, soften your forehead, and release any tension in your jaw.

Allow yourself to just flow with the natural rhythm of your soothing breath. Breathing in . . . and breathing out . . .

Let's begin.

Allow yourself to go back into the past, to the first time you can remember feeling sad.

Where were you?

How old were you?

What colors or smells come to mind?

What were you wearing?

Who was around you?

Where in your body did you feel the sadness?

What made you feel sad?

Look into the eyes of yourself at whatever age you are in this first memory of sadness. What do your eyes say?

Take a moment to feel into your energy and sadness.

When you learn to breathe into these feelings, you're making a choice to ensure that sadness doesn't take the driver's seat, but instead, you can honor all emotions that come up. Our society has trained us to think that difficult emotions are bad, but suppressed emotions are the only kinds of emotions we should worry about. All emotions are beautiful. We must honor them and give ourselves the space to feel all emotions within us. For we are nature, and nature contains both sunshine and rain. And we contain both happiness and sadness—sometimes all in the span of the same minute.

We must learn to observe the sadness. Sink into the sadness. Localize the sadness. And touch into the core feelings that were born in our childhood so that we can understand ourselves and thus free ourselves from the bondage of repressed feelings.

Be very proud of yourself for doing this work. You're doing a great job.

Take another deep, full breath in and hold for three counts: 1, 2, 3. And exhale it all out through your mouth for five counts . . . with a beautiful sigh: 1, 2, 3, 4, 5. Great work.

As humans, we face situations that may trigger emotions of sadness that we don't know how to fix right away. Maybe a sad song just played. Maybe your partner had to cancel plans. Maybe it's something more serious. Maybe you're grieving the loss of someone you love. And many times, something in the moment might be reminding you of something from your past.

It's easy to try to push away or get distracted by sadness, so much so that you become sadder, stressed, tense, and even sick.

Notice if you're feeling sadness about something that happened today or something that goes back to your childhood. Continue to breathe as you reflect . . . breathing in through your nose and out through your mouth. Wonderful.

Now localize a recent feeling of sadness. If you begin to feel anxious about this, rest assured that this is a temporary exploration. Take time to recreate the situation that made you feel sad and hopeless. Who was involved? Where were you? What particular action created this sadness? Does this remind you at all of your earlier memory from childhood? There is no right or wrong answer. Simply observation.

Breathing in and out . . . continue to take deep, full breaths in and deep, full breaths out.

Observe the emotions that arise from this experience without reacting. Now imagine you are sitting in front of a waterfall; the water brings you back home and speaks to your soul. As the water falls down onto the rocks below, visually throw your thoughts and emotions of sadness at the water as if you were throwing pebbles. Watch them fall with the water and wash away into the river below. Honor each pebble with love and reverence, for sadness is a sacred teacher. As you watch them wash away, focus on your breath as the anchor that keeps you grounded.

Meditation is your way to learn about yourself and heal this sadness. This will help you approach your problems differently, and with greater compassion and understanding.

Allow those thoughts to keep washing away with the waterfall. Let the attachments of fear, judgment, overanalysis, or pain from your sadness be washed away with the cleansing water. Focus on your breath. You are healing. You are coming back to your soul home.

When your mind wanders, bring it back to the waterfall. Use your breath as the anchor. Breathe in. Breathe out.

(Pause for fifteen seconds.)

Before you finish this meditation, take a nice, deep breath. Breathe in for a count of 1, 2, 3, 4, 5, 6. And breathe out for a count of 1, 2, 3, 4, 5, 6.

We call ourselves back from all times and all places. We call ourselves back from all times and all places. We call ourselves back from all times and all places. We are here now.

Whenever you feel ready, move your fingers and toes gently. Gently open your eyes and take a moment to come back to your surroundings. Congratulations on finishing this meditation. Feel free to revisit this technique anytime you want to feel the sadness and localize it to release it in a healthy way.

Part 3

Last, we will explore the feeling of loneliness and the first time that loneliness made its way to your door. Remember, we are touching base with these feelings to get to know how they are continuing to run us and to show up in your life. We want a healthy relationship to difficult emotions so that we can process them and cope with them in more effective ways.

Let's get started by finding a comfortable position, seated or lying down. Place your hands on your lap or by your sides. Just take the next few moments to settle in to the meditation, wherever you are.

If you've recorded this or are listening to my guided meditation, gently close your eyes. Take a few deep breaths here. Slowly breathing in . . . and slowly breathing out. With each exhale, start to let go of any tension you're holding. Relax your shoulders, soften your forehead, and release any tension in your jaw.

Allow yourself to just flow with the natural rhythm of your soothing breath. Breathing in . . . and breathing out.

Let's begin as I always do. Say to yourself, "I call myself back from all times and all places. I call myself back from all times and all places. I call myself back from all times and all places. I am here now. I call myself back home today, for however far I have strayed. I call myself back home today. Back home to my soul home."

Allow yourself to return to your body in this moment. Feel into your emotions. Give yourself permission to explore the feeling of loneliness. So often, we run from the feeling or act it out. This is your chance to feel into the feelings so that you can face them, nurture them, hear them, and localize where they are living in the body and nervous system. You will get a chance to encounter the trauma that lives below this very strong emotion. As we bring this into awareness, shifts can be made. Healing occurs.

When you learn to breathe into these feelings and navigate where they exist in your inner emotional terrain, you're making a choice to ensure that loneliness doesn't take the driver's seat. You can become more aware of how it affects you and thus make shifts so that you can move toward a greater sense of connection.

As humans, we face situations that may trigger emotions of loneliness that we don't know how to fix right away. Maybe you feel isolated within a community you are a part of. Perhaps you feel misunderstood by friends and family. Or maybe you worry that you will never have the close, intimate relationships you long for. Underneath these emotions of loneliness are colors, sensations, memories.

It's easy to obsess and focus on pushing away loneliness, so much so that we become more annoyed, stressed, tense, distracted, and even sick. Let us go to the root now, to feel the loneliness that perhaps you have suppressed.

Allow loneliness to come forward. If the idea of bringing forward loneliness makes you feel a sense of panic, take comfort in the fact that this will be temporary. Think back to your memories of loneliness as a child. Perhaps one memory stands out. Don't think about it too much; just let what wants to come, come. Give yourself permission to breathe and go back into time to remember your first experience of the sensation of loneliness. Think about the details of that moment. How old were you? Who was involved? Where were you? What did it smell like? What did the air feel like? What particular experience made you lonely?

Continue to breathe in and out, giving yourself that ease as you do this deep and powerful work. Let the breath nourish you as you go there.

Where in your body do you feel the loneliness?

What color is the loneliness?

What are its textures or shapes?

Go into the feeling and explore the core of the loneliness and how it shows up in your body.

Allow symbols to come up that represent this loneliness in your body.

Observe the emotions that arise from this without reacting.

Now, imagine you are making contact with a beautiful, large tree. As you sit close to the tree, you can feel the comfort of its branches and leaves offering shade, and the softness of the earth offering you a beautiful, cozy place to sit. This tree is your friend, and its supportive roots stretch deep into the earth beneath you, giving you support and sustenance. Lean back against the tree. Allow your feelings of loneliness to simply sink away into the earth, to be alchemized by the roots of the tree, and to feed the soil with energy that can be transmuted into nutrients. Feel the sense of lightness that replaces this loneliness.

As you watch your feelings of loneliness float away, focus on your breath as the anchor that keeps you grounded.

(Pause for fifteen seconds.)

Meditation is your way of transforming loneliness into stillness and serenity. This will help you to approach your problems differently, and with greater compassion and understanding.

Allow your thoughts to keep melting into the earth. Let the attachments of fear, judgment, overanalysis, or resentment that arise from your loneliness dissolve into the strong and supportive soil. Focus on your deep breath. You are healing. You are coming back to your true soul home.

(Pause for twenty seconds.)

When your mind wanders, bring it back to the tree you are sitting with, and into the earth beneath you. Use your breath as the anchor.

(Pause for thirty seconds.)

Breathe in. Breathe out.

(Pause for thirty seconds.)

Before you finish this meditation, take a nice, deep breath. Breathe in for a count of 1, 2, 3, 4, 5, 6 . . . And breathe out for a count of 1, 2, 3, 4, 5, 6.

Call yourself back home from all times and all places. You are here now.

Whenever you feel ready, move your fingers and toes gently.

Gently open your eyes and take a moment to come back to your surroundings.

Congratulations on finishing this meditation. Feel free to revisit this technique anytime you want to feel the loneliness and localize it to release it in a healthy way.

Embodying Safety, Love, and Joy

After you finish this meditation, look at the diagram below. Where are you holding feelings of anger, sadness, and loneliness, whether they are present realities or past memories? What are the sensations you feel (*e.g.*, heat, constriction, panic, numbness, etc.)?

Draw in the diagram below what you felt during those three different somatic journeys. If you have different color pencils feel free to use those as well. Get creative with what came up for you. Any words, or ages, or symbols, or names and write them all down in the diagram. Seeing where these emotions live in our body allows us to heal them.

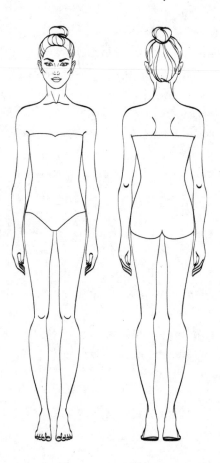

Now that you know where you are holding these emotions, you can focus on guiding more love, attention, and breath to these places in your body that require your utmost compassion and attention. Over time, as you work with your emotions, you will notice that you have more space in these body parts to express and feel other emotions, including safety, love, and joy. Filling yourself with these emotions is a crucial part of rewiring your nervous system to feel wholeness in the wake of trauma.

Unfortunately, trauma dysregulates the body. It can move you into a state of hyperarousal (which I call panic mode) or hypoarousal (feelings of emptiness, depression, and low energy). And when we are stuck in trauma, it becomes easy to oscillate between these extremes. Dysregulation can lead to all kinds of coping mechanisms, from addictions to alcohol and substances, to workaholism, to disassociation and "spacing out." Thankfully, there are practices that can help us become somatically resensitized to safety, love, and joy.

As you continue to listen to your body, offer yourself the experience of safety—which you likely did not receive at some pivotal point in your life. Thankfully, you can do so now. Place your hand over your heart and say, "I'm here for you, [insert your name]. I will never leave you. You are safe, and everything is going to be okay." Do this in times when you don't feel safe. And consider a simple act you can take that will make you feel safe—perhaps this would be talking to a close friend about your feelings, or drawing a hot bath, or doing anything else that connects you with a visceral sense of safety.

You can also do the same with both love and joy. I especially recommend loving-kindness meditation, a contemplative practice that encourages the cultivation of unconditional love. You can do it for others, but it's especially beautiful when you do it for yourself. Give yourself care, tenderness, and friendship. Place your hand over your heart and feel your mind and body soften into the experience of pure love, which is your ultimate and core identity. Breathe in and out from your heart center. You might feel some blockages at first, but that's okay. Drop beneath any self-judgments to a place of unconditional love for yourself. Then say out loud, "May I be happy. May I be free. May I be at peace. May I be able to live in this world with joy and ease."

You can also allow the experience of joy, which is very much connected to love, to arise here. You deserve to have feelings of aliveness, engagement, pleasure, and exuberance in this very moment. Often, trauma can negatively interfere with our ability to fully sink into deeper enjoyment of our lives, but it doesn't have to be this way. Place your hand over your heart and connect with the deepest parts of your soul. Then allow yourself to think of everything in your life that gives you joy, even if it's as seemingly minor as the smile of a child you saw on a playground. Everything counts. Allow gratitude to fill your heart, for where there is gratitude, joy is magnified. And remember that joy is not an escape from your life. It is not about living in a state of perfection either; it is about recognizing awe, wonder, and goodness, as well as the interweaving of positive connections in your life.

Allow all of this to feed you, Diosa. More than anything, hold the awareness that it is possible to grow and to heal in the wake of our trauma, and to come back to life despite the mini-deaths you might have previously experienced. I know this from firsthand experience.

You contain the world in your body, in your bones. Safety, love, and joy are your birthright. Allowing yourself to incorporate them into your life will require patience and perseverance, but I promise that the road to liberation will lead you to the restoration of your wholeness.

Tools for Trauma

It's important to connect with a variety of tools that help you to face the effects of trauma in your life. The reality is, it can often be hard to simply be at peace. This isn't only because of past conditioning, but because of the way we are designed. We are porous beings rather than self-contained pods of organs and sensations. Even if we wake up feeling totally unfazed, chances are that our internal landscapes respond to even the teeny-tiny fluctuations in our emotional ecosystem. In other words, if a storm's a-brewing over there, I'm likely to feel it over here . . . sometimes before I realize that's what's happening.

I offer the following healing tools to you.

Grounding: Connecting with the earth is such a powerful way to bring ourselves back to the present moment, and to feel connected to a solid sense of reality. Panic that arises from being retraumatized or triggered can send us into a whirlwind of disconnecting emotions, but the earth is always here to gently reconnect us. In fact, the vibration of the earth is harmonious, because plants are naturally self-healing and not prone to having their bodies act as permanent energetic dumping grounds. Trees are particularly powerful teachers when it comes to demonstrating how we can live in the world in a way that is both deeply rooted and infinitely flexible. When you're feeling either high-strung or down in the dumps, sit with your back against a tree, as I instructed in the somatic meditation. As you feel the supportive weight of the tree against your body, imagine the feelings of panic or anxiety being drained out of you like a toilet flush. As it is sucked deep into the earth, imagine the energy being alchemized and sent back out as brilliant light, recycled back into the plants around you to help them grow. It's a simple visualization, but you might notice yourself emerging with more clarity and ease.

A simpler version of this is connecting with the sensation of your body making contact with the ground. You can simply stand with your feet firmly on the ground, knees softly bent, and feel your weight sinking into the earth. As you breathe in and out, remember that you are here. You are present. You are alive.

Additional tools for grounding include carrying a stress-relief ball and squeezing it as needed when you want to connect to the moment. You can also use grounding crystals by holding them in your hands during visualizations and simple breathing exercises. Crystals I've found to be effective in grounding your body and mind include:

- garnet
- hematite
- obsidian
- onyx
- black tourmaline
- smoky quartz

Aromatherapy: Ever since the ancient Egyptians anointed their royalty with fragrant oils, people have been using them for therapeutic purposes. Aside from making your home smell delicious, they present an unobtrusive way of calming your nervous system and putting your ship in order. Spruce, pine, white fir, cedarwood, sage, frankincense, and lavender all anchor the body and emotions while providing gentle stimulation and detoxification. As always, you want to be mindful of the oils you are using. Verify that the oils are sourced responsibly and that they are not endangered. We must always honor and respect our plant medicine, herbs, and oils, and the lands and the peoples they come from. Asking permission to use the plant/oil is also a wonderful practice to incorporate as you begin to use these ancient healing plant medicines.

Bodywork/Massages: Having a regular massage practice is very helpful in releasing trauma on a physiological level. If you can't afford to get regular massages, get a tennis ball and roll the soles of your feet over it. You can also place the tennis ball on the wall and lean your back against it, squatting so that you can go up and down against the wall, with the ball rising and descending, releasing tension from your body. Be extra careful to avoid the spine. You might also want to get a foam roller, which can help you release tension and pain from the fascia in your body. Often, inside of our fascia lives our trauma. This is why when we do yoga or intense workouts we might sometimes feel a sudden surge of emotions being released from the body.

EFT (Emotional Freedom Technique) Tapping Exercises: Tapping is a wonderful tool that I have found to be helpful in my personal life. I would highly recommend working with someone trained in EFT, especially if you have been diagnosed with a mental health disorder. I highly recommend working with a trained clinician rather than practicing EFT on your own. I work with Dr. Rossanna Massey and highly recommend her as a practitioner. The practice allows you to tap on certain meridian points of the body that are related to stored emotions. You also work with loving affirmations and scripts as you tap, to release trauma and memories that have been trapped in the body. Below are some helpful tapping points in the diagram and scripts to use as you tap:

"Even though there are parts of me that feel unsafe still, I am willing to completely and fully love and accept myself."

"Even though I am scared to let go, I am willing to completely and fully love and accept myself."

"Even though there are parts of myself I reject, I am willing to completely and fully love and accept myself."

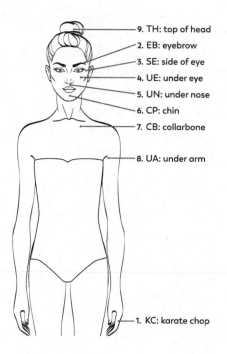

9. TH: top of head
2. EB: eyebrow
3. SE: side of eye
4. UE: under eye
5. UN: under nose
6. CP: chin
7. CB: collarbone
8. UA: under arm
1. KC: karate chop

(thetappingsolution.com, created by Nick Ortner)

EMDR (Eye Movement Desensitization and Reprocessing): EMDR is a nontraditional form of psychotherapy that is especially effective when it comes to treating post-traumatic stress disorder (PTSD). An EMDR therapist moves their fingers back and forth in front of the client's face, asking them to follow the motions with only their eyes. Simultaneously, the client is recollecting a painful or traumatic incident in their life, including emotions and bodily sensations. Over time, the therapist asks the client to redirect their thoughts to more joyful ones. I highly suggest finding a trained therapist who practices EMDR, which is a breakthrough therapy with a powerful body of research to back its efficacy.

Resourcing: This is a deeply powerful practice of creating safety. Trauma makes the body feel unsafe, and although it can take time, trauma can be healed. Think of things you like to do that make you feel safe. This is all about getting your mind and body into a frequency of safety. The goal then is to feel the panic and bring the body back into a sense and state of "I am okay," so that when the triggering feeling occurs, you can offer yourself reassurance.

Soulwork

Take a moment to reflect on the somatic meditations and how the experience was for you. Using your journal, write down your responses to the following questions:

1. During the somatic meditation, what did you notice when you went back into the feeling of anger? What sensations and memories arose for you?
2. What did you observe when you went back into the feeling of sadness? What sensations and memories arose for you?
3. What did you observe when you went back into the feeling of loneliness? What sensations and memories arose for you?
4. Where in your body do you tend to hold these sensations and memories?
5. What did you learn overall from the somatic meditations?
6. How did it feel when you did the suggested exercises for experiencing the feelings of safety, love, and joy?
7. What are some of the tools for trauma in this chapter that you have used or would like to incorporate into your self-care practices?

Mantra

Then is not now. And right now, I am here, safe and grounded in my loving arms.

Soul Ceremony
Sacred Healing Touch
In this ceremony, you are going to treat yourself to a massage or spa day. If you are on a budget, you can simply get some coconut oil and massage your own feet, taking special attention to breathing, inhaling and exhaling with each point you touch on your feet.

This connection to nurturing your body is key when you are rewiring your nervous system. You did deep work by locating the traumatic feelings and memories in your body; the other side of this work is soul rest. After such intensive healing, you must reward and celebrate yourself. If you can find a massage therapist that also specializes in shamanic work or healing energy work, that would be a bonus! But this is something that can be done at home with just you. No need to get fancy.

The key here is to practice loving, present, kind, gentle touch. As you touch your body and massage yourself, repeat to yourself, "I am safe in me. I am healing deep, and I allow myself to experience a moment of pause and relaxation."

I also recommend getting an organic lavender essential oil to rub into your palms; you can also mix a drop with organic coconut oil if you are not allergic and use it to elevate your relaxation experience. Scent and touch are underutilized tools in healing trauma, and they are both deeply necessary when healing the energy body and nervous system.

Be sure to continue to practice these rituals as you continue along on this journey. They will be deeply supportive and will offer you consistent nurturing as you do this important soulwork.

The grounded practices in this chapter are meant to be used as tools in your soul medicine kit. Go on a quest to finding the resources that are available and work for you. I became obsessed with healing and loving myself up because I knew that as I committed deeper to my healing, the better my life became. Healing my trauma and continuing to tend to my emotional and mental state is my priority—because when it wasn't, I died a spiritual death. I now know the cost of not making myself a priority. I can't gamble my life that way anymore. I mean, I guess I can—but I choose not to. The rewards of the soul path have been far more sustainable. Trust that as you commit to this deep work, you are setting yourself up to win. This work is the bedrock of a life beyond your wildest soul's dreams. Be proud and joyful knowing that you are healing. Such an honor and privilege to be doing this work together.

Then is not now.

And right now, I am here, safe and grounded in my loving arms.

#iamdiosa

CHAPTER 6

Wounds to Wisdom

"I can be changed by what happens to me;
but I refuse to be reduced by it."
—Maya Angelou

There is a power that lives within us. An ever-burning soul flame. A flame that alchemizes the pain into purpose, the wounds into wisdom. I believe that our unique life path is given to us. I believe that we each have soul contracts and lessons that we must learn as beings on a spiritual journey in this human flesh. I tell people all the time, I wouldn't wish trauma or pain or difficult lessons on anyone, but I can't say that I know many that haven't gone through some shit. Some more than others. And I can't help but think that those of us that have been burned to ashes enough times have more of a sense of the reality of nature. For nature is death and rebirth. And if you taste more of death, then you taste more of life. *La Diosa de la muerte*— the Goddess of death—knows that from the ashes she rises and from death comes life.

Your wounds carry wisdom and lessons. The verbal, physical, and emotional abuse I experienced I wouldn't wish on a soul. No child deserves to be called names or hit or suffocated for not waking up to get to school on time. No child deserves food shoved in their face because they are full. But since I went through these fucked-up traumatizing events, I decided that I would use them to make me stronger, wiser, and more compassionate. I didn't have a choice in having these awful things happen to me, but I have a choice in deciding to not let them break me down and stop me from living. As a result of me healing these wounds, I get to heal those that have gone through similar experiences not just from my clinical experience as a therapist but from my real-life experiences as well. I get my Diosas on a soul level, because I am them. And nothing can take away the power of someone getting you on a deep in-the-bones and core level.

This doesn't excuse the behavior. This doesn't make it okay. This doesn't take away the shit show. This doesn't make your abuse "meant to be." No, prevention needs to happen so parents aren't parenting through fear and hostility anymore. But since you went through it, let's work with it and get the medicine from it for you and others.

When life hands you something difficult, might as well make something of it. Don't waste that shitty situation or traumatizing event without making use of it to heal yourself. It must be alchemized. You deserve that. One of the most profound moments for me was when I was telling my therapist about how I had gone through so much and I was pissed about it. I was crying hysterically— ugly cry—*mocos* coming out of my nose. I told her I was angry that I had been burned and broken so many times. I remember being on my balcony in Puerto Rico, weeping in a little ball on the floor. I had just found out my partner at the time had been cheating on me. He had a whole other secret email where he would speak to his ex, he would call her weekly, and they even met up and had sex. I was heartbroken. All of what was safe was now foreign. My world was crashing. My bones were aching. And again, I felt the familiar energy of death at my doorstep. I was just tired of it. You know, sometimes as humans we just get fucking tired of going through shit. And I was exhausted. As I cried to my therapist, I said, "Is this what my life is going to be forever? Never-ending, open, gaping wounds? Never-ending heartbreak and deceit?" And in that moment of my crying, a mirror that was leaning on the wall tipped over. Glass everywhere. It startled me—still on the phone with my therapist—I am telling her what is going on and I pause. I look down and see the mess around me, the mess within me. I look at a piece of the shattered glass, and I see just a piece of myself. Not my whole self—but just a piece of me in this tiny shattered glass. I told my therapist, amid tears, "This is the perfect representation of where I am. I see the wound—I see just a part of me. I want to feel whole again."

I felt raw and vulnerable and desperate for change. I needed to make this mean something more. I needed to find the medicine, the lesson, the wisdom. My therapist told me: "It is imperative for you to make this mean something. Don't waste this. Use it. Transform it." And I felt it. I felt it in my core. I turned from hopeless to hopeful. I became determined to heal and learn and gain my spiritual lesson. From that day forth, I vowed to myself to never waste a shitty situation and not learn from it. That shitty deceit made me learn to trust my gut. I remember I felt it and I knew it, but I ignored it. That shitty situation helped me to come back home to myself and choose better partners. It helped me to see that I could be strong and live on my own. I felt stronger with each lesson that I extracted from one of the biggest heartbreaks of my life. The heartbreak became a breakthrough.

This message of wounds to wisdom reminds me of Diosa client Marita. She found me on Rachel Brathen's platform yogagirl .com. She resonated with my videos on healthy love and how to spot toxic love relationships. Our journey began as it always does—with an open heart and a desire to heal. Here is Marita's story in her own words.

The Journey Home

"I laid crumbled on the floor. The warm tiles felt like comfort to my skin and I had no desire of ever getting up. I used to feel it all and now I didn't feel anything. I was numb, but the numbness was worse than the pain. I was so tired. But most of all, I was tired of being tired and feeling so alone in this world. This is my journey on healing that which I thought could never be healed, finding my way back home to myself, and at long last, rising.

I grew up in a home with a lack of love where I did not feel emotionally safe or held. I did not know how to receive love or give it. I was sensitive and felt so much, but I didn't feel safe to be who I was. I hid more and more of me and my feminine essence and began leaning on the masculine characteristics instead.

More than anything, I wanted to feel and be free. But instead, I learned how to hide and suppress my emotions, guard my heart, and move away from my intuition and my soul gifts. I was conditioned to believe that strength was holding it all together and being in control.

As a highly sensitive person and empath, I wanted to save everyone, but I had no boundaries. I could care for everyone else; I just did not know how to care for myself. This became my way of life. I took in other people's pain, so I could lessen it for them, but carried a weight on my shoulders that eventually became too much to carry, and by twenty-four, I fell apart. The breakdown was a spiritual awakening and a starting point for a new life for me.

Things started to change, I started to change. And three years later, I gave up the life I knew to face the unknown, finally answering the call of my heart, and I set out to explore the world seeking to find my truth. At age twenty-eight, I moved to an island in the Caribbean, and for the first time in a long time, I felt alive.

I was on a new path, the path of the heart, but I still had so much to learn and unhealed wounds were still my driving force. I would continue trying to save others, searching for love outside of me. I ended up spending five years in a highly toxic and emotionally abusive relationship.

He was emotionally bankrupt. I was, of course, going to help him. The relationship soon turned toxic. I didn't know where I ended and he began, it was all a blur. I felt obligated to help and support him. I was in a relationship with his potential, what he could be, and I was clinging to this image. I felt responsible for his happiness. I felt responsible for making the relationship work. I felt responsible for everything, like I had felt so many times in my life.

The 'saving of others' had been the story of my life, but it was all so different when it now was the person I loved. I lost myself completely in trying to save him.

I put all the love I had into him. I love so deeply, and I gave him all. And the worse it got, the more love I tried to put in. If I only gave a little more, it would change. If I only could be better, or different, I wouldn't get cheated on so much, and we would be happy. All of my strength and confidence slowly washed away. I gave and gave and gave until I had nothing more to give. Then I was slowly dying. And then the guilt came. For walking this Earth. For every single thing I did. Guilt made a home in my body, and I stopped living in so many ways.

I was stuck in the feeling of unworthiness and being hard to love. What I had was what I deserved, I had convinced myself of that. The more powerless I felt, the stronger the attachment to him grew. I couldn't stand the thought of being alone. I didn't know who I was without him. The fear, the pain, the constant disappointments, the tears. Fighting to make it work. The drama. It was all I knew.

Emotional abuse is like living in a prison, but with the door wide open to walk out. Sometimes I would walk to the door feeling the light of freedom touching my soul. I could hear his voice: 'You can't do it.' 'You are all alone.' 'Who do you think you are?' 'You are nothing.' I longed for freedom. But I decided that wasn't for me. I walked back into safety, into what felt like home, which was abuse.

Since I couldn't get myself out, all I could do was pretend to be happy, pretend that the hurt didn't happen and make the best out of it. I made excuses and tried to live with it. I justified it all, I made up lies which I told myself and others. So many sleepless nights and tears of pain. It was a roller coaster.

Through it all, I lived my life and served as a healer, yoga teacher, and holistic health coach. But I lost myself and my intuition, my strength, my dignity, my freedom—I lost all of it. I even began to feel like I was losing my sanity. I spiraled off into a person I didn't recognize.

'It feels like an addiction,' I once told a friend. Little did I know that it actually was.

I lived in a fantasy world of happy endings. Addiction does that to you. I didn't see the reality anymore. I had made up so many lies that I no longer knew what was true. I tried so hard to fix it and just make it work. Then I wouldn't be such a screwup and failure. 'I judged myself for not being able to leave; I was so hard on myself and developed a sense of self-hatred.

In my many attempts to escape the relationship, I relapsed again and again. I was looking for comfort when I felt lonely. I didn't know how to hold and love myself. I'd grown to lean on the very thing that was tearing me apart.

Things were now worse than ever, and it was affecting all areas of my life. I had been in and out of depression many times over the past years and fought so hard to keep things together. There were so many positive things going on in my life and with my work, but I was absolutely dying on the inside.

More than anything, I wanted to be free from this person and what haunted me so much. The past and the pain and get out of this tragic pattern. I had such a hard time accepting what had happened to me, accepting life and facing reality. I just wanted it to go away. I begged for it to go away and wished that I would wake up and realize it was all a bad dream. I just wanted to be free and I just wanted a new life. Away from all this. I did not want this to be part of my story.

'Please send someone my way who can help me.' I prayed for help, and when Christine showed up on my radar a couple of days later, I knew she was the answer to my prayers. I'd finally come to terms that I needed help, and when I asked for it, it showed up so quickly.

I cried when I said, 'I don't think I can ever be free. It's too messy. There is so much pain. I am so lost.'

I was open to trying. Even though I really didn't believe that this darkness would ever turn to light.

But it did. Christine gave me strength when I had lost mine. She spoke for me when I had lost my voice. She screamed with me and she cried with me. She took my hand and led me onto the path of healing. She never let go, and for that I am always grateful. I leaned on her strength, and knowing that she was there kept me going.

I now had awareness around myself being a codependent and love addict, and with that, I could also begin to heal. In three months of working together, I finally felt free. It was a dream come true and I was so happy and so proud of myself.

Shortly after, I relapsed. And after cutting all contact again, I had yet another relapse. I leaned on Christine for support and she held me with such love and compassion, so I could hold myself the same way. In love, no judgment. I wrote a letter to the Universe and it went something like this:

'I'm tired. Okay. I just wanted to tell you that I am really fucking tired. I'm tired of healing and growing and hurting and feeling. Fuck, don't ask me to feel, because I have done nothing but feeling and now what. It makes me so angry! I'm frustrated! I'm pissed off!! I have died over and over again and tried to crawl my way out and was so lost and confused and heartbroken and I didn't even fucking know which way to crawl! All I ever fucking wanted was to be free. To be happy again. To find my way back to who I used to be. The girl who wasn't scared to love or to live.

'For months now I've done everything I can possibly do. Every single day. Haven't you seen what I have been doing!? I've had daily conversations with you, and I've expressed so much gratitude. I've told myself every single day that I can fucking do this, and I can. And I've felt great. Haven't you seen all that I have been doing and how hard I have tried!?

'So now I'm scared that I'll be fine but then wake up one morning and not be. And that the longing is back. I just want to be free. Do you understand? More than anything. I just want to be free.'

I felt that I was losing control again, that the addiction and obsession took over. Little by little, with support and by taking it one day at a time, I moved through it once again. This was my last relapse and I was never in contact with him again.

This abuse and addiction, it was old stuff rooted in childhood trauma. I carried an emptiness within, a void I so desperately tried to fill. A fundamental belief that I was not enough, worthy or lovable. And as long as I kept replaying the story of not being enough, I would keep attracting men who would confirm this to be true and reinforce the wound.

I ran away for so long. The wound got messier and messier, and I was terrified to face it. I just wanted it to go away, by itself. But the only way to find liberation was facing that which I wanted to avoid. As long as I was running, it would control me and keep me prisoner. It was only by moving through it, feeling it, welcoming it, that I found freedom and harvested the lessons.

I wanted others to give me the love I refused to give myself. The way back home was the way back to love, my own love. Being able to give myself this is the greatest gift of all. I now nourish this love and let this shine.

Healing is never easy, and it's messy. It is scary to lean in to the wound and allow it to bleed. It takes courage to sit with the shadow and peel back layer by layer until you get to the deepest parts long buried within.

But dear God, is it worth it all. I got my life back. I found my way back to my soul and reclaimed by feminine power and sexual sovereignty. I found love, I found freedom, and I found peace.

I was not being punished, nor was I forgotten by the Universe. I was worthy and strong and lovable. It was all within, waiting for me to return.

I am forever thankful for that which cracked my heart open; it taught me how to love.

I am forever thankful I had to navigate the darkness; it's how I found my light.

I am forever thankful that I asked for help; it's how I learned the true meaning of strength.

And, you know, you're never the same after you rise from the ashes, leave your old self behind, and walk away. You're not the same and never will be. The story is finally yours."

Your Wound as Spiritual Wisdom

Marita is now teaching around the world, sharing her message of healthy love. Leading yoga and meditation circles and using the wisdom she gained from her love wound. This is my favorite thing about this work—that it works if you work it. And as you can see, her story wasn't a path of linear healing but instead one of ups and downs. This is the real work. Not the glamourized spiritual self-help work. It's not that its easy and you will never get triggered again and life still won't happen on life's terms . . . but that we can and we do heal. We can rise above impossible situations and have an amazing life. This is our birthright. We are given these wounds to heal them and rise.

There is nothing that your soul can't alchemize. Pain to purpose.

Wounds to wisdom. It's what the divine and your soul were made to do.

This is key in being able to own your strengths by learning from what has happened.

Below are some examples of wounds to wisdom, taken from Diosas that I have worked with throughout the years:

- Being cheated on . . . to learning to trust my gut when things feel off
- Being left or rejected by a partner . . . to learning that I can take care of myself and be happy on my own
- Getting an STD . . . to learning that nothing can take away your worth and that your sacred energy is a treasure to be shared with only those deserving of it
- Being abandoned . . . to learning that I can't be abandoned, for my soul shall never forsake me
- Being abused . . . to knowing that abuse is about the wounded person and not a reflection on my worth

If you need help with this, take a moment to call on your spiritual guides. Ask for guidance to reveal the wisdom in the wound. Find the sacred space.

1. Take a moment to find a quiet space where you are alone with you. Perhaps in nature or in a cozy part of your room or bathroom, even. Light a candle. Light some incense. Set the mood. I love to play relaxing flute sounds to ground me; perhaps that will help you as well.

2. Breathe. Placing one hand on your belly and one on your heart, take a moment to feel into you. Breathing through

your nose and out through your mouth, inhale for three counts and exhale for five counts. Continue to breathe until you feel yourself connected.

3. Now ask for your spirit's guidance. When we need guidance, we must ask for it. It sounds simple, but oftentimes when we are feeling stuck and overwhelmed, we swirl deeper in the chaos and the pain and forget to ask for spiritual assistance. When you pray, you are in that exact moment surrendering. And when you surrender, you connect to the inner wisdom and the voice of the soul. In that moment, an invisible bridge appears between this realm and spirit realm. It is here that our ancestors live, as well as our angels and guides. It is here that your soul is alive.

"Divine Mother, Diosa, Higher Power, Jesus, God/Goddess, or whatever you feel called to say . . . Guide me to lift the veil off the wound and access the medicine and the soul healing that lives beneath it. I am ready and I surrender to the wisdom that awaits. Show me that which you guided me to, so that I may use this to grow, to heal, to lead."

In the moment of praying, something shifts within. Anytime we are willing to give it up to Goddess, we shift our perspective and our cells in our body—feel it. I believe that spiritual guidance is one of the most powerful tools that we can use. And the best thing is, we don't need anyone else. It's you and the divine, and you can call on the divine at any time.

You can track the moments the wound is triggered in a notebook. This will increase awareness and consciousness to the behavior. Track what is happening at the moment:

- Who did it happen with?
- What time of day?
- Did you sleep?
- Did you eat?
- Were you sick?
- Had you gone to therapy or had any type of self-care?
- Were you on your menstrual cycle?

Be curious as to what factors were part of that moment.

Then use the prayer to see what can be living beneath the wound. Instead of running or rushing through that moment, breathe through it, feel into it. Honor it as holy, for all emotions are messengers and should be honored as such.

My wish is that as you do this, you remember that there is nothing that your soul won't help you with. It's your forever companion in this life. Life is a series of ups and downs, slipups and fuckups. Life happens—so don't be hard on yourself. Instead, give yourself permission to be human, but allow yourself to return to your soul goal. You are stronger than you know, wiser than you can imagine.

Soulwork

After exploring your emotional triggers, the wounds connected to them, and your greatest wound, it's important to see wisdom carried in those wounds. Using your journal, write down your responses to the following questions:

1. What is the wound?
2. What is the medicine on the other side?
3. How did you grow from the experience?
4. What was the part of your personality that matured as a result of the situation?

Note: For the wounds that are abusive, I don't want you to minimize them and make them be okay. It wasn't okay. Instead, I want you to claim what you had to make medicine. For example, my abuse made me be more intuitive to others that also have gone through abuse, and now allows me to lead souls around the world to healing deep traumas and pains.

Mantra

I allow myself to embrace the sacred medicine within my wound.

Ceremony
Mirror Exercise

This chapter is really about honoring the wisdom in the wound. At times we get lost in the wound through no fault of our own, but in that, at times we forget to reclaim our power, our worth, our magic. When we make eye contact with ourselves, we remember to love ourselves and see into the temple of our own soul. Find a moment when you can be alone with you. Go into a room where you have a mirror, where you can see clearly into your eyes. This will be an eye-gazing session, soul to soul, eye-to-eye with you.

Breathe as you stare deeply into your own eyes. Eye gazing is a deeply spiritual ceremony, and to do it with yourself is an act of devotion and deep self-love. Many feelings might emerge from being this intimate with yourself. Do not run from the feelings. Simply breathe into them, allow them to move through you, and release and feel all the feelings. Stay present with you. Eye to eye, soul to soul. Begin to say the following out loud while still continuing to look at yourself in the eyes:

> I love you.
> I know you have been hurt by the wounds, but you have so
>   much medicine in you, Diosa.

You are so strong and resilient. Wow, I am in awe of you.

Sweet child, you can rest easier now.

Take the lessons and let them be your wings.

Take the wisdom and let it be your courage and your offering
     to the world.

I love you.

I am proud of you.

For all you have been through, for all that has hurt you,
     I love you. I am here for you.

Let yourself feel the strength of your feet that have carried
     you this far.

What a gift you are.

A walking miracle.

I love you.

I love you.

I love you.

Breathe and allow yourself to feel the power of saying these words to yourself. Wonderful work, Diosa. Ground yourself by breathing deep and exhaling out. Repeat 3x and get a nice glass of water or tea to relax. Journal on how this experience was for you and what you gained from this ceremony.

This process of finding the wisdom in the wound is a lifesaver. It infuses hope in hopeless places, life where only death was. Empowerment where disempowerment once lived.

Your life is yours—unique and special and designed strategically for you and only you—to grow and heal and become who you are meant to be. These wounds become places of massive growth—if we choose for them to be. Choose to get the wisdom from the wound. Grow from it. Evolve. Give back. Rise, Diosa, rise—especially if the wound was big and deep and causes you massive harm. Don't let anything stop you from rising, you deserve to live your soul life even if someone's darkness tried to stop you from doing so. You are now ready to move into the next initiation: living in alignment with the soul—the light. The lessons are here for you to embody and live them. In the next chapter we will discuss the reclaiming of your intuition and the ways your soul might speak to you. It is there that you will receive guidance to stay aligned with your soul.

I allow myself to embrace the sacred medicine within my wound.

#iamdiosa

PART II

The Light:
Living in Alignment
with the Soul

CHAPTER 7

Soul Alignment

"To me, a witch is a woman that is capable of letting her
intuition take hold of her actions, that communes with
her environment, that isn't afraid of facing challenges."

—Paulo Coelho

Part of healing is reconnecting to our gut and our intuition. When we are injured emotionally, physically, sexually, or mentally, we subconsciously begin to not trust ourselves. We begin to doubt ourselves. Some thoughts that run through our heads are things like, "If I were intuitive, I would have known. I should have known better. How did I think that was okay? I don't have good intuition or gut instinct at all. I am stupid. I don't know shit. If I knew, I wouldn't have been hurt. My intuition would have guided me out of this, but it didn't, so my intuition doesn't work."

The mind tends to make stories and go on mental projections based on what it knows, and if you think about it, it makes sense to think that your gut isn't working because something bad did happen. But the mind is often thinking extremely black-and-white; it isn't capable in those moments to see the nuances. To see that perhaps you did feel something off but you numbed it, or perhaps you knew something was dangerous but you actually were powerless to do anything because you were too young, or too broke, or too scared to leave for fear of getting hurt. These are all valid reasons for your defense mechanisms to come in and try to protect you.

Fear vs. Gut

(Trigger warning for the following.) This conversation about intuition and repairing the connection to the gut reminds me of my client Sally. She was married to a man that she loved but also felt insecure with. Because of her tendency to be insecure and untrusting because of her earlier childhood trauma, she didn't know if she was "being psycho" or "being intuitive." That is a common dilemma that many of my clients come to me with: how to know. What I have come to realize is that the wound that needs to be nurtured needs to be nurtured no matter what, so it doesn't always matter if it's intuition or not. It is key and imperative that we understand that. No matter if the person is cheating, lying, or absolutely trustworthy— the confusion that we feel within ourselves needs to be healed. Therefore, we work with what we have and take it from there.

So what did I know to be true about Sally? I knew that she had a history of childhood abuse, sexual abuse, and verbal abuse. I knew that she had a shitty relationship with men because her father was a mentally sick man who was a pedophile and abused her. I knew her tendency was to pick men that were untrustworthy just like her father because, as a result of the abuse, her self-esteem was fragmented. I knew that her fear and anger were at an all-time high because of the untended wound. But I also knew Sally was intuitive as fuck and I trusted that something was up.

Instead of having her choose from this very black-and-white perspective of "Am I being psycho?" or "Am I being intuitive?" I honored both and helped her to see there was something within her begging to be loved, nurtured, healed, and only then would she trust herself enough to know what was going on. Two simultaneous spiritual lessons were occurring:

1. Learning to trust herself and her intuition without judging herself as "psycho," "angry," "crazy," or "insecure."
2. Learning to calm the wound of insecurity, pain, anger, and fear from her childhood of abuse.

As she started to accept the two lessons without forcing herself to rush, she began to see that she wanted to heal her responses for herself. She wanted to manage her fears for herself. She began to comfort herself, and instead of punishing herself for feeling that way and yelling and getting herself worked up to the point of sickness, she began to go to therapy more often, work with me on the spiritual level, and do yoga. As she gave herself more space to heal and tend to her own internal psychological terrains, clarity began to settle in.

She began to share things on our calls, like, "I am getting less angry. I am allowing myself to really focus on my childhood abuse and the effects of it in therapy, so I can know what is true for me while I also work on the parts of me that I don't like and don't want to carry anymore."

I could hear that the focus returned to what she could heal within herself, and I was proud because this was the only way she could trust herself to make the right decision and leave this relationship for good. My gut knew that he was cheating, but it wasn't aligned to share that information yet. My spirit gives me guidance as I do healings, and it was clear when it said, "She needs to go through this initiation and discover the truth once she trusts herself again." My job was simply to guide her as she healed her childhood abuse, regained her peace, and worked on her reactivity.

She came to me again in our following session and said, "I have been more relaxed, and it's been feeling really good. I am making real progress with my anger. I am feeling less psycho and I really like it. I feel like there is something still up and I am beginning to see that—even in my calm state—I sense something is off. Except this time, I feel a sense of guidance and groundedness. I feel secure in me."

My eyes were glowing. Things were clicking within her. It was a very good sign that she had a sense of peace while simultaneously knowing something was off. Here, it was evident that she took care of her soul lesson to heal her reactivity and insecurities for herself *and* sense through her intuition that things weren't okay. Now she could trust herself and reconnect to her primal feminine inner knowing.

This is how we reestablish connection to our intuition: by doing the work and then realizing, "Yes, even in my secure state, my gut is speaking. This isn't my insecurity or psycho-ness; this is my truth." But one must not skip the trials to get there. One must go through the fires of the questioning to arrive at the centered knowing. And Sally committed to the work.

In that peace, she was guided to the information that she needed. She was ready to see the truth. She saw the messages, conversations with another woman, sexual photos, all the proof she needed. But she didn't do this without doing the work that she needed to do. Had she skipped that part, she would have gone into the next relationship feeling insecure and looking for a quick fix—constantly searching and looking for proof she would be hurt. Instead she went inward, waited until she felt secure in her, and then from that security let her repaired intuition speak.

When the intuition is injured and we make decisions from that place, we will never do so fully aligned.

When she asked for a divorce, she spoke with security, clarity, and calm, knowing that she was ready to leave. She felt empowered and proud that she did the inner healing to work on her side of the street so that she could leave with having accomplished her spiritual lessons. It wasn't fear that drove her now—it was her self-love.

Think about situations in your life that have occurred or that are happening now. Are there situations that you are confused about?

When there is confusion, return to the root of the wound. Return to comforting yourself. Return to healing yourself. Once you feel secure and calm, then your intuition can be repaired and speak. From this place of clarity, you will get your answers. Do not rush this process.

Take a moment to reflect on an area of your life where you have confusion. Maybe it's that you feel you aren't being loved by your partner, but you have had the tendency to be needy in the past. Before you act, pour more love on yourself. Do radical self-care, go to therapy, go to meetings, get a massage, meet up with girlfriends, take time to pray, journal, work out. *Love yourself the fuck up!* Then, once you have given yourself what you seek, you will have the mental clarity to distinguish if indeed you still feel that you aren't getting the attention you need. From that place, you can have a conversation with your partner with love. But the lessons that you need to learn must be attended to before you can trust your gut again. By dealing with that first and coming from that place of your cup being full, you will always have a better conversation, a better result. And there is *nothing* better than the feeling of knowing you did your part before you have those conversations.

I remember being so proud of myself when I finally cracked the code in dating. I was sooooo insecure when I wouldn't get a text back. But since I knew I had a history of codependency and fear of abandonment and being needy, I couldn't always trust my gut. My gut was still too tied with my fears, so it was unclear.

After speaking too soon, sounding crazy, and just generally acting from that place of the wound, I decided to try something different. I said to myself, "What's most important here is not the trigger but my reaction to the trigger." I leaned on the proactive formula. I decided to focus on *only* my reactions, no matter if the person was off, wrong, shady, inconsiderate, etc. This was hard as fuck. My pride was going buckwild. Like, "YO, you gonna let this mother-fucker think you are punk? *Una boba, a pendeja*!? Tell him the fuck off."

And then I would have to speak to myself and be like, "Listen, chill, maybe he is a motherfucker, but there is some deeper shit go-ing on, and until I can know the difference between whether it's me or them, I won't trust myself. I've got to know I am not crazy by calming my responses—then I will be guided. I'm onto something. Give me some time and we will figure it out. And I will say some-thing to them when I'm ready. Don't worry."

Then the hardest part was not saying shit—practicing the power of restraint of pen and tongue. And sitting in the discomfort of not saying anything when a guy waited until the last minute to confirm plans, or not responding to a text from a roommate when I felt she was being mean. As I did this more and more, I began to become calmer. Instead of feeling like a victim and like I was being ignored and abandoned—like the inner child going crazy as if I was being left by my dad all over again—I felt like a motherfucking grown-ass Diosa, sitting on her throne and observing what I liked and didn't like. It wasn't this guttural pain and rejection. It was a simple obser-vation and conversation.

I was getting it! Things were shifting. My energy shifted. I could see more clearly, and my words became clearer too.

I then felt ready to communicate my truth. Sometimes the mir-acle was that I was being cray and my childhood wounds were run-ning the show in a way that was destructive, so I was glad I didn't speak. Then the other miracle was that sometimes I was spot-on and the only thing that needed to shift was how and where my com-munication was coming from. I was able to share with ease as a woman, not with terror like a child in fear of being abandoned.

"Hey, I really enjoyed our time on the last date. I wanted to be transparent about something though. I much prefer having plans confirmed with time so I can make time in my schedule;) I am a busy lady and love a man who is his word and honors my time too;) When I didn't hear from you, I made other plans tonight. I was looking forward to seeing you, but this style of communication does not work for me. Hope you understand."

Here I was, secure and communicating from a place of empowerment and intuition. Had I spoken before, I wouldn't have had the gift of giving myself the comfort I needed and security I needed. Once I did, my connection to my gut was back and I was provided with the words to express myself.

In the rooms of Alcoholics Anonymous, they say, "You intuitively know how to handle situations that once baffled you," and through my commitment to self-love and soulwork, I was being guided and it felt good.

As you face obstacles, take this lesson with you. This doesn't stand when you are in an abusive relationship; this is for situations when you are safe, working through triggers, trusting yourself, and distinguishing the voice of intuition from the voice of fear. When in danger, you get professional help, make a safety plan, and leave. Beyond that, though, remember to keep coming back to this lesson— may it take you far and wide. It is a lifesaver and a tool every Diosa needs in her toolkit.

Let Your Soul Voice Communicate with You

The cool yet counterintuitive thing about tapping into your intuition and soul voice is that it's not something you need to learn how to "do." It's more about getting out of your own way and connecting to the deep feminine part of you that is in her full Diosa genius when she is simply "being."

Just because it's about being doesn't mean that it isn't tricky, at least at first. Most of us are taught that we must need to constantly work toward self-improvement and accomplishment, but the truth is, your soul voice is something that has always been with you. It lives below the neocortex of the brain, which is the center of the conscious mind. It is the part of you that "knows without knowing." It is ancient, wise, and will never steer you wrong. Your capacity to access your truth is connected to your capacity to become still, listen, and receive.

Thankfully, your intuition is something that lives in the vessel of your body and your five senses, although it has the superpower of communicating information in seemingly esoteric ways. Unfortunately, while the intuition is always embodied—in our gut, our heart, the way we can feel our "yes" and "no" fluttering somewhere in our solar plexus—it can be super-hard to access when our bodies have undergone trauma and we are in a state of contraction and constant hypervigilance. From this place, it can be tough to trust or even notice the cues our body is trying to give us.

There are plenty of ways to coax out the still, small voice within (or that gut feeling, or whatever you want to call your intuition—it's different for every Diosa!). Below are some of my favorites.

A process of re-collecting yourself: It's totally normal to take on other people's shit, including their fears, desires, beliefs, etc., and to mistake them as being ours. I like to engage in a daily practice of emptying myself of such influences, including those I unconsciously pick up from people, places, public transportation, TV, social media, and anything else I encounter during the day. I do this by simply imagining these influences leaving my body through a grounding cord that connects from my root chakra down to the core of the planet, almost like I'm flushing a toilet. Then I call back my soul parts from anywhere I've left them by simply imagining them reintegrating into me as light that enters different parts of my body, wherever my energy needs to go. I always end up feeling more peaceful, clear, and grounded afterward, which makes it so much easier to tap into my soul voice.

Dreamwork: Our intuition speaks to us all the time, and the language of dreams often shows us what we need to know in symbols and rich visuals. Ask a clear question at night and rest with that question as you fall asleep, intending that your soul communicate with you through dream images and messages. If you don't tend to remember your dreams, or if they were too fuzzy, pay attention to the feelings that are with you as you wake up, as well as any words that rise into your awareness, since your soul voice can also speak to you that way. I love a process from Dr. Clarissa Pinkola Estés: She suggests writing out your dreams and then replacing any nouns (birds, feet, shoes, etc.) with your own symbolic association with that word. For example, maybe in your own personal symbology, birds translate to "a sense of freedom" or "a messenger between the spirit realm and the human realm." Over time, you'll have a better understanding of your own library of symbols, and your dreams will provide you with massive insight into your life.

Divination: I love working with simple forms of divination, also known as the practice of seeking information about the future or the unknown through different strategies. Every ancient culture has its own form of divination, from the Chinese I Ching to the Nordic Runes. Indigenous cultures also use dreamwork and shamanic journeying as forms of divination. I like the following practice of divination, because you need only a coin: Ask your question before you are about to flip the coin, and determine what your heads and tails will be beforehand (for example, heads for yes and tails for no). Compare what you were expecting and wanting with the answer the coin gives you. If there's a discrepancy, how does that make you feel? If you'd prefer to work with more in-depth messages, you can also pick out an oracle card deck with beautiful images, which can be a wonderful way to unlock your own intuitive powers and offer language to the rich metaphors of your inner world.

Asking for signs from spirit: I have a beautiful story about the power of seeking signs from spirit. Not long ago, I silently communicated with my deceased maternal grandmother, my Grandma Maria Luisa. She is one of my spirit guides and someone I turn to in moments of confusion or wanting confirmation that I am on the right path. I wanted her confirmation that my next steps were blessed and approved by her. I was very specific. I asked Grandma Luisa, "Show me a peacock feather, within the next few hours, as a sign so I know I am on the right path." I then proceeded to get ready for my photoshoot, with a photographer named Federica, who I met on Instagram, that offered to shoot me. I met with Federica, and we went to her adorable NYC apartment. There she shows me a peacock feather! She tells me that she felt this divine guidance to use the peacock in our photo shoot. I was being guided. Spirit was working through Federica to reveal my divine sign from my grandma. Immediately, I felt so happy knowing spirit had my back. Making a clear request by asking for a specific sign is powerful, because our soul voice and the voice of spirit often communicate via symbols (yours doesn't have to be a peacock feather, of course; you can use the first animal, number, or word that comes to your mind). When these moments happen, you might get the chills or feel a deep sense of spiritual guidance and protection. I love these God moments. I shared with Federica what I asked from my grandma, and how within hours she delivered the sign through her. We were in happy shock and filled with gratitude. Sometimes we need those divine winks from spirit. This is a great way to get that spiritual support and nudge to keep on going.

Free writing or free drawing: For those of us who tend to live in our heads way too much, free writing and free drawing can be powerful methods of allowing our souls to speak through our hands. I love the rich, poetic messages and pictures that come through me when I'm not trying to control what it is I want to say. It's like clearing a space for your true voice to communicate with you—and often, you'll be delightfully surprised by what she has to say. Take a pen and paper and begin to write whatever is on your heart. Don't stop your pen and continue to flow. Do the same with an image. For example, you can use the prompt: "Soul, guide me to draw an image that symbolizes what I must do next. What energy I must embody to take the next step?" And then get your pen and paper and flow with what image emerges. Also note, everyone will have a particular way to tap into their intuition and guidance. Practice some of the ones mentioned here and use the one that most feels aligned for you.

Listening to what your body wants: This is a simple yet powerful way to live an intentionally nourishing lifestyle—by checking in to see what your body wants. What does she want to eat? How does she want to move? What kinds of activities would best nourish her? Often, simply asking the question "Will this sustain me or exhaust me?" about a food or a particular exercise or a person you are thinking of dating will give you immediate feedback—maybe through an image in your mind, or a specific feeling in your body. I generally associate contraction and tightness in my body with "no," and a feeling of expansion with "yes." But experiment with this, and give your body full permission to talk to you. Better yet, when you get a clear response, act on it! So often we alienate the wisdom of the body by neglecting it, which can make our intuitive knowing harder to access in the long run.

Spending time in nature: The great Diosa lives in nature, so be sure to connect with it often, even if that's only through a walk in the park or a stroll through a botanical garden. Famous artists and scientists have talked about turning to nature when they are in search of answers to their biggest questions. Something magical happens when we are communicating with a tree, a river, a mountain. Being in nature gives us enormous perspective (after all, most trees are older than us, and many mountains have lived through

the rise and fall of countless civilizations) and has the magical ability to give us clarity and a greater awareness of the big picture.
Nature is vitally calming too—something our often-overloaded
nervous systems need in order to relax and open the lines of communication to our inner being.

Tapping into breath and stillness: This doesn't mean rigorous daily meditation, although that doesn't hurt! But as often as you
can, find time to get away from the distractions and busy-ness of
your daily routine to simply be with yourself. I love taking out five
minutes to consciously breathe and be silent over a cup of tea. When
I still the constant influx of my mind, I am able to rest in the vast-
ness and peace of my true self. And believe me, the best messages
bubble up from that place!

Of course, all of the aforementioned tools are just suggestions. What
works for you is dependent on who you are. For example, I know
that because I have an addictive personality, certain forms of divination won't work for me—because if I have them around, I will
constantly refer to them any time I need to make a decision!

This isn't about getting external validation or depending on a
tool to give you the right answers. The true source of answers is *you*.
Your most precious intuitive wisdom lives within you, and while
everything I mentioned offers a doorway to that powerful knowledge, remember that Diosa speaks to us in multiple ways. Find what
works best for you and make a practice of daily connection. I promise, you'll feel the difference.

Soulwork

Reconnecting to your intuition and gut feeling is key to living in
soul alignment. Using your journal, write down your responses to
the following questions:

1. What is the situation that usually triggers the most confusion in trusting yourself? For example, "When it comes to relationships, I never know if I am being too crazy or if I have an actual boundary that needs to be met."

2. What is the feeling in your body when you know that you are in alignment with your gut? Perhaps the difference is you are not in your head, but instead there is a sense of knowing and feeling in your gut. Notice the bodily sensations and make note of them so you can discern in the future.

3. Name a situation when you were confused about something and unsure if your intuition was correct or not—and you came out being correct. You want to look for evidence of your intuition working here.

4. What is one self-soothing technique you can do to get yourself into a state of neutrality to hear your intuition? For example, talking to a friend, repeating a mantra, listening to relaxing music, taking a walk, using any of the tools in the previous section of this chapter, etc. Choose a self-soothing technique that feels good to you.

Mantra
I give myself the space to breathe and ask for guidance so that my intuitive voice can resonate through me.

Ceremony
Soul Alignment
Here you will be guided to tap into deeper realms of the spiritual and connect to your spirit guides. This can be something you

believe in deeply or you connect to as an archetype that will stand as a guide to keep you in spiritual soul alignment.

While writing this book, I did a shamanic soul journey to connect to the soul of the book, and I was taken to this beautiful and majestic room. There was this ancient elder there beyond gender—a being of light and dark and wisdom and wounds. A being that has always been. I was told, "You are the keeper of the patterns. You hold keys for the book of patterns. Your gift will be to help people unlock the patterns holding them from their soul and truth and divinity."

This was a powerful moment for me. As I continued to pray and meditate, I received guidance to pray to Santa Clara, Saint Clara. Clara, related to the word *clarity*. "Santa Clara, *aclarame esto.*" "Saint Clara, clarify this for me." The veil lifted, clarity revealed, was the message I got. Again, I was being guided.

Sometimes, the guidance comes in a spirit animal. I asked for my spirit animal to be revealed for this soul book journey and I was shown "mystical crane." If you ask, you will be guided to not only your human support squad but also your spiritual support squad. This is where the spiritual merges with the practical. This is a key element to truly living this life of my dreams. When I got sober, my sponsor told me, "But for the grace of God, I am sober." God's grace opens doors. The Great Mother's spirit guides you when you are lost. Always, there is spiritual support available for us. We simply must ask and connect.

Take a moment to light a candle. Go to your altar. Connect to your soul. Breathe and drop in. Play music. I love Native American flutes to truly tune me in to spirit. When you feel ready, ask to see your spirit guides for this journey. Notice what they feel like and ask them what loving messages of support they have for you on this journey so that you may stay in alignment with spirit.

Ask, "How will I know when I am in alignment with soul?" and let them respond. And even if you don't hear anything, here is an

answer to that question: You will feel good when you are in alignment with soul. So if nothing comes up, don't fret. Simply surrender,
focus on feeling good, and keep asking your highest self to be there
by your side, moving forward to make clear and conscious soul-
aligned choices.

Your soul has all the answers you seek. Beneath the confusion and
the fear is a well of pure knowing, of unlimited spiritual support and
guidance. Seek your soul—she is seeking you. Ask for divine signs
and be led. This chapter was all about listening to spirit to be in
alignment. It's easier than we think—when we get still, we can hear.
Make stillness a priority—make connecting to soul a priority—and
watch how magical your life becomes. Ask for guidance: Soul, lead
me to be in alignment with you. Show me divine signs, guide me—
I am here open to you. "Your intuition is now repairing and you are
beginning to not only hear but listen to the voice of your soul. Continue to practice asking your soul for guidance and listening to the
guidance you hear to stay aligned.

> *I give myself the space to breathe and
> ask for guidance so that my intuitive
> voice can resonate through me.*
>
> #iamdiosa

CHAPTER 8

Intimacy with Self

"Eventually every woman who stays away from her
soul-home for too long, tires. This is as it should be. Then she
seeks her skin again in order to revive her sense of self and soul,
in order to restore her deep-eyed and oceanic knowing . . ."
—Dr. Clarissa Pinkola Estés

There is a place that exists beyond this realm. It is a place that is of sky and earth. It exists in moments with just you and nature, where time disappears. Moments of sacred meditation, masturbation, prayer. It can be a physical space or not.

This soul home is a space of restoration and remembering. It is a place of truth, of God, of Goddess.

When we disconnect from this space of our soul home for too long, we dry up like a prune. We walk around with dead eyes, and it feels as though you are lugging around a dead corpse. In some ways, you are. When a woman is disconnected from her soul home, she is disconnected from herself and thus her light, her Shakti, her truth.

There are those moments too when we are in between: neither here nor there and not clear at all. Actually hazy as fuck, feeling lost and unsure. These moments are often ones where you must choose—there is a path opening, and the opportunity is to go the way of the soul or not.

Soul Skin

Now that you have dived into the core of your wounds and explored the connections from your past pains and traumas to your current life, self-esteem, and relationships, it is time to replace the old with the new. You have shed old skin, as does a snake. It's important that you cover this raw space with a new pelt of skin: soul skin.

The soul skin is the true skin of the soul, rather than the fake, mundane skin. It keeps our soul home intact: the place within that is connected to Source, truth, love, and wisdom beyond this realm.

What we have explored in our core wounds and traumas shows us the ways that we lose our connection to our soul home, our soul skin, and thus ourselves.

An abusive parent or a fucked-up relationship can cause this wounding of your soul skin. We are each vessels of light and energy, and when people take from this spiritual bank of light over and over again, we become spiritually bankrupt. Imagine if you keep taking money from your bank account without putting any back in; you will eventually go negative: The account will be overdrawn, and you will get charged fees until you put money in it. If you don't, the bank account gets shut down. Our spiritual bank of light is just like this.

I remember feeling that way; each time I went back to that fucked-up guy or got nasty with someone and acted out of my pain, it was as if the light was leaving me. I was moving further away from who I wanted to be. I was moving further away from my soul.

Here is some medicine to take on this journey, today and always:

- Am I moving closer to the woman I want to be, or further away from the woman I want to be?
- Is this bringing me closer to my soul, or further away?

The further away we are from our soul, the more hazy we are. The more lost and confused we are. In more than eleven years of working with women, I always hear women say, "I want to remember me, before he abused me," "I want to love myself again and feel complete in myself," "I want to do things that reflect my self-worth so I can have healthy relationships starting with me." They say these words, because their souls know.

Getting to Know the Fragmented Self and the Whole Self

I lived in a wounded victim self for the majority of my life. I was an innocent child born not with a clean slate but with an old soul that felt more connected to the cosmic realms than the mundane world. I sensed more than what I saw with my physical eyes. I would tell my mom things like, "Mom, I have dreams of people's hands and in the dreams, the hands tell me about the people." I would cry intensely while watching commercials of orphaned children. I would force my mom to let me talk to homeless people to show them love and hear their story, wanting them to feel seen, loved, worthy, and divine. I hated the suffering, and I wanted more than anything to be part of making it go away.

Then I became the victim of trauma, and little Christine was hurting not only for the world but for herself too. My parents got divorced. My childhood had love and chaos. Name-calling, punching walls, hitting. I felt so lost and sad and lonely. I was filled with feelings that I didn't know how to process. I was put down for the smallest mistakes, and I couldn't help but feel that I was somehow a fuckup and that I was to blame.

Even when they're wise or mature, children are limited in what they can understand emotionally. Children don't have the capacity to process anything other than "This is all happening because of me."

And, of course, it wasn't my fault, but rather it was my family's generations of abuse and addiction and trauma and violence and cheating and dysfunction and unprocessed trauma pouring into me. I was the recipient of it. I was drowning and didn't know what to do with it all.

I wrote poems.

I rebelled.

I begged for it to stop.

I rationalized.

A child shouldn't have to go through that, but we often do because our parents aren't taught how to manage emotions.

And so I went on to replay those patterns as a teen and as a young adult. Looking for love in all the wrong places because my brokenness was dying to be filled. Attracting unavailable men, abusing them, and being abused. It felt like home: nice and then chaotic. Punch a wall and then say sorry. It went on and on.

It wasn't until I hit thirty and met the same man in a different body yet again that I knew I had to change. It wasn't only their fault; I was abusive too. But I didn't have to live this way.

I went to therapy and to Co-Dependents Anonymous, and I finally stopped the cycle. My sobriety was the next evolution and all the work was sticking. It changed my life and opened the doors to a new world and a new happy, joyous, free me.

Often, the way you know you are ready for a new version of yourself—to move closer to your true self, reunited with your soul skin—is that you get sick and tired of being sick and tired. You feel sick in your gut, maybe even depressed. You start desiring more, and an internal voice starts saying that this isn't good enough anymore.

The trouble is our psyche is comfortable in the known, no matter how fucked-up it is. We become safe with the comfort of knowing. Uncertainty means we don't know, and we aren't in control. Who likes to be out of control?

So we cling to what we know, even if we know we don't like it. We feel scared of the consequences of trying something new. We feel scared of the work we must do or how it will look to have faith.

The fragmented self is stuck to fear and anxiety. It is stuck to cultural perceptions and family perceptions, ones that no longer serve them and are not the true self.

If we are acting out of alignment with our soul, we are fragmented.

If we are acting in alignment with our soul, we are whole.

This is the goal:

How can I embrace and love and heal all of me? Accept *all* of me? Darkness and light.

How do you know you are choosing from your wounded, fragmented self?

- A feeling of caution or a red flag arises.
- A sickening feeling in the gut says, "*No*, don't do it."
- A warning goes off in our nervous system.
- Something just feels "off."
- The choice is made in an attempt to get a high in the moment, but it brings shame, guilt, and pain.
- Your behaviors are done in a manic, anxious, or needy way.
- Your choices bring you closer to hurting yourself versus healing yourself.
- You find yourself speaking in a tone that you would never, as a healthy adult, speak to a child in.

How do you know you are choosing from your empowered soul self?

- You feel a sense of ease.
- There is feeling that you are honoring yourself.

- Something just feels "right."
- The choice is made knowing that it may not be that
  easy in the moment, but it brings self-esteem, joy, and
  peace.
- Done from a space of honesty and truth.
- Takes you closer to loving and respecting yourself.
- You would treat a child that way.

As we go on this journey of self-discovery, as we become more intimate with ourselves, it's important to remember that it is truly a journey. It is not linear. It is not easy. It is painful and confusing, full of doubt. It requires letting go, trusting, having faith, and moving forward one step at a time, or even just one moment at a time. Sometimes we know what is right by doing what is wrong. We must stay committed through all the bumps and distractions—and there will be many.

Whether it's someone honking the horn or calling us with bad news, or getting an unexpected email or bill—we must keep returning back home to our soul. This is how we remain connected to ourselves. We must be still. We must surround ourselves with reminders of soul.

Because the journey is worth it.

The more we choose from our soul and put ourselves in spaces that activate the soul home feeling (no matter where you feel it—it is personal for everyone), the more intact that soul skin becomes, the more "YOU" you feel and the more alive you feel.

Sometimes it's the wound that chose the people in your life and the situations, but the only way you'll be able to trust yourself in whether or not you need to leave that relationship is for you to trust that you've done the work on that wound. If not, you'll constantly be questioning: "Is it that bad or not?" "Am I being too sensitive?" "Is this me or is this them?" You'll keep doubting yourself, and you won't have the confidence because you haven't done the emotional work to know what's you and what's not.

You might keep saying to yourself, "Maybe I'm being too needy," instead of knowing that you are really claiming your desires. By doing the work, you'll know what's too much, what's not enough, etc. You'll know, "No, that person hasn't been consistent, this doesn't work for me," rather than "Am I bugging? Am I being too needy?"

Go beyond "Am I right or are they right?"

Know how to set boundaries. Know how to give yourself what you need.

If you notice that your wound is constantly being triggered, it might be good for you to remove yourself while you do the deep work around this trigger. That might mean celibacy, going to an AA meeting, etc.

I remember the moment when I realized, "No, I'm not being needy, this is what I desire and deserve." Move from shaming yourself about the wound to "I need to work at it *and* I get to have my desires."

We have injured instincts when we are deeply wounded in certain areas, but you can begin to trust yourself only when you take steps toward healing that wound and treating it like an experiment in self-love. What if, just for one week, you try something different, really trust your gut, asking yourself in situations, "Do I actually like this?" When interacting with others, are there any red flags, inconsistencies, etc., that arise that show the person might be untrustworthy? Are their words and actions in alignment? When you really sit with yourself and place your hands on your heart and your belly, ask yourself, "Do I trust this person's intentions?" Listen to your body and where it leads you. How do they show up in the world? Are they fake, shady, honest, open, etc.?

At a certain point, you get to choose the triggers you want and the ones you respond to. You get to claim them. You don't have to put yourself in emotional landmines where you're constantly being triggered and think the goal is "How many triggers can I heal?" There are calmer terrains that exist for you. Triggers are part of life, but you don't have to stay there longer than you want. Don't believe that you deserve to have them constantly activated because there's something wrong with you.

We have been robbed of worth, joy, peace, love, and self-esteem in many moments. But the good news is there is a part of us that is indestructible, no matter what earthly pains you have gone through. This is our soul home.

This doesn't mean that our earthly traumas will not need to be tended to, with proper healing and therapy, because they do. But this is to offer real hope. We are more resilient than we know. Wiser than we can imagine. And worthiness is sewn into our bones.

As you allow your soul to lead, your life becomes better than you could imagine.

Your soul has a plan. The ego will resist and get mad. It will demand proof and debate with you: "It isn't that bad. I should just suck it up a little longer." But the soul will tell you otherwise: "You must leave that relationship, you must quit that job, you must start that practice of daily prayer." Your soul knows.

Remember, your soul is speaking. Listen.

Soulwork

Take a moment to breathe in all that we have explored in this chapter. Using your journal, write down your responses to the following questions:

1. How have you been robbed of your soul skin?
2. What brings you into that soul home space of peace and remembering of divinity and your truth as divine?

3. What actions bring you closer to your soul home?
4. What actions bring you closer to your pain?
5. Who brings you closer to your soul home?
6. Who brings you closer to your pain?
7. What wisdom does your soul whisper to you?

Mantra

I allow my soul to lead the way. I surrender and I am *Soul-led*.

Ceremony

Diosa Bath

In this ceremony, you are going to bathe and allow yourself to be nourished in your own Diosa divinity. Baths are a saving grace for me, and oftentimes my deepest spiritual work and ceremony have happened during a bath. If you don't have a bathtub, you can be creative and use the shower instead. There is not much to "do" here—there is not a lot of effort required. This is a time to be still with your soul and hear the wisdom of your heart.

Below are some ingredients you might use, but you can add what feels best for you. The key here is to connect with your desires and your own divinity. Trust yourself to choose what's right for you in the moment, what will be the most nourishing and supportive.

Diosa Bath Ceremony Ingredients

- milk
- honey
- holy water (you can bless the water yourself or get it from a botanica or church)
- flowers (choose colors that mean something to you during this time)
- magnesium

- Epsom salt
- lavender oil

You are magic in skin, Diosa! Your soul skin is your truth, your protection, your connection to the cosmic world. Protect and honor the soul skin on your sacred bones. You are a sacred vessel, a being clothed in stars. Honor what brings you closer to your soul and choose that. I constantly remind myself and my clients of this question that I will repeat so that you take this with you and carry it within your heart: "Is this bringing me closer to the person I want to be or is this bringing me further from the person I want to be?" A profound question to help you pivot back to truth, clarity, and soul. In the next chapter, we'll discuss the moments when we slip up and choose the quick fix—when we choose the option that brings us further away from our soul. Why? Because that's real. In working with clients over the years, I have witnessed the flow of healing. And I like to make healing grounded and attainable so that you are not discouraged when you slip up. When we normalize the healing process, shame is removed from the nonlinear cycle of healing. There is nothing better than having a realistic healing plan to set you up to win.

Let your soul choose the people,
places, and things in your life.
Live a soul-led life.

#iamdiosa

CHAPTER 9

Dust Yourself Off and Try Again

"Don't ever stop believing in your own transformation. It is still happening even on days you may not realize it or feel like it."
—Lalah Delia

Diosa, you are in the midst of a deep healing process, but make no mistake: The path is going to snake around in spirals and loops, and then some. Healing is not linear—it is messy and chaotic and up and down and all around. When we are on the path, we often forget about the inevitable ups and downs. However, growth is not just about constant accomplishments and peak experiences. Things will definitely go south and fall off track at times.

Unfortunately, the disappointment that we feel when this happens can often result in a great deal of self-blame and self-shame. The negative ego traps us into believing that we somehow messed up and that everything we touch is eventually going to turn into shit. This is what I call "negative death energy"; rather than channeling the positive manifestation of destruction that leads us to re-birth and resurrection, we can feel like we've run smack into a dead-end road.

As I was writing this book, I came face-to-face with the powerful lesson of dusting myself off and having to try again—often! It's funny how spirit works sometimes. Here I was, writing this book about healing deep, loving yourself, and coming back home to soul, and it was as if the wounds I had worked so hard to heal suddenly made a comeback. I can joke about it now, but in the moment when an old wound rears its ugly head, it can be extremely painful, not to mention alarming.

This is the very moment when a major breakthrough can occur, but of course the inner critic will cut in to wreak havoc on our vulnerability and rawness.

Some of the evil things my own inner critic said included: "Should you even write this book? I mean, yeah, you have come far and helped a lot of people, but now here you are getting triggered again. You couldn't have learned that much, right?"

Son of a bitch. This inner critic knows how to go innnnnn. (Insert ghetto girl clap.)

It didn't stop there, but continued to jab in the needles: "You really didn't heal; it was all a lie. Give up. You're a fake."

Ouch. Right where it hurts most.

And last but not least, essentially sealing the deal: "You should just give it all up. Throw in the towel with writing, and tell your fiancé you should just be alone."

Note: I said this out loud and for a moment believed I really should give it all up. It's so helpful to have loving, supportive people around you who remind you of the truth instead of the lies that the voice of fear will spread. My partner comforted me by reminding me that I was upset, which meant I wasn't thinking clearly, which meant it was all too easy to give in to that fear voice that was attempting to discredit me for all the work I'd done—all under the guise of wisdom and common sense. My partner reminded me of how much I had grown both as a healer and as a woman in this relationship.

Still, despite those humbling reminders, it was painful to see myself falling off track from my usually grounded, centered, confident Diosa self! It was also frustrating and, at times, humiliating.

In the middle of my "I'm the worst and should just say 'fuck it' to everything" rant, my partner and I literally looked up to see a heart-shaped cloud in the sky. It stopped me mid-rant and brought a smile of awe to my face. I know how spirit likes to show off—and while spirit also wants us to continue doing the deep and dirty work of healing, it is always for our highest good.

I knew in that moment that I was being tested. Here I was at this pivotal point, both professionally and in my love life. Suddenly, I had the two things I'd always desired right at my fingertips, and I was a mess. Just when I felt like I couldn't possibly figure all this shit out, I received that beautiful sign from the universe. And it seemed to be saying loud and clear, "Stick with it, girl. There is love and healing here."

After that kind of validation, what better time to sit down and write a chapter about healing?

One of my favorite things about how I teach is that I do it from a sisterhood level. I allow myself to be raw and vulnerable and share the real deal of what is actually going on within my heart and in my life. This gives me full permission not to be perfect, but instead to share the pitfalls, bumps, and lessons along the way—with fellow sisters, friends, and soul *hermanas*.

That inner critic was trying to have me zoom into all the negative character defects in a judgmental and self-defeating way instead of focusing on my immense growth. In truth, I had not only transformed my life over the past eleven years, but I grew by leaps and bounds in the last three years in particular after I made the decision to get sober. Now that I was free of the self-sabotaging behavior that came with numbing and acting out with alcohol, I was a better communicator, and I approached my life with more softness and acceptance. So when the inner critic came at me, claws out, I had to remind myself that I was damn worthy of writing this book and being in an incredible, supportive relationship! I had to remind myself that spirit wanted me to share my unique voice with the world as a Latina woman and healer. I had to remind myself that spirit wanted me to be in my partnership with Fernando not only for ourselves, but also so that we could heal others through our love and show them what was possible.

Believe me, I had to really sink into the truth in such a way that it became concrete—because when I slip up, my ego and critical voice tend to take center stage and become much louder than those words of encouragement and affirmation.

As I share in this chapter, it is precisely those moments when we most need self-compassion. We need to rest in the understanding that healing is a hard and convoluted process. Just as years of AA taught me, you can't just skip the steps. I knew this when I was healing my love addiction and codependency, as well as my addiction to alcohol. But just because I had learned all of that, I still had to relearn it. New lessons arose as I opened up to my soul purpose, and with that, a new learning curve. Growing into our aligned soul selves requires patience. Through these growing pains, we cannot and must not abandon ourselves. We must be willing to tend to the land and care for the seeds that we have so diligently and lovingly sown.

So let me tell you, Diosa: Relapses and slip-ups do not erase your success. If anything, they can offer you a greater sense of perspective, appreciation, and compassion.

I share this so you know that you are not alone, and neither am I—we are doing the soulwork together. Instead of trying to avoid the falls on the journey back home to soul, let us prepare for them so we go in ready and able to bounce back faster.

In my journey as a therapist and spiritual guide for over a decade, I know that I have to prepare my clients, and you, for those moments of relapse, when you feel like you aren't strong enough to keep going; for those moments when you wonder if the journey is really worth it at all; for those moments when you will fall hard and feel your fragility and humanness. The journey of self-love will confront us with the entire range of human experience and emotion. Don't turn away or deny these moments, because they can be truly character-defining.

One of my favorite quotes, which is often shared in twelve-step groups, is "Life on life's terms," meaning that as life unfolds, we have the opportunity to face the challenges and rewards that life presents.

While we can contribute to a healthier healing journey through patience and self-acceptance, it is also true that the healing itself has its own process and flow, which we must surrender to. We can show up as best as we can with the utmost compassion, gentleness, and awareness of the constant rise and fall of our emotions. When we get in touch with the felt sense and texture of these emotions, we can acknowledge that life is a river of constant change. Even our internal landscapes are subject to this change, which is always working for our highest good.

I like to remind myself that the very energy of the healing that is occurring within me and within you is an intelligent source. It goes where it needs to go. In those spiritual dark nights of the soul, when you believe you are so far from where you need to go, I invite you to reframe your experience: Consider that spirit is testing you to build your character and heal you on a deeper level.

I feel it even as I write these words. I am being stretched to accept more . . . to be more loving and trusting . . . to exercise faith in the ever-expanding quality of life. My container is growing and stretching so that I have the capacity to hold more miracles and blessings— meaning I must set down the baggage that I've been carrying.

Fernando reminds me of this whenever he tells me, "*Mi amor*, be light with me."

Sometimes the heaviest shit comes up precisely so that it can be cleared. In those moments, have faith that spirit is gifting you.

The key is to embrace all of your emotions, because none of them are "wrong." Go inward and become aware of the emotions you feel in your peak moments (including joy, hope, confidence, sassiness), as well as the emotions you feel in that downward spiral (such as depression, numbness, isolation, anger). Now think of how you feel in those in-between moments, which mark the majority of our human experience (this might include curiosity, boredom, frustration, and any number of possible states). Familiarize yourself with the quality of your inner world. Trust that knowing yourself by heart will allow you to close your eyes, take a step forward, and navigate this rich and fruitful space with power and grace.

Activate Your Healing Process

As I was thinking about what it means to heal the soul wound and the process of falling off track, it reminded me of the journey to healing any addiction, which I think is helpful to understand. Psychoeducation can offer us immense clarity about how healing works on a scientific level.

On the next page is a diagram that highlights the process of the cycles of change.

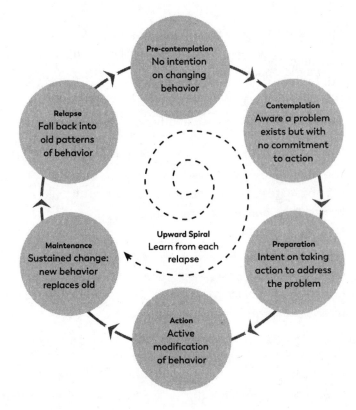

The Cycle of Change, socialworktech.com, adapted from a work by Prochaska and DiClemente (1983)/Ignacio Pacheco

Another example that provides some context and understanding, so that we can offer ourselves more gentleness as we heal, is considering the four phases of healing a physical wound. Basically, when we experience an injury to the surface of the skin, the body moves through something that is known as the "cascade of healing," a necessary process that allows our tissues to heal. This process includes four distinct stages:

- **Stage 1:** Hemostasis—This is all about stopping the bleeding. It's the first stage of healing a wound, and it's all about

damage control. This is when blood coagulates, blood vessels constrict to prevent excessive bleeding, and a clot forms
to seal the wound.

- **Stage 2:** Inflammation—At this stage, bacteria is destroyed
  and debris is removed from the wound in order to prepare
  the bed of the wound for new tissue. This is a phase when
  we might experience heat, pain, and redness, which are created by white blood cells, growth factors, nutrients, and en-
  zymes. This phase can last for several days.

- **Stage 3:** Proliferation—At this stage, the wound is cleaned
  out and covered by new tissue. The wound contracts, and a
  new network of blood cells is created so the new tissue can
  receive enough nutrients and oxygen.

- **Stage 4:** Maturation—This final phase can differ from person to person and is often impacted by such factors as
  environment, genes, infection, etc. This process is remark-
  ably complex. The cells that were used to repair the wound
  are removed by programmed cell death. Scar thickness
  is reduced, and the area of skin around the wound becomes stronger as the tissue gradually increases in
  strength and flexibility. This process usually occurs twenty-
  one days after the injury but can continue for more than
  a year.

I loved reading the above, because it reminded me of the process
of healing emotional wounds, as well. This process can also be broken down into four stages:

- **Stage 1:** Hemostasis. This is when you stop the emotional
  bleeding in your life and remove the toxic people, the self-

sabotaging patterns, the blood of the wound. This is the key to crisis management.

- **Stage 2:** Inflammation. We move into the next phase, which is cleaning. This is when we develop the necessary awareness to sort through everything that needs to be cleansed, removed, and released. It's also when we receive tools and spiritual medicine that act as balm for our soul wounds. We are likely to experience a lot of pain in this phase, but that's not a sign that we're backsliding; our wound is simply being touched and cleansed.

- **Stage 3:** Proliferation. This is a stage when we experience rewiring in the nervous system and our patterns. We recognize the triggers and the pain points and work to avoid them, as we use our tools to feed the new neural pathways necessary for the maintenance of a healthy emotional and spiritual state. In this phase, there is new blood, and we are made anew.

- **Stage 4:** Maturation. The actual maturation process varies widely. Whether we relapse (especially if we are in a toxic environment) or find ourselves managing mental illness, the key is to be patient with ourselves. This is when we develop the wherewithal to build our emotional strength.

I want to stress that the process of relapsing is totally normal and an integral aspect of the healing journey. It isn't needed to heal, but it is common and not to be feared. Just as you can reinjure yourself with physical healing, it is possible to reopen wounds that you didn't realize were still present within you. I always remind my clients that it's totally okay, and they're doing an amazing job, regardless of what they might think.

No matter our perceived slip-ups, we can learn to pivot back to our center by developing north-star soul goals, which remind us of the ultimate course that we want to stay on. "Not messing up" isn't human, and falling off track gives us the valuable opportunity to forgive ourselves. I am talking about deep forgiveness in the moments when our souls are not aligned with our actions . . . when we send that text message that we know won't lead to anything constructive . . . when we scream at our partner or child rather than practicing patience . . . when we fall into the vortex of insecurity and constant comparison . . . when we backslide into old habits and addictions in order to feel more ease, even though we know it's only temporary.

All of this requires self-forgiveness. For when we shame and blame ourselves, we decrease access to our vital life energy. The best way to regain momentum and energy is to practice forgiveness.

This is not a sentimental practice. It is one that requires radical honesty and integrity, both of which are needed to see ourselves with clarity, understanding, and compassion, and to say, "I did something I'm not proud of or that I don't like. It isn't what I wanted for myself. I give myself permission to come back home to self, to come back to the parts of me I know I want to cultivate, because they are the parts that will lead me to my north-star soul goals and to wholeness."

It's so dope to recognize the relationship between the healing of physical wounds and the healing of emotional wounds, because it gives us more space to hold the healing process with all its complexity. We start to see how all of nature and existence is connected, and processes and phases are necessary for the rhythm of life. Storms occur, things happen that are unexpected, and yet the most we can do is pivot, flow, and handle life on life's terms. There is a certain peaceful surrender we can relax into when we can accept this part of the process. We don't have to grip onto things that don't serve us, like self-hatred and self-blame. We can rest in the peace and awareness that our healing will continue to unfold in its own time and season.

The Get-Back-on-Track Formula

By now, you have a clearer understanding of some of your own emotional triggers, so let's plan for what you can do when you find yourself falling off track and reverting to unhealthy emotional patterns.

It's very easy to be hard on yourself, especially if you have a past history of trauma or were surrounded by people who were hard on you. Let yourself be soft on yourself . . . to see yourself clearly. Remember that you are not fucked-up and awful. You shouldn't just give up or stay stuck in a rut. These feelings are natural, but they don't emerge from your truest truth—they emerge from that destructive inner critic who wants to hold you back from pursuing your best life.

We must be aware that there is a primal energy that is rooting for our destruction, and one that is rooting for us to thrive. Simply by being aware of this polarity, which permeates all of nature, we can learn that we are fully equipped to manage it and to be our own best cheerleaders in the process.

Call out those voices as they arise: the voices of the inner critic, of blame and shame, of alienation. They are a program that has been handed to most of us by unconscious people; they are not the truth.

This is your chance to pivot back to center by using a simple but effective question:

"What is the truth here?"

We must become stealthy ninjas when it comes to discerning the truth, for when we fall off track and our progress is derailed, the number of lies waiting to ensnare us can be overwhelming. If we can accept this and be prepared for it, we will be better equipped at handling whatever comes our way. We will do what is necessary to move beyond the lies.

Use the following guide whenever you need to get back on track and rebuild your energy and self-esteem:

1. Recognize the "acting-out behavior" that is hurting your self-esteem. Write it down if that helps you to own it.

2. Own that you desire to change the behavior. "I desire to change this behavior and pivot back to center." Say this out loud and write it down to get behind the shift.

3. List how the behavior is hurting you and/or others. It is helpful to do this so that we get clear on how and why the behavior isn't working. In AA, they use the phrase "keeping it green," which is all about maintaining perspective and remembering why you never want to revert to old behaviors. Being able to keep yourself "right-sized" and humble is key in pivoting back to your soul goals.

4. Commit to making a decision that helps you feel good and healthy again. You might say, "I commit to coming back to surrender. I accept this doesn't feel good and it's hurting me and others. I desire to get back on track. I honor that I am out of alignment, and I choose to come back to center. I choose to come home to my soul. I desire to shift and come into a healthy feeling place." As you say this, you are allowing yourself to remember the truth of your soul goals.

5. Optional: Share this new commitment with someone you trust—a friend, a Diosa sister, a therapist—to really seal it. If you don't desire to, saying it out loud to spirit and writing it in your journal is a great way to honor your commitment to self and soul.

6. Invite your soul voice in. Say, "Soul, I have relapsed with my goal, and I need guidance and help to get back on track.

I know this behavior [insert harmful behavior to self or others here] is hurting me and hurting [insert name of person/people], and I desire to stop. Guide me to see what I must see to change what I must change. Guide me to a tool that I can use and an energetic shift I can feel to bring me to completion with this soul lesson." Inviting in spiritual support allows for your energy to recalibrate as you get support from higher consciousness and dimensions.

7. Now take a moment to pause. Write down what your soul voice guided you to do, or perhaps it was simply a feeling that soul guided you to feel. Free-write some guidance to see what emerges.

8. Write down one step you can do daily that will act as prevention against your acting out. For example: sign up for weekly therapy, or wake up every morning and repeat to yourself the goal "I choose to be proactive over reactive, and I practice this muscle in every situation of the day." Small steps add up, so recommitting to a daily step will allow you to put positive momentum and energy toward the you, you actually desire to be.

9. Celebrate yourself for each step. Give yourself positive self-talk: "Baby girl, you are doing a great job!" Take yourself out for a nice coffee or tea, or get a new journal or crystal you have been wanting when you hit a milestone.

10. Every night, note three things that made you proud of yourself that day.

11. Finally, write out your soul goals again, and write or read out loud the following: "I recommit to my soul goals, and

even if I fall off track, I promise my Self and my Soul to get
back on track with forgiveness and grace. I deserve
healing. I am worthy."

Use this each time you need an extra dose of self-love to get
you back on track. Remember, your soul is your adviser, and
you can take time to come for guidance as you need. Great work,
Diosa!

Your Emotional Safety Plan

As a therapist, I'm very familiar with helping clients with suicidal
ideation create "safety plans," which are basically a set of written
instructions that they can create as a contingency plan for the times
when they are seriously considering harming themselves. Instead of
carrying through with those actions, they can turn to the safety
plan, which contains a series of simple steps that can be followed,
one by one, until they are safe. Safety plans are wonderful because
they can deescalate a stressful situation or incident, and they don't
require excessive problem-solving or trying to figure shit out when
emotions are running hot and high.

Aside from the guidelines above to get back on track, I suggest
having an emotional safety plan in place that's all about preventa-
tive care to keep you from acting out of maladaptive or unhealthy
emotional patterns. I think of this as being like meal prep for the
soul—simple reminders that keep us in alignment with the emotionally healthy state we want to nurture.

Safety plans are a wonderful template for the moments when we
are experiencing a lot of intense emotions. Just as safety plans for
people with suicidal ideation are not about banishing thoughts of
suicide, an emotional safety plan is not about denying your feelings.
On the contrary, it helps you to own your thoughts and emotions
instead of hiding or running from them. Researchers have demon-

strated that when people who are thinking about suicide have a safe space to share their thoughts and feelings, they are less likely to act on them; likewise, by acknowledging what you are going through (to yourself and/or a trusted friend or therapist), it becomes easier to create a plan that helps you to manage overwhelming or self-defeating thoughts and feelings.

I always suggest creating your emotional safety plan from an emotionally neutral state, because when you are super-worked-up, you can't think clearly—more often than not, you will be scattered or swinging from one extreme to the next. Begin to draft your own safety plan by noting to yourself the kinds of feelings that can trip you up and send you into emotionally unhealthy patterns. What are those feelings? Sadness? Loneliness? Depression? Rage? What happens when you let those feelings take you over? Do you withdraw from loved ones? Indulge in old addictive patterns? Neglect your physical health and well-being? Finally, what are some specific ways you can calm yourself and come back to homeostasis when you're under siege by these emotions?

Below is a simple template for an emotional safety plan:

1. Name the thoughts, feelings, triggers that usuaully make you feel off track emotionally/mentally/spiritually.
   Example: When I'm lonely or hungry I tend to feel unworthy and sad.
   Example: When someone doesn't believe me when I am saying the truth, I tend to feel angry and sulk.

2. What are some healthy tools or coping strategies I can do on my own, if I feel sad, anxious, angry, or down to distract myself from my problems in a healthy way? This where you list healthy what I call "pattern interruptors."
   - Listen to music
   - Take a walk

- Journal feelings out on paper
- Move your body, even if it is simply stretching or doing some yoga
- Pet dog/cat if you have one
- Drink tea or water

3. Who are people that you trust and feel comfortable calling to get support when you are feeling sad, anxious, down etc?

1. Name_____Phone Number_____

2. Name_____Phone Number_____

3. Name_____Phone Number_____

4. Who are professional people/resources that you can contact when you are needing support?
   Examples:

Name	Phone Number/Website
1. Therapist Name	Therapist Phone Number
2. NYC WELL HOTLINE	1-888-692-9355
3. trybetterhelp.com/cosmicchristine for tele-therapy	trybetterhelp.com/cosmicchristine

5. List a reason(s) why you want to continue to heal and work on yourself. List some things you look forward to or bring you joy.
   Example: One day I want to be a mother and a wife, and therefore I want to continue to work on myself to be the best possible version of myself.

This plan will be there for you when your emotions are in danger of taking over your life. Obviously, when you are in a heightened emotional state, practicing the simplest acts of self-care can feel like a leap—to the extent that merely brushing your teeth takes effort.

Don't take any of it for granted. Please notice even the tiniest steps you can take, because they all add up. Continue to pat yourself on the back for everything you are doing to build yourself up. You've got this, Diosa!

As we head into the integration phase of this soul journey, this is really your time to step it up and move into creation mode for the life you want. You will set high standards, crown yourself as Diosa, and usher in joy and pleasure, sensuality and creativity, and Diosa sister love. Because when we do the soulwork, we must also remember that we deserve to expand and blossom. Now you are rising from the root and solar plexus into the heart and third eye—integrating a full experience of grounded healing.

Soulwork

Let yourself plan for the fall, because when you don't, it can be all too easy to forget what you are working toward. Using your journal, write down your responses to the following questions:

1. What are the top three emotions that get you off track (*e.g.*, jealousy, fear, loneliness)?

2. What are the top three situations that you want to create an emotional safety plan for (*e.g.*, looking at your ex's Instagram obsessively, going on dating apps from a place of fear and insecurity, acting out sexually when you are feeling unworthy of affection)?

3. What is one positive step you can take to prevent the three situations you wrote down from occurring? These should be steps that keep you connected to your healthy whole self and prevent you from acting out. In other words, they should be setting you up to win. (*E.g.*, block ex

on Instagram, spend more time with supportive loved
ones who remind you of who you truly are, go to a Sex and
Love Addicts Anonymous meeting when you are feeling
lonely, to actually nurture the wound instead of
reopening it.)

4. What are three healthy coping tools you can turn to when
you fall off track (e.g., prayer, play music and journal, go to
a twelve-step meeting or book a therapy session; I
recommend trybetterhelp.com/cosmicchristine for
teletherapy that is easy and accessible with an Internet
connection)?

Be sure to use the Get-Back-on-Track Formula in this chapter, as
well as the aforementioned suggestions for creating an emotional
safety plan, as needed, as part of your soulwork!

Mantra
Even when I fall off track, I am guided. I am resilient and I pivot
back to my soul goals and soul center. I got this!

Ceremony
Healing Through Art
Your ceremony is to create a beautiful visual art piece that represents
your resilience. This can be physical, with markers, paint, stickers,
feathers, sequins, etc., or a digital art piece. Write a mantra that
soothes you and will take you back to center if you fall off track (*e.g.*,
"If I fall off track, I dust myself off and get back up again. I am strong
and resilient, and my eye is on my soul prize. I've got this!").

Post your empowering art piece and mantra in your room as a
reminder that no matter how much you relapse, slip up, make mistakes, etc., you will get back on track.

It's incredible what happens when we are honest with ourselves and grounded in the healing process. I knew I wanted to include this chapter because too often self-help books minimize the messy, the raw, the slip-ups, and relapses and the nonlinear nature of the journey. It is essential for me as a therapist and healer to normalize the moments of messy. The moments when we forget to choose in alignment with our soul, the moments our triggers get the best of us. It is my hope that this provided you with the necessary information and confidence to know that slipping up and getting thrown off track is part of it. And that no matter the slip-up or fuckup, you can get back on track. In the next chapter, you will set high standards that will uplevel your worth, your relationships, and your life.

Even when I fall off track, I am guided.

I am resilient and I pivot back to my soul goals and soul center. I got this.

#iamdiosa

PART III

The Integration: Living the Diosa Vibes and Light in Action

CHAPTER 10

Setting High Standards (aka Not Settling Anymore)

"Don't put your soul in the wrong hands, mindset, or environment."

—Lalah Delia

I am so proud of you for all the work you have done throughout these chapters. I always remind myself and my clients that giving ourselves self-praise is key. Each time we do this, we are building our self-esteem and strengthening our internal dialogue with self.

The first portion of the book dove into the concepts and principles of core childhood wound exploration and how those wounds affect you presently. You localized these feelings in the body, befriended the difficult feelings, and learned language to speak to and transform the self-sabotage within. You also learned how to tap into the difference between your fragmented self and your whole self. Finally, you learned some scripts and some exercises to love up your inner child, alchemize the wounds into wisdom, and simultaneously honor the wound as it is so you can learn the spiritual lesson behind even the most difficult moments.

Then, in the second phase, you stepped into truly understanding what it feels like to live in soul alignment, and you gained principles for a more realistic take on healing so you don't trip up or make yourself feel worse when you fall off track—because falling off track is human as fuck!

Now that we are in the third and final phase of this book, you are ready to *soar* with your new Soul Self, your Diosa divine self, and make changes that stick.

That's right, it's time to up your standards, get to know your high soul values, and become lovingly strict with and devoted to yourself. This is one of my favorite parts of the journey, so I hope you're ready!

Match Your Diosa Divinity

Rising up to meet your Diosa standards requires a whole lotta self-love. I once read that self-love is the balance between compassion and being benevolently strict with yourself when needed. It's about allowing yourself to point out the things you know you need to grow within yourself while offering yourself the utmost love and compassion to be exactly where you are right now.

This is your time to go there. To get clear. For with clear sight, you can be more discerning about what and who you deserve in your life.

A story about my client Ana highlights this principle. She came to my annual Diosa Retreat with the intention to heal the core wounds of her earlier childhood trauma and to also release relationships from her life that no longer served her.

After having done the somatic exercise that you went through in chapter 5, and really uncovering some core wounds of abandonment and abuse from her mother, she began to make connections between her past and how it was still currently impacting her, especially in her dating life. She started talking about this guy in her life. Even though it was clear that the relationship was half-assed and that he was in no way demonstrating that he valued the relationship, everyone noticed that Ana was making excuses for him and downplaying the situation by saying that it wasn't so bad.

"I don't orgasm with him," she admitted. "I am not his girlfriend, and I know I deserve better, but sometimes it's nice, because he works out with me and sometimes buys me smoothies."

Everyone was in shock at what we were hearing. This is all she could muster when we asked her why she liked the guy! My husband, Fernando, who was my fiancé at the time, was photographing the retreat but also participating by casually giving advice and providing that valuable male perspective.

He looked at Ana in disbelief and said, "Wait, so let me get this right—he makes you feel bad but you like him because sometimes he works out and occasionally he gets you smoothies? Nothing else?"

At that point, Ana's friend Andrea chimed in from the back of the room: "Actually, Ana, he charges you to buy the smoothies, and there are times when he charges you more!"

Andrea's words really put the nail in the coffin. Sometimes you need someone else to call you out with love and say the truth you are hiding—because you are just too scared to admit how little you are settling for. In that moment, Andrea was offering us the eyes of clarity that Ana couldn't.

Of course, this can be embarrassing, but when the truth is revealed, it can be healed.

Unfortunately, I know all too well that this distorted way of viewing a relationship can be brought about when you aren't shown or told that this isn't love. It isn't what you deserve.

We looked at Ana and said, "WHAT???? *¡¡Que carajo!?* He doesn't give you orgasms, he only sometimes works out with you, and then he brings you smoothies that he charges you for? You can have a better relationship by ordering Uber Eats, watching Netflix, and touching yourself!"

We all then gathered around Ana to tell her that this experience she was settling for wasn't love. Fernando also said, "You are beautiful, smart—a Diosa, but every time you say 'yes' to something that is less than what you deserve, you are inadvertently saying 'no' to something out there that could be actually good for you."

That was one of the most powerful things that Fernando said, and it continues to hit home.

Fernando and I and all the Diosas sat with Ana to craft her breakup text to the guy. It was a back-and-forth at first. She resisted because she felt guilty and didn't want to be mean. She also hoped that things would change organically. She made excuses for a while, but little by little, she started to recognize that she was settling for scraps of love instead of the whole motherfucking cake!

Fernando ultimately crafted the goodbye text, which read something like this: "I have taken the time to think about things to be able to speak from a place that is honest to myself. I've realized that for the last few years I have been settling for a relationship that I know is less than I deserve. Today I've decided not to settle anymore. I forgive myself for my mistakes and commit to only accepting relationships that nurture who I want to be. I am clear this is the path I choose. Today I choose to be free, honest, and to love and honor every part of me, on my own. I wish you the best and no hard feelings. I ask that you respect my wishes and don't contact me again."

Immediately, she began to see that though it was an extremely difficult text to send, her soul was happy that she was finally upping her standards and allowing her actions to align with her Diosa divinity.

It is totally common in cases like Ana's to feel guilty about our actions, or to fall into the trap of believing that we must be nice to people at the expense of our own well-being. In truth, nothing is more valuable than saying no and cutting ties with people and situations that do not serve our highest self. This is not the same as being mean or disrespectful; you can still be kind even if you are letting someone go. It is actually an incredible act of love for oneself and for the other person, as allowing people to treat you badly enables bad behavior.

Ana started to feel more like a Diosa because she had to set the boundary, say no to scraps, and say yes to loving herself. She was challenged to accept the initiation of coming home to herself and claiming herself as divine, as queen, as an altar upon which to pour honey and receive blessings.

Diosa, you cannot move through such an initiation if you are in a crap relationship or crap job. You must rise up to meet your destiny. This is truly one of the most important lessons you can learn in a lifetime.

Ana gradually took soul-aligning steps, and her Diosa sisters were present to remind her that even the tiniest steps add up. Saying no to that bullshit dynamic was the same as saying yes to loving herself. By taking those steps, she began to claim her worth and honor the woman she wanted to be.

Sometimes, energetically, we are not yet where we want to be—and from that place, we tend to replicate patterns and behaviors that match that internal vibration. So, for example, if Ana was feeling insecure, then her actions of insecurity (in other words, letting in this fuckboy who wasn't giving her anything good) would occur. The trick is changing our actions to *go beyond* the vibration we are currently feeling; changing our actions then sends signals to the brain and nervous system, and our idea of our worth begins to change.

And yes, this is true even in the case of a relapse. We are perfectly imperfect humans, and making a mistake is not a problem; staying in the mistake, wallowing in it, and continuing to make it

over and over again is the problem. But if we constantly have our
eyes on the soul prize, we will continue to honor our worth and raise
our standards. Then, nobody can stop us.

I repeat here one of my favorite lines from twelve-step programs,
which my sponsor told me once: "Esteemable actions give you self-
esteem." Through a series of actions that weren't up to par with her
standards, Ana realized that she needed to make a change. She was
brought to her bottom in the pattern of accepting crumbs of love.
Her new soul lesson would be to increase her expectations, as well
as her values.

Fix Self-Sabotaging Habits

Habit formation is a mysterious ball of yarn. Whether we are talking about brushing our teeth or biting our nails, habits make up the
unconscious material of our lives. Habits solidified into routines create the very fiber of our lifestyles. A psychological pattern that unfolds from a habit leads to a behavior, which leads to an ingrained
belief, which we are typically unaware of even harboring.

Neuroscientists have discovered that the alive, alert, fabulous
decision-making part of our brain tends to enter sleep mode when a
habitual behavior has taken over. Most of our actions are triggered
by habit, to the extent that we are operating almost exclusively on
autopilot.

Autopilot doesn't have the kind of fuel that's potent enough for
desire to run efficiently. Moreover, autopilot sucks away most of our
energy, even when we aren't mentally aware that this is happening.
This isn't to say that all automated behaviors are bad. It's simply
that they tend to keep us firmly locked into patterns that may or
may not be conducive to the cultivation of desire.

"Bad" habits aren't bad in and of themselves. Remember, it's not
about right vs. wrong. Bad habits tend to take us further and further

away from our Diosa standards. On a certain level, they are unconscious mechanisms that keep our perspectives small and limited.

In order to let our Soul lead us, we must be ruthless when it comes to cutting out those habits that keep our lives small and colorless. A toxic friend who makes us feel like we've been drained by the biggest energy vampire of them all? Time to kick them to the curb. A tendency to hoard everything, from your senior prom dress to photographs of your world travels with your recent ex? Perhaps a bonfire or a Salvation Army run is in order.

Our obsessions and compulsive behaviors give us a decent clue about where we tend to get stuck. They are like muddy ruts on the way to a destination. They may seem to deserve our attention, but in truth, they are distractions from our greatness. We know this because they have a tendency to make us feel depleted and diminished, and the aftertaste they leave is almost always bitter.

I remember, like Ana, being drawn to a man whose interest in me was sporadic and highly dependent on everything else that was going on in his life. But the effect of his intermittent attention (which I think of as love-bombing) was like experiencing the brightest, warmest sun beating down on me after a long and cold winter. Of course, there were times when I told myself that I was absolutely finished. But every time he'd send me a one-line text (with little context or indication of his feelings), I was completely overthrown.

I wasn't getting what I truly wanted in this experience: deep connection that made it safe to surrender all the way. At my core, I was doing something I said I'd never do: engaging with a situation and person that no part of me trusted.

For a long time, even though my intuition was screaming "no," the thought that perhaps things might get better always won out. How did I come to see the difference between what I really wanted and this obsession? My true soul standards made me feel expanded and alive, while my obsession made me feel contracted and small.

Bad habits keep us in a solid identity (even if that identity isn't particularly freeing), while soul standards create freedom, space, and a clean, well-lit place for expression. Sometimes they even take us into places where we never expected to find ourselves, but those places are always vast open plains rather than dark and musty closets.

You can think of bad habits as being, at their core, misplaced loyalties that were placed in us long before we became conscious of them. My insistence that "things will get better" with this man reminds me of my observations of my parents' relationship, where true affection was infrequent, but enough to scatter little spots of light across an otherwise hopeless terrain. For those of us who are used to operating on scarcity, it's way more than one could otherwise hope for.

When you haven't discovered your soul standards as the most potent fuel, sometimes the bread crumbs of pleasure can feel adequate. A habit keeps us locked in an attitude of sufficiency (*e.g.*, "This isn't what I want, but I guess it's good enough"), whereas aligning with your soul standards helps you maintain loyalty to a deeper and more generous truth.

Of course, habits are things we build up only over time, which makes them sneaky little bastards. After all, they go mostly unnoticed, swept up in other distractions! That's why it's a good idea to make a record of your habits over the course of a week. Write down the things you find yourself doing over and over. A good way to do this is to watch where you spend your money. If you see the use of your time, money, and other resources as an indication of where the energy is flowing in your life, this can give you loads of information on how you are using or abusing that energy.

Do you find yourself constantly signing up for personal-development courses, even if you never actually use them? (Again, this can be a form of escapism, especially when it comes to gathering the courage to gently set the self-help down and move toward action.)

Many of our habits may also come from a sense of obligation that causes us not to view our habits as habits at all. I always come back to the example of toxic or energetically draining relationships, like the one Ana was in. Because many of us are so tied to the notion that we should be nice, appropriate, compliant little sweethearts, we build habits that don't serve us in the long run. At the same time, the habits that keep us in homeostasis are usually things that we have a complex emotional relationship with. We might cherish them dearly (especially if they are intimate relationships), and biting the bullet and letting go are way easier said than done. The bad habit might be a boyfriend, one who's more interested in "spending quality time" with you than he is in lighting a fire beneath your feet to help shape you into the champion Diosa you're capable of being. It might be a relaxed schedule where you get up at whatever hour you want, and there's no real pressure to start at six-thirty a.m. with morning practices, exercise, business planning, and the like. A habit can be so sneaky that it takes the form of a good job that has gradually turned into golden handcuffs.

When we have a road map of our true north and compare it to our daily habits, this gives us an indication of where we are actually spending our energy vs. where we want to be. So stay vigilant, radically honest, and compassionate but firm with yourself. You're going places, after all.

Upping our standards is all about dismantling the many internal programs and patterns that have us maintaining a tangled mess of self-hating behaviors. We uncross those wires and debug those viruses when we are willing to face up to the behaviors that have kept us small, unsatisfied, and in pain. We process our histories, take inventory of those things that continue to eat away at us (such as guilt, regret, shame, and other demons), and do whatever we can to clear away the cobwebs of our past. And those of us who tend to mull over the past can choose to alchemize those shadows every time we move toward who we truly are—our Diosa self—in total approval and willingness to let go of the old stories, right in this moment.

It makes me think of how, at one point in my past, I was available to give away my labor and genius for free, or to hook up with people who didn't have time to get to know the real me. Gradually, I no longer became a vibrational match for any of that shit! In setting my value, I opened new doors and was met with situations that aligned with who I was and who I wanted to be.

Mamita, none of this is easy work. As you deconstruct those old habits, you're gonna have to be patient when you have to wait. I promise that whatever comes will always come in much better than you imagined, as long as you continue to move forward and catch yourself with the utmost compassion when you backslide.

I've especially seen this to be true with the M&M (money and men). As I set higher standards and moved toward them, I saw the zeros in my bank account increase and the quality of my intimate relationships flourish. I've also seen this in the lives of so many Diosas.

So get ready for the good that's coming your way. Check those bad habits and let the information you find help you claim your worth and your new normal.

Commit to Self-Love

We must be the ones who treat ourselves as Diosa, first and foremost. It always starts with us.

Sometimes the loneliness can lead us to settle and do what feels comfortable or habitual.

But no more! If you are reading this book, you are here to get your Diosa on and treat yourself like the lovable, beautiful woman you are. That must happen by looking at the places where your standards have been lowered so that you can raise them one by one.

Mamita, there is nothing in this world you can't do—and you deserve to craft the life you want.

Take Ana's story as an example. That esteemable action of speaking her truth allowed her to witness herself loving herself. Her saying no to settling was a massive act of self-love. The opposite—acting like her guy's behavior and treatment were okay and didn't bother her—was a massive act of self-hatred.

Settling is hating the self. Upping one's standards is loving the self.

No one wins in settling. It enables people to think it's okay to treat women poorly, and it makes you think it's okay to be treated that way. Fuck that! After enduring a hard life and plenty of hard-earned soul lessons, I finally decided that I would choose relationships that nourished me and that honored me. I went through too much to continue to perpetuate that cycle of low-vibe love.

Making a commitment to yourself in this way allows you to love yourself and trust yourself, one day at a time. In this way, no matter who has hurt you in your past, you can sincerely begin to say, "I will not hurt me. I will advocate for myself, my inner child, and my well-being."

This commitment to self-love is the true source of power that radically shifts your entire life. Because even through all the fucked-up shit, we must become resilient to say, "I am going to do the soulwork to give myself the life I deserve."

Your relationship to yourself is key. What you allow yourself to do to yourself is in many ways what you allow others to do to you. I want you to take a moment to write how you would like to be treated in your ideal world. How will your commitment to self-love be reflected in the world around you?

Here's an example: "I would love to be treated like a Diosa. I would love to be looked at with sweet and tender and compassionate eyes—eyes that tell stories of gratitude and appreciation that they finally found me. I want to be spoken to with patience and understanding. I desire to be told I am beautiful, smart, powerful, divine, sexy, perfect as I am. I desire to have someone's presence and devotion to me. I desire an honest and consistent and thoughtful partner."

Now, look at that list and ask yourself these questions:

Do I treat myself like a Diosa?
Do I look at myself with eyes that are sweet and tender?
Am I patient and understanding with myself?
Do I compliment myself and tell myself I am smart, divine,
*   powerful, sexy, and perfect as I am?*
Am I consistent with myself?
Am I devoted to myself?
Am I honest with myself?
Am I thoughtful with myself?

This practice is not meant for you to be hard on yourself about all the ways you don't do that which you desire. It is, however, about getting radically honest so you turn up the volume on your values of devotion and honesty and self-love so that you will never again allow less than that.

An important thing to remember here (and it's a slightly more unpopular view in the spiritual community) is that sometimes you can't just love yourself first. Sometimes you need the love of others to give you a template for how to treat yourself, especially if you grew up in an abusive environment in which you were not taught to value yourself.

In twelve-step communities, they have signs that read "Let me love you until you can love yourself."

Sometimes a therapist is the first person you meet who shows you unconditional positive regard, kindness, and love. Use those models to show yourself what healthy love feels like. The Diosa

Tribe was created with that exact intention: to give you a community of like-hearted souls to love and support you and be there by your side.

In turn, over time, you will learn to give all of this to yourself. Your standards will dictate not just your romantic relationships, but your work, money, spirituality, and friendships.

Expand Your Vessel

This is the part that always blows people's minds when I say it to them: You do not have to settle in your requests to the universe! As you claim your full Diosa divinity, you get to expand into believing you are deserving of more, because you are!

Knowing that you are deserving of a life beyond your wildest dream requires the expansion of your vessel. What I mean is, as human beings, we all have doubts, but when you tap into your divine self, you know without a doubt that you are absolutely deserving. The parts of us that have been harmed, wounded, and betrayed tend to talk us out of our greatness or our desire to live in our highest good; this is a protective mechanism that keeps us small, "safe," and contracted. But it isn't true. Don't rely on this as your reality.

Instead, rely on the truth that you are worthy beyond the pain you've experienced. Have the audacity to set even higher standards that honor the Diosa you are. Set even higher standards in the arena of money, orgasms, intimacy, your family life, the dreams you dare to dream. Know that as you expand, spirit/source/Goddess is there to provide you with that which is in your heart and soul. This isn't about proving yourself worthy; it is about getting out of your own way by believing you are worthy.

When you say to the universe, "This is what I want—and this is what I'm not settling for anymore," you are creating a loving boundary that will allow spirit to connect with you from a place of greater clarity. As a *bruja*, your words and intentions are powerful in cocreating the reality that you deserve.

Once you become intimately acquainted with what you really want, the universe will conspire to move you toward that desired destination. It will also become easier to not get caught up in distracting surface manifestations and glittery objects that tempt you away from your ultimate truth. For example, when you find yourself rooted in your desire to experience love, you can more easily bypass people who are clearly not going to give it to you. On the other hand, if you find yourself consistently pursuing someone who is incapable of giving you what it is you most want, you might ask if you are being honest with yourself, or if you're fixating on that love object in an attempt to keep yourself from expanding into the infinite generosity of the universe.

A desire with genuine magnitude isn't something that wants to be locked in the closet. Indeed, it longs to be expressed and met by the universe. But it's not enough to recite positive affirmations, or to demand that the world give us what we want. When we are launching our soul standards out into the world, we must do so by making tangible requests.

In moving toward what we want, we must infuse our desire with both intention (the raw and potent consciousness that lets us know who we are, what we stand for, and which peaks we wish to scale) and direction (a plan for how to get there, which includes external actions such as making requests and enlisting others to help us). Without intention and direction, our desires may as well be antiques collecting dust in the attic.

I've taken a few big risks in my life. I've been amazed at the fact that, overall, they've turned out pretty great. Every time I've taken a flying leap into the abyss of the unknown, a safety net (or a trampoline) magically appeared before my eyes to cushion the fall.

When this has occurred, I've marveled to myself, "Wow, the

universe must really have my back!" On a deep level, I believe this is true, but recently, another thought occurred to me. The universe is truly abundant. Like, dizzyingly and magically fucking abundant. So much so that we should feel like we can truly put ourselves out there and trust that, as we expand, spirit will give us exactly what we ask for, and more.

Honor Your New High Standards

As we up our standards, we up our potential for abundance, love, and health (mental, emotional, spiritual, sexual, and physical) in our lives. In upping our standards, we also begin demonstrating what we are no longer available for. For example, "I am no longer available for men who are not true to their word. I am available for men who keep their word with me."

Even after years of doing this work, there are always more layers to peel and grow through—and I wouldn't have it any other way. Because I know that the more I heal and deepen into my worth, the better and more magical my life becomes, the more authentic my life becomes, and the healthier my life becomes.

When I began to up my standards, I was so shocked! Like, OMG, it actually works! When I set standards and I express them in a clear, strong, and chill way, people listen and honor and respect me more. And the people who don't get asked to leave or simply fade away on their own.

I did this in dating. "I really enjoyed our date, but I noticed you seem to be a bit flaky when we make plans, and while I think you are amazing, flaky isn't something that I desire. I want to be transparent, as this is not enjoyable for me. I love consistency in a man. I wish you the best on your dating journey!"

I even did it with my parents. I told them, "I am no longer available for you to pick on me. It doesn't make me feel supported. I'd much prefer if you tell me the things I am doing well and allow me the space to figure things out in my own way."

The act of speaking my truth and honoring my high standards makes me feel like such a self-love badass. I love myself. I am honoring myself. I am protecting myself in a kind and communicative way. I am setting boundaries that honor my values, and I have no problem expressing them.

Of course, you'll find that as you set standards, some people will get defensive, because it requires them to change or be vulnerable. There will be times when they must admit they are being sloppy and they are forced to face their own shadows. That process isn't always pretty, and it's very likely that they will turn it back around on you and make you doubt your right to stand in your Diosa divinity. They might say, "Who the hell do you think you are?"

Please prepare for that. Understand that part of the test here in upping your standards will be that you will have to face people who disregard your standards, attempt to lower your standards, gaslight your feelings, and trap you. Stay strong during this test!

Other times, your boundaries and enforcement of high standards will create more respect and desire, as well as healthier dynamics. In the dating arena, my life definitely got better, and I activated my swagger, for sure. Because there is nothing sexier than a woman who honors her time, her body, her desires, her values, herself!

So don't be discouraged if people fight against it. If they do, they are not ready to be in your life, and you might have to make the decision of whether or not to remove them from your life or set boundaries that distance you from them. If they respect your newfound boundaries of self-love and do the work to match your new standards, then that's wonderful! But most important, it is you who must know your values and stick with them, no matter what.

Diosa, I promise that if you up your standards, you will up the quality of your life.

Soulwork

It's time to carefully consider how you want to honor your Diosa divinity and uphold your new standards. Using your journal, write down your responses to the following questions:

- Write down ten things that you are no longer available for. For example:
  - *I am not available for disrespectful relationships.*
  - *I am not available for intimate partners who fail to sexually pleasure me.*
  - *I am not available for flaky or unreliable friends.*

- After that, write ten lines of what you are available for, such as:
  - *I am available for mutually respectful, caring, reciprocal relationships.*
  - *I am available for stellar sex with partners who love to please me.*
  - *I am available for friends who've genuinely got my back.*

Before continuing, take a moment to pause. Where in your life are you lowering your standards? Are you doing so in relationships, friendships, work, money? Give yourself a second to think about where you are accepting scraps instead of the whole motherfucking cake.

- Now write a list of high-quality values that you want to demonstrate and that you also seek in the people around you. For example:
  - *honesty*
  - *loyalty*
  - *good communication*

  - *integrity*
  - *kindness*
  - *affection*
  - *selflessness*

- Next, write out a list of people you'll practice upping your expectation of these values with. For example:
  - *coworkers*
  - *family*
  - *friends*
  - *dates*
  - *intimate partners*
  - *children*

- Also consider what needs to change in order for you to live in alignment with these standards. Write out your list. For example:
  - *No longer going on dates with people who reflect low standards, and instead looking at the high-value list and using that as a barometer for whom you allow in your life*

Mantra

I am no longer available for settling. I am available only for high-value relationships that honor my worth and soul and Diosa divinity!

Ceremony

You Are the Altar

In this visualization ceremony, you are going to set aside a few minutes where you can be alone and close your eyes. Find a comfortable seat and place your left hand on your heart and your right hand over your left hand. Take a full, slow, and deep inhale through your nose. Hold for three counts, and exhale out through your mouth. Repeat this two more times and sink deeper as you breathe in and exhale out.

Imagine yourself walking up to a beautiful gold altar. This altar is made of pure gold and it is glimmering bright and shiny. On the altar there are magnificent scents that fill the room. You smell jasmine, copal, frankincense. You are overtaken by the luscious scents. Immediately your body surrenders and feels more relaxed. On the gold altar are flowers of every color: blue hydrangeas, red roses, white roses, yellow sunflowers, and the most plump pink peonies. There are fruits and candles that smell of vanilla and ylang ylang. The altar fills you with joy and regal energy. And as you look at the altar, you see yourself there. You, just like the flowers, are on the altar.

You are reminded in that moment, that you are deserving of all the luscious things this altar holds. For you are diosa. In that moment you say to yourself: "I am deserving of fruits, flowers, words of honey, and actions of truth." In this moment, you realize that if someone is coming into your life they must meet the standard of treating you as if you are that golden beautiful altar, because you are.

As you download this truth into your cells, come back into this moment and into the room again and slowly open your eyes. Great work!

The lesson here is that the people that come into your life, must add value and appreciate the divinity that you are—period and no excuses! Otherwise, they will be asked to leave. Practice doing this in your life. Notice who honors you and who doesn't. Start by honoring yourself as the sacred altar. The Diosa community is also a wonderful, safe, sacred community that will love you up until you can love yourself and while you love yourself. This will allow you to remember the truth of your divinity and embody the Diosa you are.

Get it, Diosa!!! I am so fucking proud of you for diving deep and upping your standards. When a woman owns her worth, she is truly unstoppable. There is no greater feeling than honoring and loving oneself. Reclaiming your no's so that you can welcome in your true yes's in your life is massive. You are saying, "I love myself and I refuse to settle anymore." In this space you can confidently communicate with ease and clarity from a place of empowerment versus a place of need. Your vibe is aligned with your Diosa divinity, and your swag oozes like honey. Continue to honor yourself and look at your values and nonnegotiable standards when you go on dates, when you accept jobs, when you interact with people in your life, and even in how you treat yourself. Keep those values and standards close to you so that you can check in often and practice them in all areas of your life. Now that you have owned your values and upped your standards, we are going to discuss key principles in cultivating healthy love. Ultimately, we were created to love ourselves and share that love. Relationships are the keystone of life— relationship to self, to soul/spirit, and to others. In the next chapter we will dive into some keys in you cultivating healthy love. You will explore what love attachment style you are and how to set boundaries to welcome in high-quality love. In this process, you go beyond the inner love you have been cultivating and practice how to cultivate that love with others.

I am no longer available for settling.

I am only available for high-value relationships that honor my worth and soul and diosa divinity.

#iamdiosa

CHAPTER 11

Cultivating Healthy Love

"no

is a necessary magic

no draws a circle around you
with chalk
and says
i have given enough

-boundaries"
—Nayyirah Waheed

Holy shit! The journey to arriving at healthy love and continuing to water the seeds of healthy relationships is no motherfuckin' joke, yo! It takes sooo much work. But the not-so-pretty and not-so-glamorous work is the work we need to bring to the surface and be real about.

The moments when we are in our bed about to text an ex because we are lonely . . . or when we are in a relationship and it feels like we are playing that game Minesweeper and accidentally click on a mine.

I know my insides are shockingly similar to those mines—bombs blowing up inside of me when I get triggered. Tornados of emotions whirling as my thoughts stop and overwhelm rises. I find that a lot of people cycle among these extremes of reacting to triggers: fight or flight, freeze or blow the whole fucking thing up.

To heal, we must keep it real—and my real was uglyyyyyy, boo.

There was a time when I threw shit at my ex. Yes, actually threw things at him, including a lit candle, meaning the wax splattered everywhere when it hit. I was in deep pain, and my actions showed it.

Abuse is a vicious cycle, and while I was a victim of abuse, I also learned to abuse. I am not proud of this. But this is the reality of the pain and demons and deep rage that I carried within me. I was a walking example of the opposite of cultivating healthy love. I lived in an internal battlefield. I constantly chose men who were not healthy for me, and in turn subconsciously perpetuated the belief that I was unworthy and therefore deserved toxic love. This brought out my demons big-time, and it served to stall and delay my emotional growth and healing.

There were other times I felt unsafe because of the traumas within me, and not necessarily because of the person in front of me. Discerning the difference between the two and being able to communicate in a healthy way so that I could set boundaries that would honor and protect my inner child has been key to cultivating healthier and more conscious relationships—not just with others, but with myself.

So, yeah, becoming frozen and shutting down, or running away from my problems, and blowing up were the three main gears I went into. Not cute, not healthy, not fun, not productive—but perfectly understandable, considering my story and background. And when I speak to other Diosas, I know that they have gone through similar things. This helps me feel less crazy and less alone. None of this is to minimize bad, unhealthy, abusive behavior; on the contrary, it helps it come to the surface and reveals how distorted things can become if this behavior is left unchecked and untreated.

If you can relate, I'm with you, Diosa. And I want you to be kind to yourself, even as you undergo the process of staring any ugly truths about your past behavior in the face. I know it's hard, but that's part and parcel of cultivating healthy love. Facing the emotional triggers and the wounds is part of the journey. We can't skip it or avoid it, numb it, run from it, or hide from it forever. Sure, we can for a little bit (and that is okay too, as well as a natural part of the process), because we can't change everything at once. But inevitably, we must return to the timeline of our soul and heal each wound, one by one. We must take an inventory of our life and be painfully honest with ourselves: Who did we become because of those wounds? Who did we choose? What did we let in? What boundaries did we fail to set that we can lovingly integrate into our lives today?

Healthy Attachments

Our earliest lessons about relationships inform almost all aspects of our later connections: to ourselves, other people, and the world.

Attachment Theory is an important psychological theory that helps us to understand ourselves and learn how to work with who we are and how we relate in all types of relationships. Therapist John Bowlby formulated this theory. He was a psychoanalyst who researched attachments between children and their parents. He was greatly impacted by the ethological theory, which focuses on how behavior evolves to achieve survival, as well as zoologist, ethologist, and ornithologist Konrad Lorenz's theory of imprinting. This theory revealed that ducks had an innate biological drive to attach to their parents for survival. In developing his own theory, Bowlby believed children would ideally use that original primary caregiver as a safe base from which to form a sense of internal safety and healthy attachments, which would help them to feel safer in the world at large.

This working model does a wonderful job of highlighting what happens when attachments are secure, what happens when they are

not, and the effects that all of this can have on our future relationships.

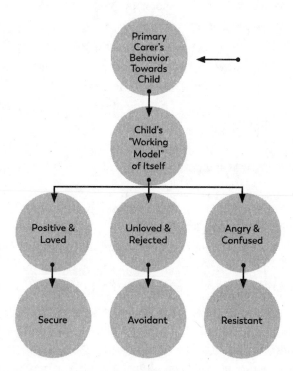

There are four patterns of attachment that Bowlby described:
Secure, Anxious Avoidant, and Disorganized.

- **Secure attachment:** Secure attachment describes children
  who feel secure and therefore are able to depend on and
  experience trust and safety with their adult primary caregivers. For example, when the adult leaves, the child may be
  upset or scared, but the child feels safe and certain that the

parent or caregiver will return. The child also knows it's safe and good to seek comfort from their caregivers. Such children feel confident in their caregivers to give them love and support if they ask for their needs to be met.

When the primary caregivers are not a safe home base, the following attachments are formed:

- **Anxious attachment:** Anxiously attached children usually become scared and show signs of distress when their adult caregiver leaves. If a parent is not consistently available, children may feel ambivalent about their safety and comfort, and therefore show distress. These children do not feel the same safety as securely attached children when it comes to obtaining support and comfort, or even expressing their needs. They are unsure that their needs will be met.

- **Avoidant attachment:** Avoidant attachment describes children who do not seek comfort from their caregivers, and instead, actively avoid them. With this attachment style, children usually don't have a preference between a stranger and their adult caregiver. This is very common among children who have neglectful and abusive caregivers. Children who are punished, abused, or not given positive reinforcement for relying on and coming to their adult caregiver will internalize that and avoid seeking help in the future. When I worked as a family therapist in the prevention sector of Child Protective Services, I encountered many children who were abused and neglected. They often displayed this attachment style. This is painful to witness and important to note, especially if you experienced neglect and abuse, as I did.

- **Disorganized attachment:** Children with a disorganized attachment style have a mixture of different emotions that seem to be the result of a parent or primary caregiver being inconsistent in their behavior. This is highly common in homes where both danger and comfort coexist. Children in this state tend toward a high degree of confusion. It's as if they are looking at themselves in a funhouse mirror, and the image is distorted, so they don't know what a healthy and true reality looks like. Conflicting messages from adult caregivers often lead to disorganized attachment in children.

Though these descriptions mention children, our attachments can continue to develop over time, and they certainly continue to impact us well into adulthood. There is a wonderful test online to find out which attachment style you most relate to: https://www.psychologytoday.com/us/tests/relationships/relationship-attachment-style-test.

If you can, take the test or take time to reflect on the style or styles you think apply most to you. This is key to understanding how you relate in your adult relationships and what you might do to make them healthier and more aligned with your Diosa divinity.

If you fall into the category of secure attachment, for example, you can continue to cultivate your relationships as they are, and to build even more intimacy, transparency, vulnerability, and trust—all while speaking your truth more pointedly and lovingly.

If you identify with any of the other three attachment styles, I suggest working on the areas that are causing distress so that you may heal your attachment style and, in turn, your relationships.

For example, if you are anxious, you could begin by seeking out consistent, safe relationships (as opposed to ones that blow hot and cold, which can be a pattern for this type). Over time, you prove to your psyche that stability and consistency are possible. This creates new neural pathways and mental constructs, which will allow you to build safe, healthy, and consistent relationships.

If you are avoidant, it's key to work on communication and vulnerability. You can start with yourself, simply by identifying your feelings and emotional state, and, over time, sharing it with others. Dig into your inner landscape and get to know and appreciate yourself. Notice when you are putting up walls, and challenge yourself to stay connected with loved ones, even when this feels difficult.

And if you are disorganized, it's likely that your primary caregivers' inconsistency in their behavior created a lot of mixed signals and crossed wires that disabled your communication skills or ability to say what you need. I suggest therapy that helps you to express your emotions, thoughts, and needs with clarity.

Doing EMDR work for early childhood trauma is also a great tool to help get to the root of the child/parent dynamics that created your attachment style. EMDR, which stands for eye movement desensitization and reprocessing, is backed by statistically valid research that supports its reduction of the effects of trauma, including psychological and physiological symptoms.

Noticing when your attachment style comes up allows you to be in a place of empowerment because you can focus on creating healthy patterns for yourself to heal the attachment styles that are causing harm in your life.

Codependency and Boundaries

For years, I suffered from codependency, which many therapists define as an excessive emotional or psychological reliance on other people. Plenty of love songs romanticize codependency with lines like "Baby I need you, I can't live without you, you complete me," but codependency in action? It ain't cute. Often, I pushed my needs completely to the side and gave my life over to my abusive and unhealthy partner. I didn't even have a life. I was consumed by fixing him and helping him, to the extent that I let go of all the things that were important to me.

Unsurprisingly, my attachment style was ambivalent. I was constantly fearful of being abandoned, and instead of doing the work to heal the childhood wound of abandonment, I acted out by begging for the love I wasn't getting. Once I discovered the attachment styles, I had a powerful framework and information on how my psyche and love blueprint were working. I was able to target the actual wound in therapy and work to develop a more secure attachment style.

Awareness allows for transformation, and the willingness to seek help to make the changes allows for the change to stick and new behaviors and patterns to be born.

We are not meant to stay trapped in our original patterns that our caregivers instilled in us; we are beyond resilient and capable of rewiring and reprogramming how we relate by choosing safe, supportive environments that model healthy love. This starts with us!

Begin to notice how the attachment styles come up in all of your relationships. Begin to nurture the parts of you that were not given love and consistency as a child. The best way to do this is to offer yourself the consistency you craved in those formative years.

I had an aha moment when I stopped looking to be saved and loved, and I instead committed to radically and deeply loving myself, to honoring my word with myself, to setting healthy boundaries, to receiving support when I needed it. This provided me with an internal security that I'd been seeking in the external world for years.

With this new awareness, I came to understand that a key element in healthy relationships is boundaries. Oh, child, I didn't know jack shit about boundaries when I was in the early stages of my self-esteem recovery! I was so desperate that I didn't even know what my needs and desires were. I didn't feel worthy of taking the time to reflect on what I wanted, what I didn't what, what I needed, what I didn't need. My desires were out the window.

I was Capitana "Save an Emotionally Bankrupt Boy"! I wanted to feed his love tank, but in doing so, I ran out of fuel and ended up mentally, spiritually, and emotionally bankrupting myself. In truth, this was not the first time; I had spent years in relationships where my needs were not present at all. Their needs and their healing were my only purpose.

When I finally did the work, I was like, "*Wow* I have been ignoring *me* for years. I have needs. I have desires. I deserve to have my voice heard. I deserve to say what I need to honor my mind, body, spirit, time, heart, money."

My worth was activated—and boundaries were my means of continuing to honor myself.

So, what exactly is a boundary? According to the IPFW/Parkview Student Assistance Program, "A boundary is a limit or space between you and the other person; a clear place where you begin and the other person ends. The purpose of setting a healthy boundary is, of course, to protect and take good care of you."

So truly, a boundary is a limit that honors your soul's truth.

Because my boundaries were nonexistent, my ex-partner's needs were so enmeshed in mine that I had no identity or sense of self. This is very common in codependent dynamics.

What does codependency actually look like? Some of the things that have been found to correlate with codependency include:

- low self-esteem
- familial dysfunction
- depression
- anxiety
- stress
- low emotional expressivity

- difficulty saying no
- poor boundaries
- emotional reactivity
- compulsion to take care of people
- a need for control, especially over others
- trouble with honest communication
- fixation on mistakes
- the need to be liked by everyone
- the need to always be in a relationship
- denial of one's own needs, thoughts, and feelings
- intimacy issues
- confusion of love with pity
- fear of abandonment

When we begin to set boundaries for ourselves, we ensure that our needs and desires don't get enmeshed with another person's. We begin to stand on our own two feet and develop methods for taking care of our own mental, emotional, psychological, and spiritual health. This is how we become grounded, emotionally healthy, and available for loving relationships with equal partners.

Before we go any further, though, I want you to ask yourself: Where do I fall on the following scale of boundaries?

- **Nonexistent boundaries:** This is classic codependency. That is, you have a tendency to capitulate to other people's wishes and desires and allow yourself to be a doormat, as long as that means you are "needed" by others. You have difficulty discerning between emotions that are yours and emotions that belong to someone else, like a loved one. You have a tough time saying no because you have difficulty letting people down. Although you are plagued by guilt and anxiety, you also find yourself getting easily drained because you're in a position where all your energy is going out but none is coming in.

- **Balanced boundaries:** Your boundaries are strong but flexible. You are able to communicate your needs with ease and transparency. You can say an authentic no, and you can also hear no from others without being triggered. You honor your boundaries but don't feel the need to define or explain them. Because you are such an honest communicator, this inspires trusting, transparent relationships with the people around you.

- **Rigid boundaries:** You're good at saying no, but this can leave you feeling guarded, defensive, and alienated. Anytime someone else wants to get close, you feel threatened and put your wall up. This probably comes from the expectation that you'll be harmed or taken advantage of, but it keeps you from having the intimacy and understanding you want.

Think about the categories above. Do some areas and relationships in your life have rigid boundaries, while others have nonexistent ones? Where do you tend to experience balance? Take a moment to reflect.

Changing people, places, and situations in your life is key to making space for a new garden of healthy relationships. It is imperative to look closely at your life and recognize how conducive the environment that you are in is to your growth, and accordingly make changes toward becoming the Diosa you want to be. Your insides are an environment, just as your outsides are. We are not all blessed with being born into internal and external environments that are peaceful and nurture our highest self. It is important to take into account our culture, our socioeconomic status, our mental/emotional health, our neighborhood and community, our family and social circle, our work, our school environment, etc. All of this affects us and how we relate to ourselves and to one another.

Okay, *mamita*, let's do some spring cleaning!

Let Yourself Be Vulnerable

If you are someone who tends to have rigid boundaries or if you have just been burned way too much to trust anyone else, the ability to be vulnerable with yourself and others can be so challenging. But it's key to the kind of intimacy you deserve.

Acts of self-disclosure can be really fucking hard, especially when you are taught to close your heart, because doing the opposite can lead to intense pain and betrayal. I, like so many other Diosas, have learned to keep my heart open and let people see the most vital pieces of my soul, even though I learned early on that this could be potentially hazardous to my health. Acts of self-disclosure felt both unsafe and unwise, which is why I learned to focus on other people's needs.

Intimacy can be so painful in this sense. And even when we don't realize it, there's some part of us that's been conditioned to believe it might die if we bare so much metaphysical flesh, covered as it is in tender wounds.

If you have not experienced the intimacy you've wanted, be gentle with yourself and consider that maybe, on some level, you haven't fully let other people in. Have you retracted? Stonewalled? Hidden behind excuses and resentment? Perceived slights in actions that were not meant to be unkind?

All of this not only prevents people from seeing or knowing you; it can also keep you from attaining your deep desire to experience passionate love. To have the delicate, most tender parts of you held and supported and revered.

The body wants survival, connection, and dignity. Usually, when we are children, it is easy to connect with others from a place of simple trust and openness. However, if you've experienced trauma or successive rejection from an early age, the body separates the idea of connection from that of safety, especially if you've been endangered in your earliest relationships.

There is nothing wrong with the desire for safety. Our experiences, after all, require a solid, reliable container for context. But I am also aware of all the times I chose to avoid conflict as an easy way out of experiencing true intimacy. And, of course, true intimacy is full engagement with the present moment—which requires a huge amount of vulnerability—and what the reptilian brain might conceive of as the very real possibility of danger. We have to get it out of our heads that connection is unsafe, especially given the evolutionary impulse to open our hearts and bodies to one another if life is to continue. We are pack animals; in effect, we aren't that different from people who existed in caves thousands of years ago. It doesn't matter if you're a triple Scorpio or insist you've chosen to be alone and are quite content to avoid any intimacy—if this is what you're telling yourself, it's a coping mechanism.

"When I finally admitted to my lover that I had successfully hidden my substance-abuse problem for years and that it had cost me my friends, family, and a promising career, I was so scared that he'd react badly," a client of mine recently told me when she was describing a breakthrough in vulnerability.

"It took a lot for me to get to that kind of sharing," she remembered. "Not necessarily because it was a big deal, but because I thought that in order for him to find me attractive, I had to be mysterious, or aloof, to make my private life off-limits. And let's be real—you can't cast a spell over a man when you're opening up to the full truth of who you are. But he just reached across the table and took my hand. And there was true kindness and love on his face—not discomfort or pity or the desire to quickly change the subject."

What we often forget is that vulnerability is sexy because it is free of false constructs or preprogrammed behavior. It is spontaneous, unpredictable, and dynamic.

Mystery is not achieved by concealing who we are but by revealing the depth of our passion and longing, sacred and uncontainable instincts that couldn't care less about social norms or us making fools of ourselves. And stepping into Diosa divinity means being attuned to what is real for us in the moment. There's no need to hide, obscure, deny, or manipulate thoughts and emotions. Instead, we can lovingly assume the risk of sharing the truth. Rather than wasting energy on clamming up or redirecting attention, we can ride on the joy of being authentic.

"I knew I had to play the game one hundred percent so that my life with my partner wasn't just empty time," my client told me.

The façades people wear are part of their voluntary musculature, those parts that have been carefully sculpted by failure, rejection, and scolding. Unfortunately, when we are interacting with those façades, we are not coming in direct contact with the people beneath them. In intimate relationships, the tendency to put an approachable face forward is a tactic that can be completely undermined when things go haywire down the line. Our partner, who was intoxicated by the illusion, is surprised when pent-up anger, sorrow, or desire are cannonballed out into the open.

Instead of hedging our bets and playing it safe in intimacy, maybe we should be pushing the envelope and getting our deal-breakers out on the table, front and center. When we reveal ourselves, warts and all, we are not depending on a tidy fiction to keep intimacy afloat; we know our relationship isn't built on a "deal" that we've unconsciously made, so we are never in doubt that love is the sole thing that holds us together.

Of course, putting authenticity into practice isn't a cakewalk. And sometimes we are too busy going for the easy thing to go for the real thing. Often, we are wary of sharing who we truly are with our partner because we can't possibly know how they will react. But to reveal ourselves, fully and unreservedly, is an act of true generosity; it is too respectful of its recipient to sacrifice truth for the pale comfort of safety.

Of course, we cannot expect that revealing who we are will magically get us what we want. It may not. But even in the midst of tension or rejection, when we choose to stop wanting something from our partner, it becomes possible to understand the intimacy that already exists between us. And this gesture of generosity is what true freedom—and, therefore, the expression of genuine desire and intimacy—is built on. In being who we are, we (ideally) offer our partner the space to do the same. We open the door of continuous discovery and feed a slow fire that is always building.

The ability to reveal ourselves isn't about a desired future outcome but about expressing our full selves in the present. It doesn't mean we will always enjoy what we have or be happy every step of the way, but it does mean that we will be oriented in a willingness to live completely in the moment by being honest with ourselves and whatever arises.

Being vulnerable can stir up some deep-seated anxiety in people when they get too bogged down in the extent to which complete self-revelation is necessary. As always, it isn't about the content you're sharing but about the attitude you have toward sharing. "The space between two people allows for the transmission of information that we don't even realize is necessary, crucial, or accessible," a teacher friend recently explained to me. "If your partner has good attention, trust that they will notice what needs to be noticed. Opening up isn't about telling your life story; it's about being present and letting yourself experience your own vulnerability. It's not about showcasing your wounds for the world to see either. It's simply about engaging in an authentic, give-and-take conversation with the other person. This means you can relinquish full responsibility and let them do some of the work."

Take some time to ask yourself the following questions: What do I most want other people to know about me? Is it easiest to share myself with close loved ones, or with strangers? How often do I make space for myself to be free and open with others? How often do I make space for others to be free and open with me? Can I open to the people in my life from a place of vulnerability and the genuine desire to share who I am? Most important, am I willing to do so?

Scripts for Setting Healthy Boundaries

We have spoken about toxic relationships in great depth. But how can you identify what a healthy relationship looks like, especially if that hasn't been your MO?

Here are some relationship *green* flags to cultivate within yourself and your partnerships:

1. Has their own hobbies and interests and takes time to do what they love
2. Is invested in their emotional, spiritual, and mental health
3. Is kind to others around them, including waiters, retail workers, their parents, and friends
4. Shows concern for the well-being of animals and the world
5. Is open-minded and curious about others
6. Is compassionate and has a big heart
7. Speaks in a kind tone
8. Honors their commitments to themselves and to you
9. States their needs openly, without expecting you to guess them
10. Is patient
11. Is open to feedback and growth

Obviously, I want you to be able to step into relationships with the kind of people who display the aforementioned qualities (including yourself!), but learning how to express boundaries takes a lot more than relationships with the right people. It's about getting 100 with yourself and flexing a muscle that might feel new to you, especially if you have rigid or nonexistent boundaries, and/or if you have had trouble being vulnerable in the past. That's why practice makes progress, and I'm offering you the following scripts and tips to communicate your needs when tension or disagreement arise.

1. Speak from a place of "I": Instead of focusing on the other person "doing" something to you, focus on how you are feeling as the result of this interaction. Don't blame them; instead, take responsibility for your experience and needs.

2. Get curious about the other person's reality, especially if they are unwell and completely off base: You can note this for yourself and not take it as an attack on you or engage with it. However, if you are dealing with someone who is well and you are in the midst of a conflict or disagreement, simply remain curious about their reality and perspective. Really ask questions about their thought process and see if you can understand where they are coming from.

3. Ask the other person when is a good time to speak: Instead of diving into a difficult conversation, you can give yourself and the other person ample space and time to step into it, at a time that works for both of you. This kind of respectfulness sets the stage for the conversation to come.

4. Place a request in a sandwich of love: For example, "Love, I am feeling a bit overwhelmed lately with all the tasks in

the house. I know you are working a lot and work hard for me and the family, and I appreciate it so much. I also would like to request that you can pack lunch once a week for Dean when he goes to school, so I can get in a little more self-care time. This would really be helpful for alleviating my stress. Again, thank you for all you do for me and Dean. I love you and appreciate you." In this case, there is a clear request: "Can you pack lunch for Dean once a week?" sandwiched between acknowledgment of her partner's hard work. She both requested her needs and validated their hard work. This is a great way to communicate a need while also providing a cushion of love and appreciation.

5. Decline offers: If you have a hard time saying no, keep it simple and add a thank-you. "While I would love to go, I won't be able to make it. I have too much on my plate right now. Have an absolutely amazing time!" Again, simplicity is great, and don't feel the need to explain or justify your decision.

6. Communicate an insecurity to your partner: For example, "Lately I have been feeling a bit insecure, and I feel rather vulnerable bringing this up, but I want to communicate a fear I have. A story I am making up in my head is that you don't find me as attractive as I used to be. I know this might not actually be true, but my mind has been rather hard on me lately. I want to share this with you because it's been weighing on me. And I have a feeling it isn't true, but I'd love to talk about it." Here, she is owning her own insecurity, and instead of projecting it as real or blaming or attacking her partner, she is saying, "The story I am

making up is this, and the mean things my mind has been saying include the following." The approach is honest, empowered, vulnerable, and free of attacks and projections. This is key for having healthy conversations that navigate difficult insecurities or feelings that might arise in a relationship.

7. Setting boundaries with parents: For example, "Mom, I know you worry about me and love me; however, your fears are making me feel more nervous versus excited about the choices I am making. I know your intention is to love and support me, and this doesn't make me feel that way. I ask that instead, you trust me to make my own decisions so that I can feel trusted by you." Claiming agency and responsibility in your life can be challenging when it comes to dealing with parents. But once again, asserting your needs as well as your competency in determining what it is you need is critical when it comes to taking a stand against meddlesome or disempowering parental attitudes.

8. Setting boundaries at work: For example, "Hello, Mr. Ramirez, I would like to have a conversation regarding the overtime I have been doing. Let me know when you have time to schedule a meeting. Thank you." And during the meeting, "Mr. Ramirez, I want to bring up something that might have gone overlooked with all the new hiring and projects. I have worked extra hours this week and have not received overtime payment. Here are X amount of hours I worked during these dates and times. I would like to be compensated for them. And since it seems we are getting busier, I want to suggest an idea that might benefit the

company and my overall productivity as well, as I sense burnout coming on with all these late hours. My suggestion is to hire an intern that can help me twice a week with the extra tasks. Let me know your thoughts. I feel this would be of great benefit for me and the company." This is especially effective and powerful, because not only is the person in the example setting powerful boundaries and standing behind her worth, but she is also suggesting a win-win solution that stands to benefit more people than just herself.

9. Reject shaming: For example, someone says dubiously, "You really think that's a smart idea to leave your husband and kids for two weeks to go on this spiritual retreat?" A good response could be, "I am clear on what I need for my mental and emotional health. It is a priority for me. It sounds like you might have fears and judgments about my choice, and while I love you, I am going to ask you to not project your fears when I am expressing something that I am excited about." Again, a totally clean request without taking on someone else's fear and judgment!

10. Decline offers that don't meet your standards: For example, "That sounds like an amazing experience. However, I have to pass. My current rate is ten thousand dollars, with flight and accommodations. Should another opportunity come up with a bigger budget, I would love to discuss! Thank you for thinking of me." Be clear about your rates and don't settle for less. Be gracious and appreciative, but firm all the same.

11. Admit when you aren't ready to have a discussion: If you feel you are not ready to dive into a dicey talk, you might

say, "I value your feelings; however, at this moment I am overwhelmed and not in the proper space to have this discussion. I will let you know when I am feeling up for talking."

12. Set time and energy boundaries with friends and dates: For example, "I love meeting up with you and I know you tend to be late, but since I am leaving from far away, I'd rather you let me know beforehand how much more time you need so I know when to get there and don't have to wait for you," or, "I would love to hear about what's been going on with you but have had a long day and need time to recharge. I would also love to have a balanced conversation where I can share too. I know you have been very stressed and I will always be there for you, but I have also been going through a lot and would love to feel seen and heard, as well. Can we have a proper chat when I am recharged, perhaps tomorrow after work?"

13. Cut into a heated disagreement: It's absolutely your prerogative to exit a conversation where it feels you aren't being heard, or where people are talking over you or imposing their beliefs on you. For example, "I know this topic is getting heated, and I feel like we both have different opinions, but that doesn't mean we have to be unkind to each other. What do you say we take a moment to breathe and we agree to disagree on this one? I respect that you disagree with my opinion, but I don't want us to force our opinions on each other."

14. Don't accept offensive jokes: When someone is joking about you or others in a way that you don't feel

comfortable with, be clear that this is unacceptable. For example, "I don't find jokes like that about my body or other people's bodies funny. I ask that you don't joke that way with or around me. Thank you."

15. Be honest about your "no": For example, if someone asks you to let them borrow a prized possession and you don't want to lend it to them, you can say, "Sorry, but I don't feel comfortable lending this to you because it's really expensive and I'd rather not risk it."

16. Cut off an unhealthy relationship: When someone is treating you in abusive or unfair ways, you can say, "I am no longer going to engage with you and speak with you when you address me with language and a tone that is hurtful for me."

Practice using some of these scripts, especially if you are faced with a situation that you know could benefit from healthy boundaries. And please know that no matter how much you practice, while it might open the doors to communication and resolution with some people, not everyone will honor your boundaries. Some may resist or reject them, shame or guilt-trip you, or insist that you aren't being loving. Don't let any of this deter you. Boundary-setting is leading by example; it creates mutually beneficial relationships that allow for even greater empathy, compassion, respect, and authenticity— and at the same time, it works to remove toxic people and influences.

When you start practicing boundaries, you step into connections that honor your Diosa divinity. Your internal environment begins to match your external environment. The love that you display toward yourself as you step more decisively into your soul goals will be mirrored in the people and situations around you. Moreover, it will lead you to cultivate communities that value secure attachments and model healthy ways of being together—of demonstrating true intimacy instead of Band-Aid love.

Soulwork

Let's go inward and do a deep assessment of you. Using your journal, write down your responses to the following questions:

- What is your relationship like with yourself? Loving? Distant? How well would you say you know yourself?
- What is your external environment like? Home life? Family? Friends? Work? Community? Social environment?
- Who are the main characters in your world? Name them.
- What are their qualities? Do they support keeping your wounded child scared and disempowered, or do they support your higher self and the person you want to be?
- Is your external world safe or chaotic? What about it makes it feel safe or chaotic?
- What kinds of boundaries do you have with respect to time, energy, relationships, money, work, family, etc.? Are they balanced, nonexistent, or rigid?
- What about your physical boundaries around your body, sexuality, and how much space you share or feel safe with in your relationships?
- What about conversational boundaries? What do you feel comfortable sharing or not sharing?
- What about content boundaries? How much time do you spend on social media, online, or watching TV? How does this make you feel?

- Now think about relationships in your life that might feel extra-challenging. Go through each relationship one by one.
  - *Do you feel drained after speaking with this person consistently?*
  - *Does the person assert their own beliefs and make you feel bad about yours?*
  - *Do they constantly take and not give?*
  - *Do they not invest in their own growth but place their continuous issues on you?*

Based on the scripts and other information in this chapter, write down ten boundaries that you will practice enforcing in the future. For example:

- I will have a heart-to-heart with that old friend who takes up all my time and asks for tons of favors without giving me much in return.
- I will cut short conversations that make me feel uncomfortable or that are overly intrusive.
- I will no longer make excuses for dates when they show up late without giving me ample time to change my plans.
- I will limit my phone conversations with close friends to thirty minutes and set a timer so that I can move on to other important things I want to accomplish during the day.

Mantra

I love myself enough to honor my boundaries and needs, and to give myself the love and security that I didn't have when I was younger. I am now only available for interactions and ways of relating that lead me to my highest good.

Ceremony

Love Vision Board

Create a love vision board that embodies the core of the energy and the words that you want in your ideal love (or if you are already in an intimate relationship, the ideal friendships, community, etc.). Take magazines or images and cut out pictures and words that stand out to you. In addition, write down any key words that are important to you in cultivating healthy love.

Be sure to not focus on the superficial, but instead tune in to the depth of the soul of the partner you wish to call in. Choose images and words that evoke that depth. For example, I chose a beautiful image of a cosmic couple with the words "Divine Partnership." I wrote down words like *my ready love* and focused on images that made me feel safe, loved, happy, spiritually clear, and calm.

In addition, I want you to go out and find a pair that evokes that feeling of healthy love within you. This can be a wooden statue of a couple hugging, or an image of two animals. Find a representation that gives you the feeling you know you want to cultivate. Finally, let go of anything that holds any old stale attachments from the past— such as old letters and photos, or an ex's clothing. Energetically, this is all stuff that has to go! Clear out the old and make room for the new. You are ready for epic love and connection, because you are doing the work to come into healthy attunement with yourself. Amazing work, Diosa!

You did not come here to mess around, and it shows! This chapter is key in shifting our lives around. It's difficult to do this soulwork solo, but even more difficult when we have other humans in the mix! I knew that this book needed practical steps to discussing how to cultivate healthy relationships, set boundaries, and communicate better. This soulwork is meant to heal ourselves and then share in that healing dynamic with others. It takes practice, so no one get discouraged—if it doesn't come easy at first. But progress is what we are aiming for in practicing these tools. The gift of life is that as we heal within, our external world begins to shift as well. You have learned about attachment styles, communication scripts, and boundaries. Use these and revisit this chapter as needed when things come up in your romantic relationships and any relationships in your life. I believe that it is in our relationships where our deepest spiritual work is done. This is often where we do the deepest soulwork. Allow your vision of love to fill your body and your mind and align yourself one day at a time to that vision of love that you have. Become that which you seek.

I love myself enough to honor my boundaries and needs. I give myself the love and security that I didn't have when I was younger.

I am now only available for interactions and ways of relating that lead me to my highest good.

#iamdiosa

CHAPTER 12

Coming Back Home to Self: Diosa Rituals

"Walk as if you are kissing the Earth with your feet."
—Thich Nhat Hanh

Diosa bella, preciosa, divina. You are so fucking badass!

You have been committing to this work and digging deep. You are realizing your triggers and making the real steps to heal and move into your true identity. This isn't easy work—in fact, it's the hardest work that most people will do in a lifetime, because it requires finding your own blueprint to self-actualization. And yet, still, you chose to do it!

As we come to this phase of the healing, this is our time to practice all the rituals we've amassed for self-love and sensuality and joy and pleasure. We get to come into a space of deep enjoyment. Sometimes, when we are so used to doing only the heavy lifting, we develop the misunderstanding that healing has to be hard, and that we have to go around excavating all the dark, hidden caves of our psyche. We get stuck in the underworld, and we forget that there must be a balance of dark and light. It's not about going to extremes of avoiding our shadow, nor is it about romanticizing it and wallowing in our suffering. Many religious doctrines emphasize martyrdom and giving up all pleasures, as if that is what's going to make us "better" people.

Diosa, you have nothing to prove to anybody. This isn't about playing in the Pain Olympics and wearing your hardships on your sleeve. The road to healing isn't about self-victimizing all over again. Yes, there is always dark shadow work to do, but getting addicted to pain is a weapon of the ego as well, and it's something to be mindful of.

I had a massive shift when I realized that I was addicted to learning the hard way. I relished the heaviness and the shadow work because it made me believe that I was accomplishing something big. Can you believe that? My pain became a barometer for what I believed I was receiving from the healing journey. If things felt easy, it seemed to me that maybe I was doing something wrong. I truly believed that suffering was the only way through, and that my ability to manage the suffering meant I was making progress.

I understood that a great deal of the spiritual lexicon that over-emphasized love and light was missing some depth, but I had to admit that it also contained a medicine I had been afraid to embrace. There was a part of my fear that was still scared to truly surrender to spirit. To truly let go and let God/Goddess. I was almost afraid to enjoy the blessings, as if the light would somehow take away the depth I'd come to find in my darkness.

But we all contain both light and darkness. Our ultimate identity isn't about choosing one over the other. It's about recognizing our wholeness and allowing ourselves, body and spirit, to settle in to the new seasons. It can't be winter forever!

It's interesting that even in our healing, we can become addicted to thinking we are broken instead of celebrating and enjoying life. Life shouldn't be a long and difficult road through one's past traumas. In fact, while trauma-informed therapy and spirituality are absolutely vital to our growth and healing, our healing, is incomplete without acknowledgment of our innate resilience and capacity for joy.

We are beings of joy, of sensuality, of pleasure, of connection. At the end of the day, we are absolutely doing the work so that we can be happier, lighter, freer, and so that we can share our joy with the world around us.

Let Yourself Thrive

My annual Diosa Retreat is a deep healing retreat that I describe as spiritual surgery. People have told me that their lives were saved during a Diosa Retreat. They have walked away from violent husbands, made the choice to not kill themselves, healed childhood sexual abuse, and so much more.

It is my greatest gift to witness these miraculous shifts. And in that, I also remember asking myself, "Now what?"

All of these women were making these shifts and finally learning to love themselves, and they needed to know what to do next. What were they going to replace the abuse, suffering, addiction, and depression with? After all, if we don't fill our lives with new habits and activities, we often end up reverting back to what we've always known.

But I didn't know what to do next. I was good at getting out of the shit show of abuse, but I still didn't know how to integrate pleasure, or how to embrace peace. I had become really good at digging into the bones of abuse and pain, but what about the thriving? What about enjoying the fruits of my labor? What about teaching other Diosas to make a space for joy?

It was almost as if I was still holding my breath, holding on to dear life for everything I had fought for. I was still scared that the other shoe would drop at any moment. I was still in the grip of the paralyzing fear that all the good could be taken away.

The Diosas kept saying, "I am so grateful for you. I learned to love myself and walk away from this toxic man. And now I'm ready to go big. To enjoy life. To cultivate peace. To step into my soul purpose. To create more abundance in every way: financially, spiritually, in my relationships, sensually, creatively."

And so I was guided to do the same.

I created the Soul on Fire Diosa Mastermind for women to up-level and step into their soul's purpose. Not only to survive but to thrive. I created it for them, for me, for us. We learned together, side by side. I remember during the first ever Diosa Mastermind Bali retreat, we were scheduled to have a workshop on abundance. Up until that point, I had a super-long schedule. I worked backbreaking hours, from seven in the morning to almost one at night. It felt deep and necessary and like an integral part of the process.

And here I was, teaching this "next level of stepping into pleasure and feminine abundance" type of retreat. When the class on abundance arrived, I was super-stressed because we were still at the beach and the schedule had completely gone off track. I felt I wasn't teaching nearly enough, as I had planned. And beyond that, I was exhausted. I didn't want to disappoint the Diosas.

I brought it up in full transparency and said, "We are supposed to go to the abundance workshop, and I am feeling bad because we are off-schedule and I haven't given you all the tools I'd intended to."

At that point, they all looked at me with love but with an expression of "Girl, you are bugging."

One of the Diosas said, "Diosa, this is the abundance you want to teach us. You are teaching us by being in abundance with us. We are on a gorgeous black-sand beach in this beautiful private restaurant. We couldn't be learning more about abundance."

I was in shock. My teachings had been so intense that I didn't know how to register that sharing a topic as charged as abundance with my fellow Diosas could be as simple as sharing this beautiful location with them. Something in me had simply not been wired to believe that life could be this easy. I'd been trained to believe that I had to work hard to heal myself, and to show others the way—and that exhaustion was my reward at the end of the day for all the effort I'd put in.

But what if the journey wasn't about effort at all? What if it was simply about embodying Diosa—in all her creativity, pleasure, sensuality, and receptivity?

My teachings were shifting, and life was showing me that there was another way.

There is life after trauma, and sometimes it's hard to enjoy it when you finally make it out of a war. There was a theme of more sweetness presenting itself, more ease, more flow, more chill. So as you can imagine, my ego was bugging out. "I'm happy. Joyful. Easy. WTF is this? Is it for real?"

And yes, it was real. And it was essential for me to own that lesson so I could bring people to fully integrate joy and understand that life isn't just an eternal uphill climb toward "something better." What's the fun in that? Life is not about mere survival. It's about allowing ourselves to rest in the safety of spirit and learning to trust that we deserve ease, love, abundance, and flow—just as the universe has always intended for us.

Maybe you would think it's easy to embrace something so beautiful, but when hard has been your default, surrender can be the most challenging step. I was called to shed even more of my layers, and the old aspects of me that were clinging to difficulty. Clinging to difficulty is a form of resistance that prevents us from being receptive to the universe's gifts. So, Diosa, it's time to keep shedding—and yes, that requires even shedding the identity that got you out of the chaos. She served you well, but that was a means to an end—to welcome in the state of Diosa ease and grace you have always been meant to embrace.

This chapter is in devotion to ease, to love, to pouring honey, to dancing wild and letting our spirits be free. Let's choose ease. Let's accept once and for all that we can put down the burden of our suffering. At this stage especially, life gets to be easy and fun.

Prayers for Peace and Ease

On the journey toward surrender, we need to be in partnership with spirit. Even when surrender does not feel natural to who we are, we can appeal to spirit to come to our aid, just as a loving mother would to her child.

As I wrote this book, spirit tested me to live out the principles I wanted to teach. I was given my soul's deepest desires: the love of my life and a book to express my soul's work to help women and souls around the world. And yet, here I was, still scared to surrender, lean back, and enjoy. I was holding my breath in some ways. I was meditating, but I wasn't truly available to the pleasure in my life. I knew that I needed to reach out to a power that lived beyond me, and to ask for the divine assistance I needed.

These words came through me as a reminder to be lighter so that I could carry the blessings that were pouring from me: "Thank you, Great Spirit, for all the blessings. The blessings hidden, the blessings revealed. Thank you for it all. As I write my soul book, I am coming to face the deepest parts of me. I am being called to shed skins and asked to rise higher. For someone that has been through so much abuse, trauma, and betrayal, it's scary to finally have it good. It sounds counterintuitive—like, wouldn't I be happy to have all my wildest dreams come true?"

Life will ask that we keep expanding so that we develop the capacity to hold more blessings. My soul spoke and asked me to release the weight I was carrying so that I could be filled by her more deeply. So I listened. And I continued to reach out whenever I felt bereft of answers, or when I felt that wall of suffering and hardship contracting around me.

I share this with you, as it gives me comfort, and I pray it does for you too. In times when you need to be reminded you deserve peace and ease, repeat the following:

"Spirit, Great Mother, help me to rest in the ease of your grace. Let me surrender and dance free to enjoy the fruits of my labor. Let me taste the sweetness and be overwhelmed with joy! Let it run through my every pore. Let me rest with faith and certainty. Joy, fun, and ease are available for me. I am finally free. I am free!"

Tapping into our creativity, into fun and sensuality, are pivotal for the wild and blissful Diosa to truly come alive. When we are so used to living in the darkness that we don't remember what to do in the light, we must be gentle with ourselves. After all, so many of us were forced to grow up before our time, and we had little to no space to play and fully explore the range of our emotions and expressions. Repeat the prayer above as often as you want to, and always give yourself compassion. This is your time to play, my beloved.

I also want to share some key Shakti Diosa tools to activate pleasure, bliss, and abundance in you. A powerful mantra from my Sri Vidya Tantra lineage, as taught by my teacher Psalm Isadora and then by Amma from her Guruji, is the Lalita Tripura Sundari mantra, also known as the Panchadasi mantra. Tripura Sundari means the triple Goddess. Sundari means "beauty." It can also be translated to "Goddess of the three realms."

Lalita translates from Sanskrit as "She Who Plays." With her holy mantra, we are allowing ourselves to embrace the medicine of play, of honey, of sweetness, of bliss, of abundance. The mantra allows us to activate key parts of our chakras to awaken the divine knowing of what we deserve on a cellular level. Use this mantra to help you recalibrate to the frequency of joy and play: *Ka E I La Hrim Ha Sa Ka Ha La Hrim Sa Ka La Hrim.*

This mantra is to be used with honor, devotion, and respect to the culture, people, and lineage from which it emerges. This beautiful mantra was passed down to me, and I now share it with you because it is meant to be here, as a tool that will lead you to greater levels of playfulness, joy, freedom, and expression. Please use it with absolute love and reverence.

I love this mantra deeply because I feel its effects on every level of my being. I see how in letting go, in dissolving, I become even more of myself. I give birth to myself.

Each new level will require a shedding, a release, so that you can hold more blessings and step into the truest manifestation of yourself. You are not your suffering. As a manifestation of the Goddess, you are meant to be a vessel for more joy, more love, more forgiveness, more compassion, more stillness, more fun, more reverence, more ease, more faith, more trust, more surrender, more miracles.

So let go of a little more today. Offer your prayer to the universe and ask for help releasing a burden that you have on your heart so that you can make room for the joy and bliss and play that are here for you to experience.

Diosa, I ask that you take in the beauty of this world: the sky, the earth, the trees, the fruit, the ocean, the abundance. Really take it in, because it is a manifestation of the divine and a reminder that you were made to be in a state of ease. Look at the way the moon meets the sky and how the sun rises! There is a method to all this magic, and it occurs without effort. It simply is.

This is the new evolved Diosa soul-on-skin-and-bones version of you. You get to play and rest now, Diosa. You get to enjoy all aspects of your life. Give yourself this gift.

Sacred Shakti Sensuality

Sensuality is closely related to joy; however, patriarchy and modern religions have tied so much shame to it that we have forgotten the innocence and power of inviting in sensuality as a form of healing.

Pleasure is one of the most impactful ways to heal. Let pleasure be your new teacher. Let play lead you to the new phase of your healing. For Lalita is the other side of the coin of Kali. Both are sacred teachers, with immense wisdom to share. Let us lean in to the medicine of the Goddess Lalita now.

Tantra is the path of ecstasy. In tantra, and specifically in Sri Vidya Tantra, the lineage that I was initiated in, we believe that the body is where the Goddess, la Diosa, lives. When we recite mantras, like the one I shared with you above, certain points of the body get activated and thus healed and connected to the limitless energy of the mother Goddess.

When we chant, we connect to the energy of that Goddess. Mantras have helped me heal deep layers of programming, and tantra and the path of Shaktism have allowed me to see the macro universe of the sun and the moon, of masculine/feminine, of shiva/ Shakti, within my own body.

Embracing the connection between pleasure and healing is a new way to learn. And once we have learned through pain, which can be an amazing catalyst for change, we realize that we must also learn from the teacher of pleasure.

Start by connecting to your body and breathing. Take a moment to embrace yourself as Diosa. Set the space for you to connect with you: the wild feminine, the primal animal body, the Goddess. Light candles and some incense, and put on some sensual music that connects you to your body. This is your time to reconnect in a safe way to the innocence of sensuality.

This goes beyond the sexual. Sensuality is quite literally about connecting to the source of creation: the same energy that birthed the universe and makes the sun rise and set within us. It is where matter and spirit kiss and entwine. Breathing and remembering that your body is alive and that la Diosa lives within reminds you that healing can be as simple and beautiful as loving up your body and giving her pleasure, recognizing her divine origins, and coming back to praise at your own altar.

Take it slow as you reconnect to sensuality. So many of us have been traumatized in our physical bodies and our expression of sexuality that we might feel numb, or like any touch—no matter how gentle—is torturous.

Featherlight touch is a great start. Simply breathe and gently trace your fingertips along your hands and arms. As you slowly touch your hands, allow yourself to go where it feels good—perhaps this is over your face or lips or heart. Let yourself flow with this body love meditation. Continue to breathe and bless every single part of your body with each stroke. Love yourself with each stroke. Whisper words and mantras of light, vitality, and acceptance to the neglected parts, whether they be breasts, belly, hips, calves, genitals, ass. Embody the Diosa.

When we do this, our Shakti light turns on little by little—and when that light turns on, there's no going back! You will naturally embody happiness, connection to spirit, and your full vitality. And now you are absolutely ready to light the fuck up and make your life magic. This is your birthright!

If you feel ready to go deeper, I recommend mindful masturbation and sacred self-pleasure. As you touch your own erogenous zones, you can consciously slow it down, breathe, and connect to the energy of the divine. This isn't about "getting off" and burning through your sexual energy; it's about patiently stoking the fire of your own turn-on. Think of a light expanding in your sex organs, like a sun shining brighter and brighter, allowing you to feel safe within your own arms. Relish every sensation. You are savoring your sensuality for you and you alone.

The closer you are to your sensuality and pleasure, the more in touch you are with your power—and the more in touch you are with your power, the more selective and mindful you will naturally become about who deserves to be in your life and inside of your heart and body.

The work of reclaiming your sacred sensuality is deep, ancient, and powerful. I hope that you allow it to awaken parts of your being that will open you up to the pleasure that is yours, as a living embodiment of Diosa. As Nikita Gill says in her book, *Wild Embers*,

"Some days
I am more wolf
Than woman
And I am still learning
How to stop apologizing
For my wild"

Rituals for Continued Growth

I view this entire dream of existence as something that was cooked up in the cauldron of Big Mama's body and soul. And in the work I have done with ancestors, spirit, and even my bright and glowy future self (who has a lot of delicious messages for me when I tune in), I always come back to the same belief: The innate cosmic intelligence is always communicating with us, and she wants nothing more than for us to take our rightful place in the glorious totality of creation.

Of course, as much as I appreciate my ego—which helps me maintain strong boundaries, get my bills paid, and ensure good hair days—it can be a trickster when it comes to taking the Divine's hand and allowing her to lead the way on this wild ride of life.

Although I, like so many other people, was raised with fear-based thinking, my intimate encounters with life have shown me that the universe is essentially on our side. It is intimidating and

dark only when we view it as a distant and remote thing, and ourselves as separate and powerless pawns in a game whose rules we
cannot comprehend.

But the more we surrender to our lives and recognize our connection to everything around us, the more present, powerful, and
joyful we can be. I've found that we just need constant reminders in
our lives in the form of meaningful rituals so that we can actively
connect with spirit and know it's on our side.

So many people are indoctrinated to step into rituals only when
the going gets rough, and we neglect to express gratitude and appreciation for our lives when we are happy, nourished, inspired. Don't
make this mistake. Create rituals in your life that let you simply check
in with your Diosa self and spirit. For instance, during the new or full
moons, on specific days of the week, or daily, feel free to express
gratitude for all that the Divine has given you. (The universe especially smiles upon creative offerings in the form of dance, art, and
poetry.)

Here are some of my fave rituals for connecting with the joy of
spirit.

Movement as medicine: Twerking, booty dancing, and hip
circling are all part of a primal movement that is in the bones of my
ancestors, as a Latina/African/Taíno with roots in Puerto Rico.
This movement of the hips is the spiral of the circle of life. It is the
drumming of the body that awakens the spirit of joy, life, animus,
Shakti, creativity, soul. We must move and stir honey with our hips
to remember we are alive. I suggest you make a movement medicine
playlist and add songs that allow you to move in ways that remind
you that you are Diosa. Play with dance. Watch yourself in the mirror. Get lost in the movement. Drop into the primal animal body
and breathe as you move and dance and play.

Song as prayer: *"Me abro mi alma hacia el cielo. Las mariposas vi-
enen y se duermen en mi corazon.* Fly free, butterfly, fly free." I sing this

as I sway from side to side, letting my soul make songs that are ancient and yet new to me on a conscious level. I play by allowing the spirit realm to meet me in physical reality, in the vibration of my being. Song is the bridge to get me there. They say that singing is like praying x 3. Make songs from your soul and sing to the heavens. Cry and release in your songs. Let yourself get bigger and bigger as you pull words from the invisible realms within. Create *cantos del alma,* or songs of the soul. In a sacred ritual called *temazcal* that I participated in while in Mexico, with a healer of mine, Maria Luisa, I sweat and released as I sang. It was cathartic. Another spirit moment here was: I was led to this healer and her name is the same as my grandmother. Coincidence? I think not! It doesn't matter if you think you can or can't sing. Just sing! Let your song erupt from your soul and the deeper voice within. Let it be a song that you made up, or a song that resonates with your soul. Singing is the most ancient way to pray. Take time to sing.

Journaling as freedom: Writing is a practice that allows you to unlock spiritual doors and powerful emotions that live within you. Take a journal and pen and write what is on your mind and heart. Write your feelings and also let this be an opportunity to ask Spirit for guidance. Ask for clarity. Ask to release and let go. Ask to connect to Source. As you write, allow your words to tumble out of you without censorship so that you can purge and release. This is a way to pour out what is in you. Journal to get to know yourself. There are gems within you that can be released only when you write. Be a channel for your deepest thoughts. Whether it's pen to paper or fingers to keyboard, write daily if you can, so that you can sort through the wealth of information that lives inside you and make some sense of it all.

Art as healing: Whether you write poetry and short stories, take photos, paint, sculpt, dance, or sing—let your creativity flow through you! You are a manifestation of divine creation, and as

such, you are intrinsically creative. Making art from the soul alchemizes pain and feelings. It adds aliveness to your daily existence.
It infuses your bones with soul and color. Each time we participate
in creating art, we are working to deeply heal our own and others'
wounds. We are merging with the truth of our joyful, always-
creative state. If you are hesitant to create, sign up for a new class,
perhaps a pottery class or a writing class. Read Julia Cameron's incredible book *The Artist's Way* to reclaim your own dormant artist
self. Take a dance workshop. Allow yourself to commit to including
art in your toolkit of healing.

Prayer as connection: Make an invitation to the Divine, however you envision it. The more specific your invitation, the better.
(And don't worry if your invitation is about "petty" human concerns—
honestly, nothing is too petty for the mistress of it all.) Many of us
fall victim to the notion that the universe is an impersonal, cold, and
unfeeling container for existence. But the more you actively engage
in conversation (yes, I am talking about the spoken-out-loud variety), the more you will begin to recognize the subtle energies that
point to a conscious, compassionate, and cocreative being at the center of existence. She hears your pleas. She feels your suffering. She
relishes your joy. So ask the questions you would like to have answered. Share your most heartfelt desires and hopes. Or, if you don't
have anything in particular to vent about, feel free to shoot the shit
and simply have a cup of tea with the universe. No big whoop. Just
a simple chat with universal love. If you talk to her like she's your
BFF, your partner in crime, your beloved . . . she will respond. If the
"Divine" feels too abstract for you, focus on something specific. She
lives in everything, after all. Maybe, for you, she is the oak tree in
your backyard. Or the moon in a cloud-swept sky. Or your partner's
eyes after making love. Truly, if you yearn to experience connection
with all that is, you will discover that the universe has the power to
make itself known in the most unexpected places.

Seasons as rhythms: Observing the Earth's dynamic miracles at play by observing seasonal changes (including your own birthday) can be super-powerful in understanding the cyclical rhythms of creation and your very own existence. Working with fire, air, earth, water, metal, or wood can also help you cultivate a more intimate relationship with the building blocks of life.

You are free to use your imagination. Don't be limited by the suggestions above. However you choose to integrate ritual into your life and connect with yourself as an expression of creation is absolutely up to you. Just know that once you open those channels of communication, you will never be the same again. Welcome the crossing-over, which is deep, rich, and more satisfying than words can say. You deserve it, Diosa.

Soulwork

Using your journal, you're going to write a love letter to yourself.

Let's get rid of the idea that compliments, appreciation, and deep romance can exist only in our relationships with other people, as opposed to the relationship we have with ourselves. At first you might feel like you lack proficiency (after all, how often do we stop to meditate on our own value?), but try approaching this activity with an open mind.

Before the days of email, letters served as a reminder of the unwavering attention that can connect two people separated by distance. Think of the times you've received a love letter or, at the very least, something that arrived for you in the mail—that was just for you, and loaded with care and personal attention. You probably felt a flicker of something in your heart, or butterflies of anticipation in your stomach.

In our time-distracted world, the experience of this kind of deep acknowledgment is becoming more and more rare. Of course, what we place our attention on multiplies in our world, which is why I want you to offer your attention to something that is worthy of it: you. You as soul mate and as Diosa.

A love letter doesn't have to be sappy or flowery. As you sit down and write a letter of deep love and commitment to yourself, take the time to point out specific things about yourself that are powerful, moving, worthy of acknowledgment. What are some specific moments in which you revealed your superhuman powers (whether they include intense vulnerability, unseen courage, or fire-breathing determination)? If you were to take the vantage point of an adoring lover, what would you say? What would your commitment to yourself be?

And while you're at it, don't forget that this is a time to release any negative beliefs, toxic self-talk, and judgments of yourself. Forgive yourself wholly. Know that you deserve to be happy. Imagine yourself releasing the old and stepping into the new.

Don't be afraid to mention some of the ways you secretly love yourself but are too bashful to admit to, because that would mean (horror of horrors) stroking your own ego. Stroke away, boo! Get out your favorite writing utensils and some stationery (yup, you're doing it longhand), and maybe even some glitter and art supplies—and spend at least an hour in passionate written courtship with that part of you that's gorgeous, brilliant, and worthy of so many love letters.

Mantra
I am a luscious and beautiful being, worthy of adoration and joy.

Ceremony
Honey Flower Shakti Selfie
I realized early on that spirit-guided ceremonies go beyond conscious thought. I would be midsentence with a client on the phone

when I'd be seized by a creative idea, a spiritual download that I didn't consciously understand. Sometimes it would be a visual, such as an image of a sun, and my spiritual guides would advise me to tell the client to focus on the sun in their vagina and imagine rays of light shining down on them—to activate their Shakti and sensuality so that they could honor it and choose whom to share their energy with in a conscious and honoring way.

Other times, clients would be grieving, and I would be guided to tell them to hold an imaginary funeral for an old part of themselves and offer a eulogy to honor the transition. While writing this chapter, I received a specific ceremony to offer you. This is a sensual Shakti-activating ceremony. Take time to find a quiet moment and a place where you won't be disturbed. You will need:

1. organic honey
2. flowers
3. a mirror
4. a cellphone with a camera to take a selfie
5. a pink or white candle (optional)
6. incense (optional)
7. music (optional; I recommend anything by Ayla Schafer)

This is your time to adorn yourself as a Diosa and tap into that primal, sensual, innocent beauty.

Go to your bathroom, bringing your supplies with you. Get naked or perhaps leave on your bra and underwear. Place honey on the parts of your body that you wish to honor; be a living offering to yourself. Become the living altar. Play your music. Light your incense. Put on your music to set the vibe. Once you place the honey on your body and stick the flowers on, take a selfie in the mirror or set a timer to take a self-portrait. This is your time to step into embracing your inner Diosa beauty and Shakti.

You are meant to be in love with you. To worship yourself and treat yourself as Diosa. When you treat yourself as divine, you will inevitably settle less frequently—because how can you be treated as less than a Goddess when you are living in a walking ceremony and devotion to yourself?

You are the living temple. Always remember this.

Oh my Diosa! You are here. You have made it! YES! YES! FUCKING YES!

Celebrate the beautiful journey that this has been! Difficult and yet rewarding. Satisfying to the soul. Taste your progress! Mmm, that tastes like divine soul growth. In this chapter you were reminded that amid it all, there is pleasure and bliss to activate. That you deserve to feel good. That you deserve to reward yourself for every step of the way. Be like Lalita, "she who plays." Use the Lalita mantra whenever you need a reminder of invoking that play and pleasure and bliss into your life. It is a gift I offer you to take with you and place it amid the safety of your heart. Flow with the tools that you have learned and return back throughout the book to see what resonates in that moment. Take what you want and leave the rest. This book is meant to be a soul companion. To come back to and pray for your soul to be guided to a page, or to a tool that you need. Get creative as you practice these principles. Open your eyes to signs and practices to deepen your healing. I fell in love with this journey and it is my wish that you do too. For this healing that we do is a gift that never stops giving. Ever-flowing bounty of blessings. Ever-flowing bounty of love. In the next and final chapter of this journey, you will own all that you are, Diosa. All the blessings. All the soul growth. All the love. I love you so much and I am so grateful for your reading and going on this journey with me heart in heart, hand in hand. Let us take a deep breath together. Inhaling in through the nose, holding for a three count—1, 2, 3. And exhaling from the mouth—releasing all of the breath out with a smile for a long and slow five count—1, 2, 3, 4, 5. *Mmm*, yes.

I am a luscious and beautiful being,
worthy of adoration and joy.

#iamdiosa

CHAPTER 13

You Are Diosa

"She remembered who she was and the game changed."

—Lalah Delia

Wonderful work, my love. I am so proud of you for diving deep, getting raw, and doing the work needed to come back home to you, to your true self, to your soul self, to your Diosa-in-your-bones self!

You are in the best possible place to cocreate the Diosa lifestyle of your design and desire. You've stripped away the dead skin of old beliefs and behaviors, and you are now left with your glittering soul skin. The skin of your true self, your highest self, your in-alignment self.

All of this is possible when you've done the soulwork that you've been guided into throughout this book. The reward is your soul emerging from the powerful quest you have taken inward, diving deep into your own oceans to understand your wounds, the blueprints of love you downloaded from your parents, and the toxicity that you may have inherited and internalized since you were in the womb. You've set down outdated soul contracts and agreements and determined a new vision of self-love and self-reverence. You've identified old triggers, as well as rituals and behaviors that will serve to honor your new soul vows and soul goals.

You've lovingly traced and retraced your patterns, inside and out, and you have familiarized yourself with the places within that may have been concealed by shame, trauma, judgment, and fear. By plumbing your depths, you have integrated your darkness. For as Diosa, you contain the cosmic womb of darkness, which is full of its own spectacular mystery and healing potential.

And now it is time to bring your whole self to the light—to sing your wholeness into its fullest manifestation. You have collected the parts of yourself that you have met along the path and now bring them into coherence, love them up, return them to their vitality. The Diosa journey is here to help you walk (or dance) closer and closer to the woman you want to be, not the one who has been used to responding from her wounds and trauma. As a Diosa, you can reframe any story or experience (especially those that entail giving away your power) to communicate your highest standards and values.

This is your time. You are ready to crown yourself as Diosa, to embrace your beauty and riches, and to walk your soul path as your ultimate destiny.

Seeing with Soul

As we continue on this journey (which never truly ends), I want to leave you with one of the most powerful Diosa practices in my life. This requires the integration of soul ritual and practical steps. It is the fusion of magic and real work that allows dreams to come to life.

There is an African proverb that says, "Pray but move your feet." If I were to sum up my advice, it would be this: Do the spiritual work and ask how you can practically put it into action.

You are worthy of your soul's desires. Crafting your soul's vision is key once you have gone to the root and healed and loved up your wounds. You have connected the dots between how the past has affected the present, and you've begun to rewire your nervous system and pivot toward actions and behaviors that are in true alignment with your healthy whole self. The next leap is designing the life you actually want and giving yourself permission to dream big.

This is not only about diving deep into the shadow work, but it is also about believing you are worthy of stepping into a new evolution of self. For sometimes it is also true that we play small or cling to old defense mechanisms out of fear of being too bright, too seen, and too loved. So here, I invite your creative child spirit to play and craft and dream up your ideal magical soul life.

Once you have pulled out the weeds, it is time to be intentional about what you are planting in the garden of you. This is soul crafting. This is true manifestation. And it requires that you tap into your inner *bruja*, Diosa, medicine woman, shamanic magical self.

Once you know what you will no longer settle for, you must take the time to say yes to what you are upgrading to. It is crucial that when you remove something that no longer works, you replace it with something that does work. (After all, nature abhors a vacuum.) This is your time to go all out and really allow yourself to flow and dream beyond your perceived limitations. Because you have been doing the work to expand your vessel, you must fill it with things, people, situations, ideas, and desires befitting a queen. You must continue to grow and add wings to each word you speak and sparkle to each vision you create. For you are the dream maker. And you are ready for the initiation of crafting your life from soul.

Soul envisioning is different from shallow manifestation, for it is never just about the surface. A soul vision rises from the deepest depths of who you are, from the mysterious starry darkness that lies beyond the "darkness" of trauma, blanketing you in the most sacred truths. This is where the call of la alma lives. It is the call that you must respond to, for it is the divine's mission for you.

The divine has placed these dreams in you, and it is your job to find them and live them and be them. When you discover these visions and dreams, they will be your north star so that you absolutely know when you are off track with respect to navigating your soul map.

Let us go on a journey to dream up your soul life and embed it in your current reality. You may want to record the next meditation in your voice, or ask a trusted friend to speak the words to you. Find a comfortable place and an hour when you will not be disturbed. It's time for magic-making and revelation!

Soul Dream Life Meditation

Find a comfortable space for you to be with you. Somewhere cozy, quiet, and private. Close your eyes and sit in a comfortable position or lie down. If you are sitting, sit in what I call "mindful body," which is neither too stiff nor too slouchy but somewhere comfortably in between. Rest your hands on your thighs, palms facing up or down—whatever is most comfortable for you.

As you sit in this position, you begin to connect to the limitless source energy available to you at all times. It is as if you are plugging into an outlet and that light source is the energy of the divine, of God, Goddess, pure ultimate consciousness.

Turn your focus inward and go to the space of soul, beyond all concepts of time.

You are now in the limitless field of creativity, where all of your wildest dreams are possible.

If any doubts creep in on this journey, don't bug out—simply observe them. Inhale through the nose for a three count, and exhale out of the mouth for a four count, releasing and surrendering as you exhale.

It is time for soul crafting.

Ask your soul to guide you now. Invite your soul in. Say, "Soul,

I invite you to come with me and guide me. Soul, guide me to see the images of my soul's highest, most magical destiny."

Allow yourself to play and dream now. Allow the images from your soul to come forth. Allow them to float in effortlessly, as if you are crafting the most magical work of art.

Perhaps your soul is a vibe you immediately feel. As it comes over you, you feel confident, secure, loving, and connected to the divine. You notice you are smiling. You feel the warmth of the sun inside of you.

Notice the joy that is possible when you are in your soul's highest form. Notice your energy in your soul's highest form. Notice what you are wearing in this dream vision of yourself. Notice the details of what your happiest, most confident, most aligned self would wear.

How are your facial expressions and body language? Perhaps you are smiling. See your forehead relaxed and eyes glowing and serene. Notice how you look when you are deeply happy, fulfilled, and at peace.

Continue to breathe, inhaling in through the nose and filling up your entire body with prana, with breath, with the energy of light, and exhale it back out through the mouth.

Notice where you are as your highest soul self. Where are you living? In the city? The mountains? The beach? Where are you in your wildest dreams? Traveling? With a big beautiful farmhouse alone writing, or surrounded by a vivacious and loving family? Let yourself see specifically where you are and what lights you up most.

Notice the details and the smells and colors and interior design. Let yourself feel and sense the surrounding culture and people. Who is next to you? Is it the love of your life? Is it your best friend? Are there babies or a large community of like-minded people on a mission? Notice the amazing people by your side in your vision. Feel the vibration of being surrounded by soul-aligned people.

How do you feel in their presence? Alive, invigorated, supported,

safe, celebrated, joyful, loved? Feel that energy and breathe in all
the love now.

Breathe it all in, and exhale it out. Good work. Continue to play
and dream up your soul's highest destiny for your life. Don't be
afraid to go big! Allow the visions of your soul, based on your own
unique calling, to come flooding in—bypassing the limitations of
your conscious mind.

What are you doing to support your soul's mission in the world?
What is your purpose? How are you living it out? Speaking on
stages, writing a book, being a mama, traveling the world, running
a nonprofit, releasing an album, becoming a politician, going back
to school? See what you are doing to live out your soul's dharma, or
work in the world. Feel how good it feels to be living your authentic
purpose.

Breathe in that energy now, and exhale it back out with a smile.
Tap into your beauty and sensuality and body—your Diosa
pleasure. Feel how good it feels! You are activated in body and spirit.
You are feeling sexy and inspired because you have touched your
depths, and your love comes from that sacred place. Feel into that
Shakti now.

Allow yourself to add any details from your ideal dream life
now. Soak it all up. Feel into it and register all the feelings and details. Breathe it into your body and cells. Plant these visions in your
body. Trust your soul's guidance for a life beyond your wildest
dreams.

Beautiful work. Slowly come back to your senses and the room
you are in. Now journal about everything you saw and felt, being
sure to be as detailed as possible. Ask your soul for three simple steps
you can take to ground this beautiful vision into your life.

Align with Your Soul Destiny

One of the key soul lessons that I want to leave you with is that as we do this work of soul envisioning and soul crafting, we upgrade our soul destiny.

Whereas before, it may have felt that the path was one of chaos and destruction, as you practice the principles in this book step by step, new choice by new choice, prayer by prayer, shift by shift, your path will dramatically change.

If your previous "normal" was dating drug dealers, replicating childhood wounds, hanging around shitty people, and engaging in self-hating behavior, let's say you were on Destiny Path F—a long and desolate road toward ruin and self-destruction. But when you do the inner work by going to therapy, recognizing your triggers, and taking leaps toward your truest self, you are now on Destiny Path A—looking toward the expansive and star-studded horizon that was always meant for you.

I often think of it like a video game where you constantly upgrade to the next level. Living as a spiritual being in this human experience is very similar to that. When we choose to lean in to our soul lessons, or tikkun (that which we came to this Earth to repair or integrate), the klippot (in Jewish mysticism, the vessel or shell symbolizing our obstacles, which conceals the light of the divine) is cracked open. As we dive into our obstacles rather than turning away from them, the light of miracles and transformation is released. And just like in a video game, we gain light and energy by overcoming our obstacles. We upgrade to the next level, where we are capable of doing bigger and better things, and of expressing even more of our Diosa self.

We upgrade our destiny each time we perceive our obstacles as opportunities to grow. We upgrade our destiny when we go to the root and love and sing to our wounds until we heal them. We upgrade our destiny when we stand with ourselves and truly get to know, forgive, love, and trust ourselves. We upgrade our destiny when we choose in a way that aligns with soul over fear, with courage over temporary comfort, with expansion over contraction. And before we know it, we reach Destiny Path A, the one where we are in full alignment with our truth and our potential.

A video game is full of new challenges and characters at every upgrade, and life is no different. The beautiful thing about soul paths is that they are not about perfection, only progress. On such a path, you are still met with life, but you handle it with greater ease and grace, and you return to soul alignment much more quickly. Moreover, the types of problems you are likely to encounter will be aligned with the highest version of your soul self. You will experience less chaos and toxicity, because your daily maintenance of a spiritual practice and the implementation of soul tools will grow you. You will nourish and feed the beautiful cocreation of your life.

I want to emphasize that it takes a significant amount of work to get to this place. When we are operating from trauma, we simply don't have the energy or capacity to deal with life in a constructive way. We are still at the survival level of the root chakra, so our work at this stage is to simply become grounded and meet our needs.

You've done the work, baby. And now you are ready to rise into the seventh chakra of claiming your crown and embracing your oneness with spirit. I want to remind you here that this is not about "rising above" your humanity, but rather encompassing and embracing it.

I know it is hard when you are doing the work of heavy lifting, but as we explored in the last chapter, you are now in a place where the new "work" is about enjoying the gifts that come to you, just as the most regal queen allows herself to receive the riches of her life (along with the soul responsibilities). The path of soul devotion is meant to be ecstatic and blissful, just as the ancient sages and poets talked about. Believe me, blessings will come your way, so please don't get used to the struggle. You absolutely deserve to be happy.

It's time to devote your energy to cocreation and building the life you want. Let go of anything or anyone that is not worthy of you. Allow yourself to reprogram your nervous system by saying yes to your soul destiny and to what is meant for you.

All of this reminds me of how, before I began working on this book, I broke up with a wonderful man. Yes, the relationship was healthy and did not contain any of the toxicity I'd experienced from dating abusive drug dealers—so, clearly, I had upgraded. This man was always good to me, but I could feel in my heart that the relationship was not in alignment with what I wanted. It didn't contain the passion, mutual soul goals, and 100 percent authenticity that I longed for in a true and deep partnership.

Our breakup was warm and amicable, but admittedly, I was a little freaked out by the fact that I wasn't spiraling or engaging in self-destructive behavior, like obsessively checking out his social media to see if he was dating someone new. I wondered: Is this normal? Is it weird that I'm embracing the idea that it was in my highest alignment to part ways with him?

What I realized was that my new normal entailed wholeheartedly embracing a bigger version of myself, of my soul. I could actually trust my decisions instead of second-guessing them, because they came from a secure, infinitely wise part of me. I was also assured by the fact that I had shown up in the relationship as my highest self; I had been honest, transparent, self-loving, and kind. All of this meant that I wasn't hit by the backwash of regret that had usually accompanied previous breakups. I didn't need a do-over. I'd done all I could. I was finally learning my soul lessons, which meant that I could let go gracefully and embrace my creative energy in order to visualize what I wanted to bring into my life.

Brujita, can you too give yourself permission to dare to dream big? To expand your expectations? To love bigger and even more boldly? To welcome your highest good? To embrace the peace, abundance, and blessings that are your soul destiny?

Alignment with soul and spirit is the goal. So I want you to always ask yourself: Am I in alignment with my soul? And if not, Spirit, how might I return to alignment?

This is a gift that our soul gives us: the opportunity to choose to cocreate our lives with spirit. We get to be active participants in creating and designing a life that is fully aligned with soul, joy, fulfillment, and love.

Keep the Faith

When I really began to accept that I had a role in my life, and that I wasn't a victim to the experiences I'd been through, but a victorious Diosa with the capacity to change and lead a life that I love, I began to cultivate hope and faith.

As we surrender to the voice of our soul and the higher power of our own understanding, we are guided. Faith in our soul alignment fuels and fills us with energy, positivity, humility, and joy.

There is a passage in the bible that speaks to the power of cultivating faith: "He presented another parable to them, saying, 'The kingdom of heaven is like a mustard seed, which a man took and sowed in his field; and this is smaller than all other seeds, but when it is full grown, it is larger than the garden plants and becomes a tree, so that the birds of the air come and nest in its branches'" (Matthew 13:31–32).

Even the smallest amount of faith offers nourishment to the garden of self that we are cultivating. It breathes life and sustenance into our dreams. While visualizing my dreams, there were certainly times when I had doubts, but I did it anyway because it felt better to invest energy in the creation of my dreams than in the destruction of them.

I began to reflect on how much faith I had in my business and how it felt effortless even when it was hard. Even in the beginning, when it was only one person who was buying my course, I felt abundant—because the joy of building the course and helping that single person was so soul-aligned that it fulfilled me. I let that joy overcome me and allow me to keep investing in my business, no matter what. No matter the side jobs as a nanny or selling another MLM essential oil product—I kept on going. I let my dream push me forward and give me momentum.

I realized that my faith and determination to flow no matter what, all while enjoying the process, allowed my business to be successful. More opportunities came in. My visions on my dream board were manifesting before my eyes.

"Why is it so easy there and not in my love life?" I thought. And then, "What if I applied the same principles of faith and flow where it is easy for me to areas of my life that are not as easy? What would happen then?"

Part of the magic of me in my business was that I always focused on what I could offer the world—and while I had my goals, I wasn't gripping them for dear life; rather, I was in a state of true surrender. When something didn't work out, my attitude was "If it's not this, there is something better waiting for me. I only want what is in divine alignment for me. I trust Spirit" or "Perhaps not now, but if it's meant to be, I will try again in divine timing."

I trusted my gut. I allowed space. My energy was calm, trusting, patient, like the perfect rhythmic energy of inhaling and exhaling. There was a definite flow.

I realized that I wasn't customarily like that with my romantic relationships. So I started exercising the same energetic and faith-based principles that I used in my business and career with my love and romantic relationships. I crafted my vision board for love. I envisioned my ideal partner. I wrote down all the qualities he would have, how I would feel with him, who he would be in the world, who we would be together. I began to make space energetically, being very intentional about seeking therapy and healing and doing the soulwork that I listed throughout this book. I also cleared out physical space in my home. I emptied a drawer and bought a beautiful wooden carving of a couple holding each other, and I placed it on my bedroom dresser so I could see it daily and be inspired. I bought matching side tables to bring the energy of couples into my home— a principle I had once read about in a feng shui book.

I was trying it all, just as I'd done with my business—playing with and fine-tuning the process while keeping my eyes focused on the prize, but not so tightly that I would repel what I wanted from effortlessly coming in to meet me.

My dating life transformed. I began to naturally feel and be more chill and confident. I was more me, because I trusted that dating was about growth and not about meeting "the one." I removed the pressure I'd previously applied. Although I kept my ultimate goal of meeting my twin flame, my future hubby and baby daddy, my soul partner, my perfect vibrational match, I let go of my attachment to it. I focused on the fun of creating the vision of the holiest love I could dream of, in full faith that it would find me. I wrote poems and prayers to my future beloved.

Here is a simple prayer I wrote in the Notes section of my phone, to my future husband:

I pray for you my warrior
My soul mate
My best friend
My hubby and life partner
I can't wait to meet you and love you and be loved by you and do life with you
I hope you are getting all the love and healing you need in this moment
I am sending love to your heart and spirit—that you be loved and protected exactly as you need

I can't wait to meet you, my beloved—I can't wait
I've been preparing myself my whole life for you it seems, and finally in
stripping myself of all that no longer serves me—I feel myself coming
home to myself and to God, divine source, and thus, to you
Can't wait to smell you and lay in your arms and feel yes, yes, yes!
I waited for this—
You are what I have been waiting for, and I have been what you are
waiting for!
Love you, my beloved
Thy will be done, God, I surrender all of my desires to you
That you lead me to what is for me and steer me away from what is
not for me
Amen, and so it is

Xx,
Christine

I wrote that poem on April 19, 2017. Nine months later, I hit it off with a man whom I'd been friends with online and had hung out with once. He was a photographer, so I hired him to do my photo shoot in preparation for this book that is now in your hands. We felt a spark and a soul alignment, and we flowed. With him, I felt the same way I feel when I am doing and living my soul's work. Healing and helping women to come home to themselves was natural and effortless for me. I knew it was my dharma to do such work in this lifetime. I felt the same with him—he felt like part of my soul path, not something I had to struggle to fit into other aspects of my life. It just made sense. We made sense.

Four months later, we were engaged—and now we are married.

I don't believe in coincidences. I believe in shedding the layers that no longer serve you until you arrive at your soul skin. I believe in aligned actions and being guided. It was all there waiting. I just had to keep showing up, and not giving up before the miracle. I want to highlight that the miracle was me being willing and courageous to repeatedly do the soulwork necessary to heal deep, love myself, and come back home to my soul. The external manifestations were the icing on my already delicious Diosa cake ;).

So I implore you to keep showing up too. Keep showing up in the stormy nights and the lonely nights and the twists and turns. Keep showing up. Cry and then write a poem to your future beloved. Get pissed and let yourself be human and bitch and complain to your bestie and then recommit to your soul vision.

You are human and divine, Diosa. You get to do both!

Yes, you get to long for something with all your heart, and then you get to surrender the vision, knowing that spirit is cocreating it with you and gently ushering you toward your true destiny.

Soulwork

It's time to choose your light word, my love. This is one of the activities I always do at my Diosa Retreat. At the beginning of the retreat, each Diosa chooses her own shadow word, which symbolizes a wound she is working to heal, or an unhealthy pattern that she is here to deconstruct so that she can build her life anew, from a place of soul.

At the end of the retreat, I ask each Diosa to select her light word—a word or phrase that embodies the highest manifestation of her Diosa self into the world. She has done the important work of coming back to her soul, and she needs a reminder of all that she is capable of. This is how the light word functions.

On the next page, you will find a list of words in the shape of an infinity symbol. Instead of choosing a word from your mind, I want you to trust in the guidance of your soul. Soften your gaze so that you aren't able to read the words on the page. Place your finger or pen on the symbol and gently trace around it, like a sigil, which is a

One with Spirit · Multidimensional Woman · Healed · Warrior · Grace · More than Enough · Voice of Soul · Clear Sight · Worthy · Supported · Whole · Vessel of Light · Still · Shakti · Confident · Embodied · Diosa · Clear Sight · Rooted · Voice of Soul · Rooted · Seen · Empowered · Loved · Emotionally Sober · Present magical symbol imbued with power. Do this ten times, as you breathe deeply. Stop when you feel ready. Wherever your finger or pen has landed, you have found your own special light word.

Your light word is like a compass that will continually remind you of your Diosa identity and orientation toward your soul's true north. By holding the word in your heart and soul, you will always remember that you are a full, living embodiment of the multidimensional strength and wisdom of Diosa.

Mantra

I am Diosa, and it is my birthright to align with my soul destiny and live a happy life.

Ceremony

Crown Yourself as Diosa

You have done the work and are ready to go out there to crown yourself as the Diosa you are!

I love the ritual and ceremony of vows. They offer an intentional way to commit to yourself all the ways you have chosen to live your life as a Diosa. These are your values and promises to self and soul in this new initiation as Diosa embodied.

Take some time to write vows to yourself and post them in a place where you can always be reminded of this beautiful commitment you are making to your soul. Be detailed about how you want to feel and show up in the world. Below is a sample of mine that I wrote a few years back and that I found synchronistically as I was writing these ceremonies. I knew I had to include them in the book.

> I vow to honor the voice of my soul.
> I vow to listen to my intuition as my compass in life.
> I vow to love myself, especially in the moments when I feel I
>   don't deserve love.

I vow to get back up again and again and pivot to soul.

I vow to love myself as Diosa.

I vow to speak my truth no matter what.

I vow to commit my life to healing, one day at a time.

I vow to enjoy the fruits of my labor.

I vow to share the gifts of this medicine, as called by spirit
    to do.

I vow to create joy and peace.

I vow to be gentle.

I vow to be kind.

I vow to allow in only aligned high vibes.

I vow to treat myself as sacred.

*I am Diosa, and it is my birthright
to align with my soul destiny
and live a happy life.*

#iamdiosa

DIOSA BLESSINGS

Dearest Diosa, we've come to the end of our journey together, but that doesn't mean it's the end of *your* journey. Whenever you are tempted to be hard on yourself or go faster, I encourage you to pause, for healing isn't something that can be forced. The more we force, the slower the process.

Sink in, and listen to the rhythm of your unique journey. This is healing for the long run, and therefore it's okay to go slow and steady. If you feel like leaping, you can leap, but do it only if you are motivated by the deepest parts of you. Do not be hard on yourself to do more. You need not do anything but sink deeper and allow what needs to happen to happen. Being reborn is a beautiful creative process. Allow the process to unfold and unfurl you, like a luscious rose with many velvety petals.

Embodying the energy of the Diosa is about remembering that the divine is in your every cell. That the love of the universe pulses through your veins. That the elements of fire, water, earth, and air are living within you. What a walking miracle you are! Yes, you might sometimes forget, but that spark within hasn't left.

Being a Diosa is about committing to internal soul growth and never letting the suffering of the past stop us from becoming who we are meant to be. It is about inviting spirit and ritual and holiness into the most mundane moments, for life is our living altar, and our participation with it allows us to cocreate our soul destiny.

Being a Diosa is also about taking the power back into our hands and remembering that we are powerful, that we are worthy, that we are deserving. Being a Diosa is about crowning ourselves in confidence and saying, "Fuck that, I am not going to settle anymore! I am a motherfuckin' Diosa!"

It is about saying *YES* to the soul and *NO* to anything out of alignment. It is about doing the soulwork every damn day because that is what it takes. I won't sell you a quick-fix story. Healing is not a quick fix—it is a sacred journey and a lifelong art. And you, my dear, are an artist and creatrix, and I have no doubt you are beyond capable of creating a life that is full of your favorite colors and textures.

Know that this process works. It will help you to craft a life you love by being in the stillness with your soul and letting her guide the way. There is a sense of comfort and peace that will envelop you when you know you are being guided. You will see that even in the moments when you feel off-track, spirit is there guiding you to learn, to heal, to grow.

Life is happening for you, not to you. It is there to help you expand into your most divine self.

You are worthy. You are loved. You are Diosa.

You do not need to be fixed or saved by anybody. Of course, helpers and sacred allies will come along the path, but ultimately, *YOU* will save you. You will surrender to spirit and gain the power in your sword to slay the old demons within. You will own your power, your Shakti, your innate strength, and forge the way forward—with wisdom, grace, and the aura of a woman who has seen it all and still chooses to rise into her holiest self.

None of this is a formula. It is poetry in motion. It is invisible chords creating a symphony. It is the magic of the sunrise melting the foggy sky. It is locking eyes with someone and feeling love. It is mysterious and holy. Do not reduce the process to one that can be wholly explained with mundane words; instead, revel in the magic that goes beyond human understanding.

Dare to live outside the lines, and resist the urge to focus solely on the destination. Let yourself also surrender to the moment and the process. Let the unique power that is within you be unleashed. Trust that. Trust you. Let that feeling guide you to keep embarking and re-embarking on this journey. You will need that energy as you move through new stages and phases, new challenges, and new rewards.

As my love wrote,

All I've been
All I've loved
I honor and release
back into the source
back into the fountain of love
where all things are transformed.
I am ready to let go now.
I am ready to be new again.
I am

—Fernando Samalot

And I would add, I am Diosa.

Please know that this is not just a book; it is a way of life. These words are infused with soul medicine. Each page is a message from my heart to yours. From my soul to yours. Let this book flow into your life and come alive in you. Read the work, and do the work. Share your insights and revelations with me on social media @cosmicchristine or join the Diosa community at christineg.tv. A massive element of this journey is the community of badass real and raw Diosas who are joining you in sisterhood from around the world. Reach out and connect. And know that you are never, ever alone. We are Diosa!!!

A poem for you in honor of my late teacher Psalm Isadora

Rest your head beloved
No fear or loneliness can capture your light in your soul's embrace
I'm right here—holding you tight
When the fears arise and there is no one in sight,
Look within and I will be there.
Today and always pressed against your heart
Shining the way in the dark alleyways
Through twists and turns—
I will remain a constant safe space for you to stay
Rest your head beloved, let yourself be loved
Let yourself sing
Let yourself play
Let yourself rest from the hard days
You deserve this peace
This moment of release
The time has come to enjoy the sweet
Dance in the love that surrounds you
My beautiful one, you are safe.
Soar your wings and fly, it's time to see new dreams, and heights.
It's time to take flight—soul intact, courage in hand.
Familia del Alma that stands—cheering you on.
We braved the storms and have risen
It's time to celebrate the victory of the battle back home to Soul
You made it diosa! Shine the light you earned.
Star you are. Shining bright.
Te amo, para siempre.

Xo,
Christine

ACKNOWLEDGMENTS

There is no greater joy than to be able to thank all the souls that have supported me throughout my life and through this book journey. Life is a *we* thing, and without community, there is nothing.

I want to start by thanking my parents, my mom, Evelyn, and my dad, Raymond. Our journey is a testament of willingness to heal individually and together as a family. Without your hard work and sacrifice, I wouldn't have had access to the life experiences and education that shaped me. Grateful for you believing in me and always supporting my writing and my spiritual journey. Your open mindedness is a key in me being me. Love you both so much. Thank you.

To my cousin, my nightlight, Natali Gil: without you, there is no me. Spirit knew what it was doing when it made you and me. My companion through it all. The person that knows me in and out. Our spiritual tests have shaped me into the woman I am. Words can never encapsulate the depth of what you mean to me. Every conversation, every word with you is channeling directly with spirit. So much of this book comes from our deep reflections and aha moments. Forever grateful. I love you so much naki.

My puta parade, my best friends and family. How the fuck did we get so lucky? Taina, your prayers have strengthened me in times when I was weak. Jennifer, your cheerleader go-getter attitude always reminds me that I have what it takes to do big things one step at a time. Justine, my fellow spirit seeker, your journey has helped me feel less alone on so many days when I felt misunderstood. Thank you for getting me. Katie, for supporting my work and sharing it with people in your life, even when you are busy being the best momma—I see you. Anaeli, for allowing me to share my raw parts with you and accepting me; you make my weird feel normal. You are my soul sisters, my family for life.

To Steve Harris, my amazing agent that feels like family, who believed in me the moment I emailed him. Your patience and trust in me and this process gave me peace as I navigated new terrains. Thank you for reminding me to trust myself and to write until I cried when I read it. Thank you for your spirit and your work. Grateful to have an agent like you!

To Sara Carder, for being not only my editor but being a friend throughout this process. Our conversations reminded me that we are all in this together as women. Your support, your insight, your heart, they have all made this journey a true gift.

The entire Tarcher Penguin Random House team: Sara Johnson, Rachel Ayotte, Anne Kosmoski, Casey Maloney, Megan Newman, Lindsay Gordon, Alex Casement, Roshe Anderson, and Andrea St. Aubin. I will never forget how seen, how loved, how appreciated I felt the day I walked into your office. You reflected back to me, "We have been missing warmth in this field and you have the warmth that's been missing." I felt the warmth radiating from you all and have ever since. Thank you for pouring your support into me and this project.

To Sally Mercedes, for being a book birth doula for this soul project. For holding me accountable when things were due and allowing spirit to come through to speak to us. Being in Puerto Rico with you made this book possible; we allowed the soul of the book to speak loud and clear amidst birds, sunshine, beach magic, and reggaeton music.

Nirmala Nataraj, your guidance at the tail end of my project helped it all come together. You came in at divine timing with your editing magic and soulful energy. Thank you for your art and support.

To my Cosmic Life team: Nina Collier, my cosmie family that was there with me behind the scenes being my ride or die in both life and business. Without you, this and so much more wouldn't have gotten done. I know for sure Psalm sent you to me and me to you. Te amo my tantra brujita mentee forever and ever. And Jessy Dorsett, my amazing assistant that made me feel supported and held, and brought a lightness and joy into my life. Your energy has helped me grow as a leader and person. Thank you for being you. Your presence on our team is truly magic.

To the entire Diosa Tribe: It is because of you all that I do this work. Your stories, your resilience, your dedication to healing. Your open hearts and your trust in me and each other. This is all for you, for us. *Mis hermanas del alma.*

Miguelina and Wendy, for being the assistants for the deep soul-work that occurs in the annual Diosa Retreat. You are spiritual treasures to the world.

To Melissa O'Connor, for creating art and magic behind the scenes for me for years now. My business has grown because of the beauty you have brought to it.

To Christina Zayas, my sober sister who has gifted me with being a mirror and also offering the best creative ideas for my business. Thank you.

To my mentors throughout the years, who have impacted my soul and shaped my teachings: Psalm Isadora, *bruja*—though you are not here in body, your spirit lives on through me. You pushed me to get my license to be a therapist and to be disciplined in combining spirituality, therapy, and tantra. Your belief in me and all the signs you sent to me kept me going. Te amo. Terri Cole, you were my first mentor who was doing therapy differently. You helped me believe it was possible to live your soul's dreams. For guiding me as a therapist and continuing to give me invaluable feedback before any big leap in my life. I love you.

My dear therapist Krystyna Sanderson, for being my point person and helping me to untangle the webs within myself to heal, to rise, to lead.

Olga, your dedication to healing and mentorship have helped me be a sober woman of dignity and grace, one day at a time. Love you.

Dr. Clarisa Pinkola Estés, your training and your work has impacted my soul and helped me to grow as a spiritual seeker and woman. Rachel Brathen, I remember you signed me up on your platform without a big following just because you felt the medicine and the power in the work. You helped me leap in my faith in my work. Thank you. Ana Flores, you have truly helped me grow because, as you say: "When one grows, we all grow." I love you sister.

The Dove Team and Sherria Cotton, for being the first to have me step on stage and speak. You gave me faith in this work and its power.

For my little Bodhi who can't read but whose love and fluff gave me love and support throughout it all.

To all my spiritual support and guides who have led the way, and to all the other beautiful souls in my life that I didn't get to mention here—because there are so many. Know that your love and belief in me means the world to me.

Finally, I thank my soul partner, my husband, Fernando. Your support in me and the work I do gives my soul wings to fly to limitless places. I am blessed to journey through life with you. This is our book. *Te amo, mi amor.*

ABOUT THE AUTHOR

Christine Gutierrez, MA, LMHC, is a Latina licensed psychotherapist, life coach, and expert in love addiction, trauma, abuse, and self-esteem. She has a bachelor's degree from Fordham University in human behavior and development and a master's degree from City College of New York in mental health counseling with a focus on prevention and community. Through her work, Christine offers private coaching, group coaching, and transformational retreats such as her annual Diosa Retreat in Puerto Rico. In addition, Christine is the founder of the Diosahood, a global community where like-hearted women gather to heal, rise, and lead. She has been featured in *Time Out NY*, *Latina Magazine*, *Yahoo Health*, *Ebony*, *Cosmopolitan for Latinas*, *Oprah Daily*, *Telemundo*, and others. Christine currently resides in Puerto Rico with her husband Fernando Samalot, their pup Bodhi, and their daughter Mar de Luz. For more on her work visit christineg.tv and follow her on Instagram @CosmicChristine.